BEST OF

Teacher's Arts and Crafts Workshop

BEST OF

Teacher's Arts and Crafts Workshop

RUTH L. PECK

PARKER PUBLISHING COMPANY, INC.,
WEST NYACK, NEW YORK

Library of Congress Cataloging in Publication Data

Peck, Ruth L
Best of teacher's arts and crafts workshop.

1. Art--Study and teaching (Elementary)--Handbooks, manuals, etc. 2. Creative activities and seat work--Handbooks, manuals, etc. I. Title. II. Title: Teacher's arts and crafts workshop.
N350.P38 372.5'044 74-2437
ISBN 0-13-073668-6

Printed in the United States of America

About This Book

You, like every good teacher, constantly seek new ideas. You grow tired of the same old thing; you feel the need for things different and refreshing for your class. The problem is—where do you find them?

You *have* found them! This book is a compilation of the best lessons selected from *The Teacher's Arts and Crafts Workshop*. Each lesson has been proven a stimulating project which your class will enjoy doing and you will enjoy teaching. Use the easy-to-follow plans as they are presented here and you and your class will be guaranteed success.

The fifty lessons in this book were selected as the "best" not only because they represent a wide range of ideas for use with all of the elementary grades, but also because they are the lessons with which children have had the most pleasure and success. They present stimulating ideas which will lead to many hours of pleasure and profit for you and your class. They stress *thinking* as well as *doing*, and each child will finish the activity with a good feeling about himself as well as have a satisfying product.

Lessons are included which use all the basic materials—tempera paint, watercolor, construction paper, chalk and charcoal, crayons, non-hardening clay—as well as scrap materials and some of the less frequently used materials. You will find yourself doing a variety of activities—making pictures, printing with all kinds of things, making collages, constructing with all sorts of materials. You will want to fingerpaint, tie-dye, and sandcast. You will find yourself outdoors sketching or inside looking out through colorful transparencies. You will make real things, interpret realism in your own way, or let your imagination roam to things never seen before.

The author talks to you and to your class in a conversational style as though all of us were discussing each "best lesson" together. You will find yourself learning and teaching at the same time. The children in your class will enjoy themselves as they learn and create.

Each lesson contains all the information you will need to complete the activity successfully. Each lesson includes:

—a suggested grade level for the activity
—clearly stated objectives
—a list of the materials you will need to have ready
—motivation to arouse children's interest
—easy-to-follow procedure that keeps children thinking

–information you and your class need about materials and techniques
–help in commenting to children about their work
–suggestions for displaying the finished projects
–a separate listing of hints about how to make it easy for you
–frequent suggestions about how to substitute other materials.

Art is fun, and a valuable learning experience for the teacher as well as the student. You will enjoy it because you have lots of good ideas and know how to go about teaching them.

Well–here they are. Let's get started!

Ruth L. Peck

Table of Contents

BEST OF

Teacher's Arts and Crafts Workshop

1 Painting

Let's Take a Trip

Tempera Painting *(Suggested for all elementary grades)*

Objectives

1. To use a basic art medium—tempera paint—to express a personal idea.
2. To gain confidence in expressing an idea with a fluid medium.
3. To learn that each part of a picture can add meaning to the whole.
4. To translate an idea into visual form.
5. To fill—but not crowd—a picture.
6. To see that a picture with real parts need not be completely realistic.

Materials

18" x 24" easel paper (newsprint)	easel brushes
newspaper	egg cartons
tempera paint	cans of water

My father went to Florida and brought home a postcard that showed orange trees and palm trees.

Take a Trip with Paint. What can be more fun than taking a trip? Any trip is fun—whether it is to a nearby city or a far-off vacationland—or even to grandmother's house a few blocks away. For the children in your class, painting pictures of their trips may be more fun than the trips themselves.

We're going to take a trip today. Yes, we are—every one of us! Oh, we're not going to leave this room. Our trip will be with paint. First of all we have to decide where we're going. We're *not* all going together! In fact, we will probably all go to different places. So decide where you would like to go. Perhaps it will be a place you have been before. Perhaps it will be a new place you would like to visit. Perhaps it will be a long trip to another part of the country where things are very different from the way they are here. Perhaps it will even be to another country. Perhaps it will be a tiny trip—only to a store or to a friend's house. Oh, of course, it will have to be to a place you know a lot about because you are going to make a picture of it.

Talk About Different Places. Let the children talk about different places for a few minutes. Ask questions which will get the children to think about specific things. How did you get there? Who went with you? What kinds of animals were on the farm? Were there any mountains or was the land level? Were the trees there like the trees we have, or were they different?

Encourage the timid child to tell about a trip he has taken—or would like to take. Reassure the child who insists he has never taken a trip—and doesn't know about any place. Of course you've taken a trip! You came to school this morning—and that's a trip. You've been to a store—and that was a trip. Or perhaps you would like to go to some place you've read about in school—you know about that.

When at last everyone is eager to take a trip with paint, give out the supplies—except the paintbrushes. Keep them for a minute longer so no one will be able to begin his picture yet.

There's just one thing. We're all going on our trips together—even though we're all going to different places! How is that possible? Easy! We'll make a game out of it and you'll paint only when I tell you to.

Pass out the brushes and again warn them not to begin to paint yet.

How to Start. Now let's take a trip—with paint. First of all make a picture of yourself as you look when you start on your trip. Remember, if you go on this trip in the summer you will not look the same as if you went on the same trip in the winter.

Wait a couple of minutes until about half the class has finished. Then ask everyone to stop. Oh, you can come back to the picture of yourself and finish it later, but right now stop painting. Turn your paper in a different direction—maybe upside down, maybe sideways. Now I want you to show me how you went on that trip. Did you go by automobile, or train, or boat, or airplane? Or did you ride your bicycle? Whatever it was, make a picture of it. Oh, make it large because that was an important part of your trip.

Again allow a short time for painting. Wait until about half the class has finished before going on again. In the meantime talk about what the airplane looked like, or about the rails that will help us to know it is a train, or about other people we would be able to see at the bus windows. Make your questions or comments help the children to see—and to paint—more details in their pictures.

Now it's time to stop. You may go back and finish it whenever you have time. But right now we have all reached the place we are going to visit. So this time paint a picture of where you are going to stay overnight. If it is such a tiny trip that you are not going to stay overnight, you won't have anything to paint. But most of you will stay overnight somewhere. Was it in a motel, or a tall hotel in a crowded city? Or was it at someone's house? Or did you go camping? Whatever it was, make a picture of it. But first of all turn your paper again. You see this is a picture of your trip and there are all kinds of things in it, so they can be any place and any size at all.

Other Things to Paint. Continue to allow time to paint, turn the papers, and then suggest a new thing to paint. Other things that could be painted

Last year I went to England. I saw the Tower Bridge and Cleopatra's Needle

are: someone who went with you; something you saw that you wouldn't see here; something you did that was fun; something you brought home with you.

Before each new part of the trip is painted have the children turn their papers in a new direction. Have them fill the large areas first and encourage them to make big things. As the remaining spaces get smaller, the things they paint can become smaller. Relative size and position are not important.

Now that the papers are filled we will have to call our trips finished. But allow a few more minutes to complete any parts of the pictures that weren't finished earlier.

Allow the painting to partially dry while you clean up. Then let each child show his picture. Perhaps the children can guess where another went on his trip from some of the clues that are in the painting. The artist may want to add some information about his trip.

It was almost as much fun as really going on a trip, wasn't it? More fun? Well, perhaps so!

MAKE IT EASY–FOR YOURSELF!

1. Organize the class into groups of from three to six. Place sharing materials on one empty desk (or counter or table space). Sharing materials will include a can half full of water and perhaps paints. Small cans like soup cans are suitable for water containers. They are easy to handle and take little storage space.
2. Cover all work areas with newspaper. Cover the sharing desk, also.
3. Use egg cartons for paint containers. The regular papier-mache type cartons can be broken in half to provide six compartments for six different colors. In this way even the young children can carry all the paints for one group to share.
4. Plastic bottles make ideal paint dispensers. Paint in them will remain moist and ready to be used from one lesson to another. They provide a clean and easy way of filling egg cartons without spilling any paint.
5. Assign a helper from each group. It will be his job to cover all the desks in his group with newspaper. Include the sharing desk. He will give each child a painting paper (18" x 24" easel paper for primary grades or 18" x 24" manila or white paper for upper grades). A brush for each child will be put on the sharing desk along with a can half full of water. If paint is to be shared he will also get a carton of paint for the sharing desk.
6. If children are to have their own personal palettes, have a few children at a time come to an area where you can fill their cartons with paint.
7. No pencils! No preliminary drawing. Just paint.

8. Be sure the children stand to paint. It permits greater freedom of motion, makes it easier to use the sharing desks, insures fewer accidents—and results in better pictures.
9. Clean up the easy way. Have each helper collect the brushes from his group and leave them on a newspaper so they can be washed later. It is a good idea to collect the brushes first to prevent children from adding to an already completed picture. Have the helper next bring the carton of used paint to you. Empty it in the sink and pile all the cartons together, one on top of the other. Wrap them in a newspaper before discarding. If individual palettes were used, have the children leave them on the sharing desk. You check to see that they aren't too full of paint to be stacked together; wrap them in newspaper and throw them in the basket. Last of all have each child slide his newspaper out from under his painting and fold it twice. The helpers may collect the newspapers and put them in the wastebasket.
10. Brushes that are not in use should be stored flat in a box or stood on their wooden ends in a can.

In the Mood

Tempera Painting *(Suggested for Grades 3 through 6)*

Objectives

1. To experiment with line and color to express a feeling.
2. To use a fluid medium to create a visual interpretation of a mood.
3. To observe the action of paint on wet paper.

Materials

tempera paints
egg cartons
cans of water
large watercolor brushes
12" x 18" white drawing paper
newspaper

How often have you said, "I'm not in the mood for it!" That won't be any problem this time—you can create whatever mood you like.

Are you always in a good mood? Well, perhaps you are most of the time—but not *all* the time! Do you ever get angry? Of course you do! Do you ever feel sad? Certainly! Are you ever jealous? Perhaps so.

Moods of Colors. Talk about how people feel when they are happy—sad—angry—any of the moods. What colors would you use to show a happy mood? Yes, red can be a happy color. What would you use with it to make it happy? No, blue is a sad color. Perhaps you have even heard people say they were blue—meaning they were sad. Yes, yellow or white would help to make red a happy color. What would you use with red to make it angry instead of happy? When you are angry you feel like fighting. What color fights with red? Yes! Orange fights with red! We say the colors clash. Continue to talk about the moods of other colors. Sometimes a color can have different moods—just as you can—depending upon what colors are used with it.

Moods of Lines. Every picture you make has to have something besides color. The colors are put on in lines. Do lines have moods the way colors do? Oh, yes, they do! What does a line look like if it is happy? Yes, a rounding, flowing line is a happy line. It moves about in big, circular motions. Make your hands move in happy lines. Good! Those are happy lines. Would angry lines move the same way? No! You don't act the same way when you are angry, and neither do lines. When you are angry you want to hit out at things. Make your hands move in angry lines. Yes, they are lines that change direction suddenly, that hit out at things. If you painted those lines red and orange, wouldn't they look angry? Yes, you could even have some black angry lines.

Have your class gather around you at a table. Pour a small puddle of water in the center of a piece of 12" x 18" white drawing paper. Lay your hand flat on top of it and quickly spread the water over the entire paper.

An Angry Mood. Now, let's see what kind of mood I will make. I'll make an angry mood, and I'll begin with red. But I have to think what I'll do with that red—what kinds of lines I'll make. They should be ________? Yes—rough, straight, sharp, angry—lines that change shape suddenly, that hit out at things. As you talk, make a sudden, quick line on the paper. Suddenly change its direction. Immediately move to another part of the paper and again make a fast, jagged line. Perhaps it will cross over part of the first line. They look angry with each other, don't they!

Yes, the color is spreading. That is because the painting is being done on wet paper. Now change colors. Pick up a brushful of orange paint. Repeat two or three motions similar to those you made with the red paint. The lines clash with each other and the colors clash with each other. If any of the lines have begun to disappear into the wet background, repaint them—with the same angry motions.

What would you use if this were your painting and you wanted a third color? Blue? But blue is a quiet color—a sad color. Would that be a good choice? No, not at all! You are right. Black would be a much better choice. Black is a strong color that would make your angry picture even more angry. Add a line or two of black. See, isn't it even angrier? Repaint any line that has tended to spread too much. Then lay the painting to one side.

Pretend a Mood. When you are angry—or disappointed, or happy, or any other mood—what part of you shows it? Of course, your face does! So let's make another mood picture that is a face. Talk about the parts of your face that show expression—eyes, eyebrows, mouth. Eyes that are round would show surprise or happiness; slanting, narrow eyes would be angry or jealous; long, drooping eyes would be sad. Let children pretend they are in a particular mood and demonstrate how they would look. Can you tell by the mouth and the eyes and eyebrows what the mood is?

A Face Mood. Pour a puddle of water on another paper and quickly cover the whole paper with it. This will be a sad person. So I'll make his face long and narrow. Oh, he won't look like a real person because it is just a sad mood I am painting, so I can make his face any shape I want. Long blue lines are sad lines in a sad color, so if he has a long, blue face, it will be sad. Now for his eyes—long, drooping blue ovals, like that. Aren't they sad? Yes, I could give him a nose, but a nose isn't important to a sad expression, so I could even leave it out. If I put it in, it will be just a long line. Instead of giving him eyebrows, I am going to give him long, straight hair that hangs down over his face. But first let's give him a sad mouth. Yes, the corners will go down. Perhaps I will use black for that so that it will look extra sad. Now for that straight, straggly hair. Make some straight lines with blue and black paint. Paint the lines in uneven lengths over the forehead and at the sides of the face. Add a touch of blue or black paint to any large areas around the face. Yes, we can give him a neck and shoulders just to finish the picture. Isn't he the saddest thing you ever saw? If any of the lines begin to disappear, they can be repainted—to keep him sad!

Paint Your Own. Now, you decide what mood you would like to paint and whether you want it to be just lines and colors or whether you want to paint a face. You may have either two or three colors to show your mood.

When everyone has returned to his own desk, have helpers give out the newspaper to cover desks, 12" x 18" white drawing paper, and half an egg carton to each child. Have cans of water placed on sharing desks so that one will be easily available to each child. Then distribute paints. As soon as a child has the two or three colors he needs, let him go to work.

Be sure to get your paper wet—just nicely wet, no puddles. If you have too much water, push it off onto the newspaper where it won't do any harm. Begin with the most important color for your mood and put in the most important lines first. Good! You must be in a happy mood. The round face painted with red tells me so. Be sure everything else you paint makes the face even happier. Um-m, red and blue in the same mood? Red could be either happy or angry or excited, but blue isn't any of those things. Blue could be sad or calm, but red isn't either one of them. Decide which mood you want and then be sure you have the right colors. You don't even need a face to tell us those lines are happy, do you? The gay, rounding lines tell us so. They are almost giggly, aren't they? Yes, repaint any lines that begin to disappear. That will make them even more important.

As soon as the paintings are finished (it should take only a few minutes), have a quick sharing time. The paintings will still be too wet to hold up, so just walk about the room commenting about especially good things—or calling attention to something to avoid another time. You may even want to let groups of children take turns walking about the room to see all the results.

Make Another Picture—but Different. Now let's make another picture. You may paint the same mood again, if you like, or you may paint an entirely different mood. But this time change the kind of painting you make. If you made a face the first time, make just lines and colors this time. If that's what you did the first time, then make a mood in the form of a face this time.

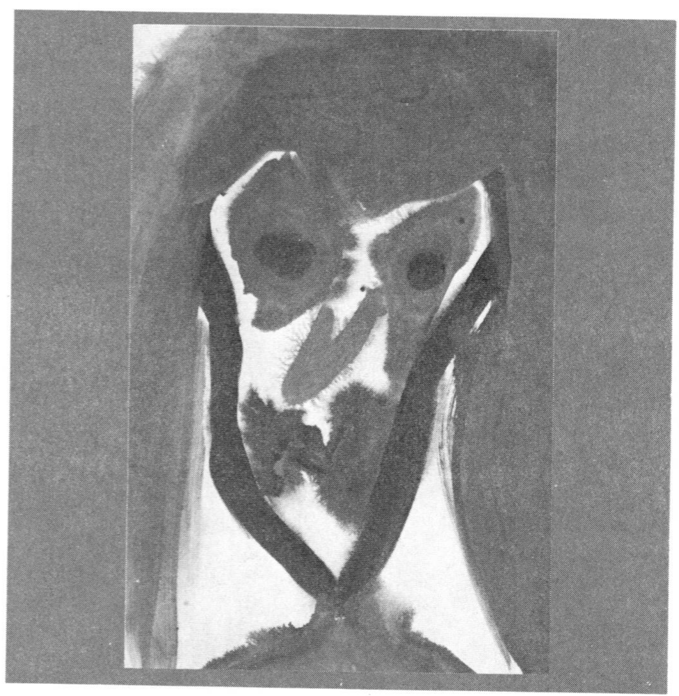

Jealous

Refill Palettes. Yes, if the mood is to be the same, you may want to use the same colors again. If you change moods, you will probably have to change colors, too. But that won't be any problem. You have extra sections in your egg carton palette, so I'll give you any other color you need. Yes, you may need another color even if you paint the same mood again. If you didn't have a good choice of colors the last time, you will certainly want to make some changes.

Let the helpers empty the cans of dirty water and get half a can of clean water. Have each child lay his first painting in an empty area nearby. Move the paintings as little as possible so as not to disturb them. While someone gives each child a clean piece of paper, make any color additions to the palettes that children want. As soon as a child has all the materials he needs, let him go to work on his second painting.

Walk about the room as you did before, complimenting, encouraging, and assisting individual children in any way they need. Remind them of the things they did well the first time and remind them of things they were going to do differently.

The second paintings will be completed quickly. This time be certain to let all the children see the work of every other child. Later you will want to make a display that will get you in the mood—every mood.

MAKE IT EASY—FOR YOURSELF!

1. Too much water on the paper causes puddles of water to form. If this happens, wipe the excess water off onto the newspaper.
2. Egg cartons make excellent palettes. Break the cartons in half so that each palette will have six sections. Use two or three of them for colors for the first mood painting. The remaining sections can be used for new

Angry

colors if they are needed for the second painting. This eliminates the need for getting entirely new palettes.

3. Plastic squeeze bottles make ideal paint dispensers for filling palettes. Distribute one color of paint at a time to anyone who wants it. Supervise the selection of colors to try to prevent a child from mixing moods.
4. Use large watercolor brushes, number 12 if possible.
5. Encourage the children to paint rapidly. The entire painting should be completed before the paper dries. Repaint any lines that tend to disappear.

That's Different!

Tempera Painting *(Suggested for all elementary grades)*

Objectives

1. To be more aware of the relationship between our sense of touch and our sense of sight.
2. To express the sense of touch in visual form.
3. To experiment with color and line as a means of expressing a reaction to touch.
4. To develop the ability to express a reaction in non-objective form.

Materials

18" x 24" easel paper
12" x 18" white or manila paper
tempera paint
large brushes
egg cartons
cans of water
newspaper

You love to feel things! You run your fingers over a piece of smooth material to enjoy its feel. You squeeze each head of lettuce in the grocery store to find the one that feels just right. You let the sand run through your fingers as you lie on the beach. You rub your hand across the silky fur of your cat. You touch all of these things.

But did you ever realize that things touch you, too? Your cat leans his body against you and rubs against your leg. That's different, isn't it!

Good to Touch. What do you like to touch? What feels good when you rub your hands across it or let your fingers sink into it? You will get all kinds of answers when you ask your class those questions.

Some children will enjoy the smooth, slippery feel of the polished surface of a piece of furniture. Others like the soft, wet feel of mud squeezing between their fingers. Another might prefer the soft, slightly rough feel of corduroy.

Like Having It Touch You. Then ask another question—what do you like to have touch you? No, you don't like it when someone bumps into you or hits you. No one ever does! But doesn't anything ever touch you that you like the feel of?

Yes, you like the feel of a hot shower on a cold morning. It makes you feel good all over, doesn't it! Other things will be suggested, one after another: warm sun on a cold day; leaves covering you as you jump into a newly raked pile of them; heat from the fireplace as you stretch out in front of the crackling flames; a gentle breeze on a hot summer day; your father holding you tight when you're afraid; wet sand oozing between your toes as you walk at the edge of the water.

Not Good to Touch. All of those things feel good—and other things you will think of, too. But can you think of anything that touched you that didn't feel good? No, we don't mean when someone tried to hurt you.

That's right! On a cold day, the wind doesn't feel good, does it! There will be other things, too: the day your pet dog came in from the rain and shook water over you; a tiny branch that snapped back and struck you across the face; a bee that got up your sleeve and stung you!

You felt all these things that touched you. Some of them you liked—and some you didn't like at all. Could you make a picture of them? No, you wouldn't make a picture of the thing that touched you—you would make a picture of how it felt. Let's see how that would be.

Think for a minute about that bee that stung you. It wasn't the way it looked that counted, was it? It was the way it ______? Felt! It didn't look and feel the same, did it? The bee got up your sleeve, and you probably didn't even see it—you just felt it.

Lines and Colors. What kind of lines would you use to show how the bee sting felt? Would they be smooth and round? Not at all. It was a sharp pain, wasn't it? So the lines would be sharp. What kinds of colors would you use? Was the pain soft and light? No, no! So the colors couldn't be soft and light. They would have to be like the pain—severe and heavy. Was the pain all over you or did you feel it in one place? That's right, in one place. But it did continue, didn't it? It wasn't just a little thing that was over quickly.

Talk for a while about lines and shapes and colors. Some of them are pleasant and relaxing and make you feel good. Round or gently curving lines are pleasant; jagged or pointed lines are sharp and unpleasant. Some things feel like round lines; other things feel like pointed lines. Some things are big and you feel them all over, and some things are little and you just feel them in one place. Some things feel like red and orange and black all at one time, but other things feel like pink and yellow. What would be the difference?

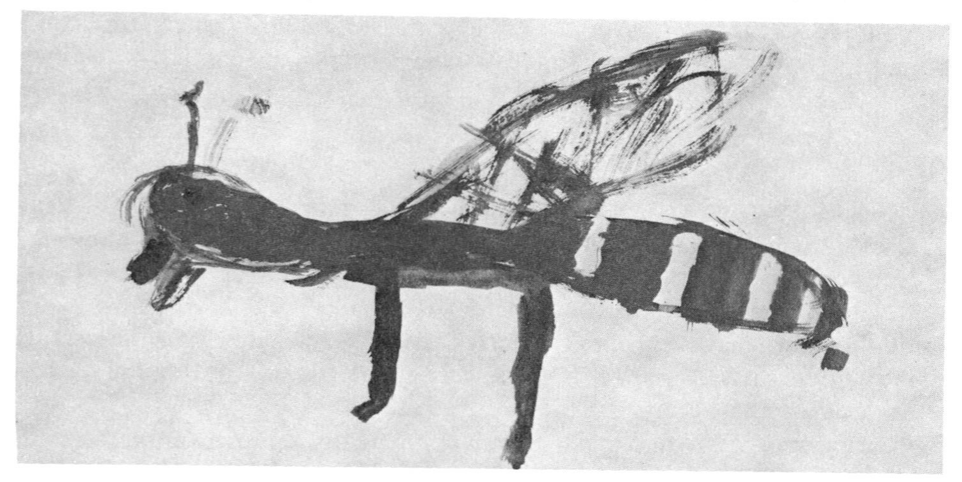

Bee Sting (thing-that-did-it)

What It Felt Like. Ask each child to think of something that has touched him at some time. What did it feel like? Give him a large piece of paper and a large brush. Have some paints available so he can choose the colors he needs. Ask him to paint how he felt.

Walk about the room encouraging children and reminding them of the things they have just talked about. Was it warm or cold? Could you choose colors that would tell us? That's a good beginning. That's big enough so we can feel it, too! How gentle and soft. It must have been pleasant. That must be something you felt in different places. Oh, that's something you didn't like! I don't think I would like the feel of it, either.

The Things They Felt. As the children begin to finish their *how-it-felt* pictures, ask them to do one more thing. On a separate piece of 12" x 18" manila paper ask them to paint pictures of the things they felt—the *thing-that-did-it*. Paint it with the same colors you used for the *how-it-felt* picture—even if they aren't the right colors for it. So you might have pink rain or a red and orange bee or a green pussy cat.

How-It-Felt Game. Now let's play a how-it-felt game. Have all the children place their *how-it-felt* paintings together so that they can all be seen at one time. If you have a large bulletin board, tack them up quickly. If there is no other place, lay them side by side on the floor. Place the *thing-that-did-it* paintings nearby.

Ask one child to pick out a pleasant-feeling picture. Have another child find the thing that caused it. Ask the child who painted the *how-it-felt* picture if the other two children were right. Then find an unpleasant *how-it-felt*—and the *thing-that-did-it*. Were they right? Keep score, if you like, and see whether the girls or boys win. It will be fun and you will be surprised how many right answers there will be.

You don't always have to go around touching things, do you? Sometimes things come and touch you—and that's different! See how it felt!

MAKE IT EASY—FOR YOURSELF!

1. Use either 12" x 18" or 18" x 24" paper for the first painting. Newsprint is satisfactory for younger children but older children should have either manila or white drawing paper.
2. Egg cartons make excellent palettes. Break each papier mache carton into three parts. This will provide containers for up to four colors for each child.
3. Plastic squeeze bottles make excellent paint dispensers. Tempera paint in them remains moist and ready for use from one lesson to the next. They also provide an excellent way of filling the egg cartons.
4. Cover all work areas with newspaper.
5. Have several cans of water placed about the room so that one is easily accessible to every child when he needs to wash his brush.

Bee Sting (how-it-felt)

Cat Rubbing (thing-that-did-it)

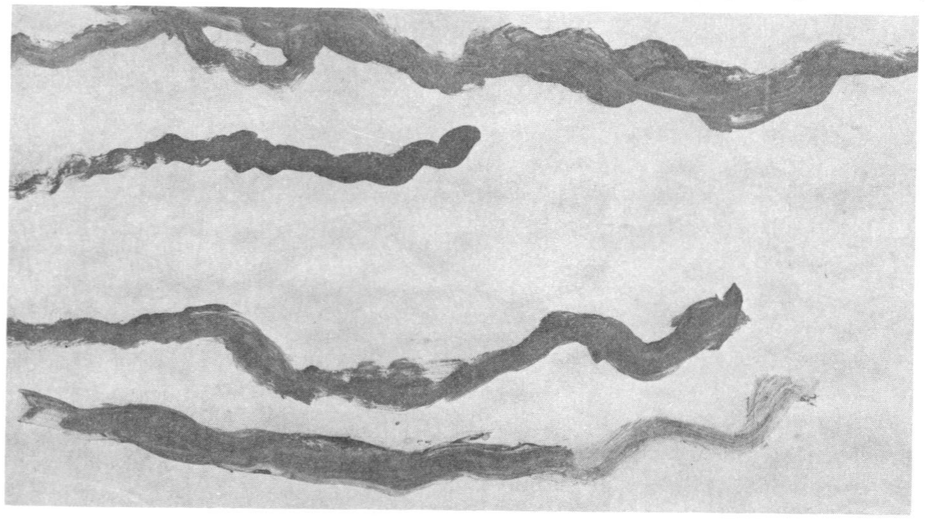

Cat Rubbing (how-it-felt)

6. Be sure the children stand to paint. It permits greater freedom of motion and therefore results in better pictures.
7. No pencils! Just paint.
8. After each child finishes his *how-it-felt* painting, have him put it in the temporary display area—tacked on a bulletin board or laid on the floor. This will provide a safe place for it to dry and will provide him with more work space while he makes his second painting—the *thing-that-did-it*.
9. Clean up the easy way. Have one person collect the brushes and leave them on a piece of paper at the sink. They can be washed later. Let another child collect the cans of water, empty them, and put them in their storage space. Have each child slide the newspaper out from under his painting and fold the newspaper into quarters. It can be collected and thrown away.

Where Is It?

Cloth and Paint Pictures *(Suggested for all elementary grades)*

Objectives

1. To be more aware of the association of sight with sound.
2. To use sound as the motivation for original pictures.
3. To use familiar materials in a new and creative way.
4. To help children organize their ideas into a complete thought.

Materials

12" x 18" white or manila paper
printed cloth
newspaper
paste and paste brushes
scissors
tempera paint
large brushes
egg cartons
cans of water

Did you ever have a sound play a trick on you? You knew what the sound was, but you didn't know where it was. You finally asked, "Where is it?"

Ask your class where they hear sounds—any kinds of sound. Everywhere, of course! You hear sounds when you're in the house and when you're outside. You hear sounds in school, in the store, at the movies. You hear sounds in your backyard, in the park, at the swimming pool. You hear sounds everywhere.

Sounds You Recognize. Do you always know what makes the sounds? No, not always, but you usually do. When you hear a dog bark, you know what it is. Maybe you even know whether or not it is your own pet. Can you think of another sound you know?

Locate Them. All kinds of sounds will be suggested, from a baby crying to an ambulance siren. After a number of different sounds have been suggested, begin to locate them. Where would your baby brother be when you hear him cry? Yes, he might be in his crib at home, but could he be any other place? Of course—he might be with your mother while she is in the grocery store, or he might be playing in the backyard and cry because he fell and hurt himself. If you were making a picture of your brother crying, you would have to show us where he was.

Talk about other sounds and where they would be. Where would the lawnmower be when you heard its loud noise? Where might you hear thunder? Did you ever hear a frog croak, or an owl hoot, or a squirrel chatter? Would they all be in the same place? No, not at all! The picture would have to tell us *where* the sound is. Would you hear an automobile horn in the same place that you would hear an electric mixer? The automobile would be outdoors, of course. The electric mixer would be in the kitchen. Your picture would have to show that.

Colors for Sounds. Have an assortment of printed fabric. Show it to the children—they'll be excited just to see the designs and to know they are going to use a different art material. Talk about the colors in the pieces of cloth. Would some of them be better for loud noises than soft sounds? Yes—some of them do look noisy, don't they? Yes, the bright colors, especially that bright red one. Perhaps you will be able to pick a color that will sound like your noise.

Explain to the class that just the thing which makes the sound—the dog, the tractor, the telephone, the dishwasher, the drum—will be made of cloth. Make it big, of course, because that is the thing which is making the sound. It's the *subject* of your picture—the thing your picture is about—so it should be big and important. It will be pasted onto the background paper.

But that will be just an empty piece of paper. What will you have to do after you have the sound object in your picture? That's right! You will have to show where the sound is. If it is a drum, you will have to show the person who is playing it. You might even want to show the whole orchestra.

Sirens in the City

Tempera Paint. That part of the picture—the *where-it-is* part—will be done with tempera paint. Show the class where you are going to set up painting areas. When they have finished the cloth—the *what-it-is* part of their pictures—they may take their pictures to a painting area to finish—to paint the *where-it-is* part.

Spread out the pieces of fabric on an extra desk or table and let groups of children take turns selecting material. Give each child a piece of 12" x 18" white or manila paper, a pair of scissors, a tiny bit of paste, and a paste brush. Remind the children again to make their objects large.

Areas for Painting. While the children work on the fabric part of their pictures, you may prepare several painting areas in various parts of the room. Arrange each area so that there will be space for two or more children to share the same paints. Cover each area with newspaper and place an egg-carton palette of paint on it. The papier mache or molded plastic foam types of egg cartons make excellent paint containers. One half of an egg carton has spaces for six colors. (You may want to use only four or five colors for this lesson.) The cartons make an easy way of distributing several colors at one time, do not tip, and are disposable at the end of the lesson. Place as many brushes at each area as there will be children working there.

About the time you have finished preparing the work areas, several children will be ready to use them. Direct them to an area and let them begin painting. As they finish, other children may take their places.

The Bird Singing

Collect Extra Cloth. While a child is painting, you can collect any material large enough to save for another lesson. You also have an opportunity to move to various parts of the room. Encourage children who are still working on the cloth part. Comment on their work to those who are painting. Urge them to put in only a few things to show where the sound is.

After the first children to paint have finished, have them bring their pictures back to their desks so that other children may take their places. Have each child clean up his own work area—put scissors away and discard all scraps. Those children who are still waiting to paint may also clean up in the meantime. The last child to paint at each area should also clean that space—set brushes in the sink to be washed later; wrap egg cartons of paint in newspaper and put them in the wastebasket.

There—the room is all back in order again! But more important than that, there is a roomful of pictures to be seen—and heard. They won't play any tricks on you, either! Each picture will show you exactly where the noise is. You won't have to ask, "Where is it?"

MAKE IT EASY—FOR YOURSELF!

1. Have a wide variety of fabric to choose from. Children may be able to bring in pieces from home. Tear the cloth into pieces 6" or 8" square.
2. If any of the cloth has pictures on it, warn children not to cut out those pictures. Instead, have them use the cloth just as they would a plain piece of colored paper.
3. Most cloth has a right side and a wrong side. Call this to the children's attention so that they will use the right side for their pictures.
4. If it is possible, have a set of new scissors to use for cutting the cloth. Paper dulls scissors quickly and makes it difficult to cut cloth with them. You may be able to keep two sets of scissors—one for general use with paper and one for special occasions—perhaps tagged *"For Cloth Only."*
5. No pencils. When young children use pencils they tend to make small, detailed, and fussy pictures. They will do much better by just thinking and cutting.
6. You may want to eliminate water at the painting areas. If you do, urge children not to stir the paint with their brushes. When they have finished painting, they may wipe their brushes on the newspaper to clean them for the next person.
7. Be sure the children stand while painting. It permits more freedom of motion and results in better work.

Whoever Heard of That?

3-D Painting *(Suggested for Grades 4 through 6)*

Objectives

1. To provide an opportunity for children to work either individually or cooperatively.
2. To use polymer as a paint medium.
3. To understand the possibility of having both realistic and non-objective painting in the same picture.
4. To experience painting on a three-dimensional surface.

Materials

boxes of various sizes
tempera paints
polymer
large watercolor brushes
egg cartons
cans for water
newspaper

Three-dimensional painting? That's impossible! Whoever heard of that! We're going to do something today that is impossible. We are going to make three-dimensional paintings!

Explain Three-Dimensional. Begin to review with your class what they know about the meaning of "three-dimensional." Anything that is three-dimensional has three directions; it has length and width and depth (or thickness). Hold up a piece of paper. It is only ____? Right! It is two-dimensional because it has only two dimensions or directions. We could measure it and find that it is nine inches long and twelve inches wide (or whatever the size is). It has no thickness—at least not enough for us to measure. But if we put a hundred or so of these papers together, the stack of papers would become three-dimensional because it would have thickness as well as length and width. Anything that is three-dimensional stands away from the surface it is on.

When you add paint to a paper does it add thickness? No, it is still flat. A painting is two-dimensional. It has only length and width.

But you are going to make three-dimensional paintings. How is that possible? There may be some strange suggestions, but probably only puzzled expressions. Give them a clue. Have you even helped your father paint something that is three-dimensional? Right! Your house is three-dimensional and you paint that. No, you don't paint pictures on it but that wouldn't make any difference. You will paint pictures on what you paint today. You won't be painting houses, though; you will be painting boxes.

Realistic and Non-Objective. Show the class the assortment of boxes you have for them—some small ones, only a few inches in each direction; some large ones, a foot or more each direction. Explain that all six sides of a box will be painted. They won't be just plain, colored boxes; they will be pictures, too. Each box must have something realistic as part of the picture, and each must have something that is totally non-objective or abstract as part of the picture. Oh, yes, one other thing! On some part of the box a part of the picture will extend from one side of the box right on around to another side—just as though it were on one continuous flat piece of paper.

There will be questions. Yes, the box picture may be mostly non-objective, but somewhere there must be something realistic. Or you may make it almost completely realistic, but somewhere there must be just non-objective shapes. Oh, yes, the whole box must be painted—no empty areas. No, not everything should extend from one side of the box to the other, but most of it may do that if you like.

Add Polymer. You are going to do one more thing that is different. You are going to change the tempera paint so that it will have a hard, shiny surface when it is finished. Usually tempera paint has a dull finish when it is dry, but this time it will look almost like enamel paint—or as though you had varnished the paint. You will do that by adding just a bit of polymer to the tempera paint as you use it.

If your class has used polymer before, they will remember that it is a synthetic material that can be used as an adhesive as well as a paint additive. If this is the first time they have used polymer, show them the white liquid and explain its uses—as an adhesive and as a medium to mix with paint. Remind them that because it is a powerful adhesive, certain precautions must be taken. The paint brushes must be wet before they are put into the polymer and they must be put back in the can of water whenever they are not being used. If even a drop of polymer spills on furniture or clothing it must be wiped up immediately with a damp sponge.

Alone or in Pairs. Explain to the class that they may each work alone or two children may work together on one of the larger boxes. Remind them that, if they decide to work with another child, they should be sure to choose someone they will work well with—someone who likes much the same things that they like, and someone whose work they respect.

Each child—or pair of children—will have half an egg carton as a palette. That will provide six separate compartments—one for polymer and five for tempera paint. You may not want five different colors. You may decide

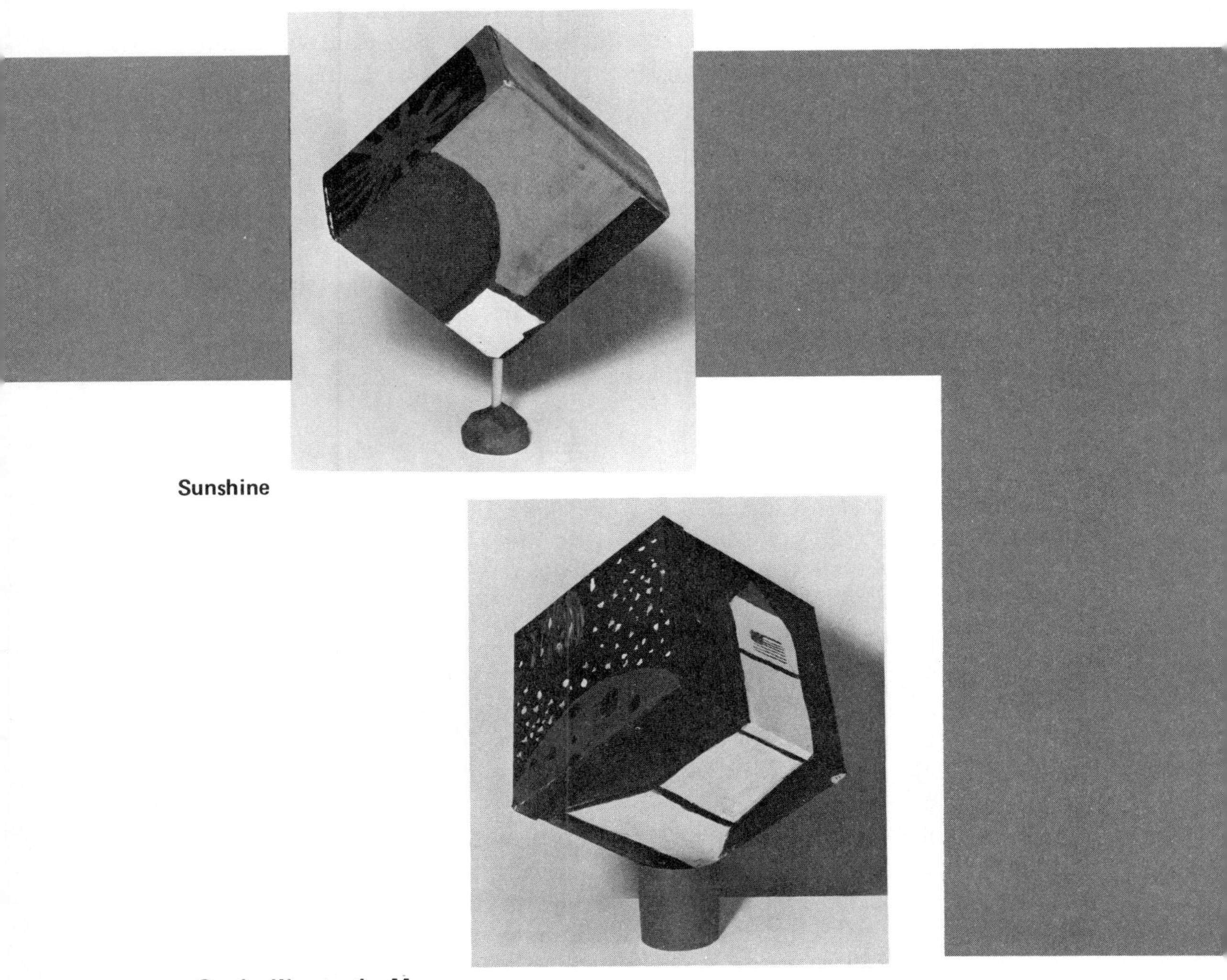

Sunshine

On the Way to the Moon

to save one or two of the sections for mixing new colors. You can decide that when you are ready for your supplies. When you paint, you will dip the wet brush into the polymer and then into whatever color you want to use. Each time you want a brushful of paint, put a little polymer on the brush before you dip it in the color.

Select Partners and Boxes. Let any child who wants to choose a partner do so, and then let them select one of the large boxes. Partners will need a few minutes to talk over ideas and make plans. While they are doing that, let those children who want to work alone take turns selecting their boxes. Children who work by themselves will have enough work space at their own desks, but partners will need a larger area. If possible let them work at a large table—or move two desks together.

Place several cans half full of water in various parts of the room so that each child will have easy access to one of them. Give each child a paint brush, and, when he is ready, let him select his paints. It will get things moving more quickly if you pour the paint into the palettes the first time. Then, as children need more paint, let them get their own from a central supply.

Children will soon be hard at work. Walk about the room to help wherever you are needed.

Have you both decided yet how to paint your box? Well, talk it over. When you work with another person, you both have to agree on what you're going to do, you know. That's right, just a little polymer on the brush with the paint each time. No, it won't lighten the color. It won't change it at all, except to make the paint shiny and waterproof when it is dry. Certainly, you can make a space capsule that extends over two sections of the box. Have you decided what the non-objective part of the design will be? That's right. You will have to wait for one side of the box to dry before you can paint the last side. Don't turn the box over on a wet side. That would spoil it, wouldn't it! Oops! Wipe up that drop of polymer with a damp sponge right away before it begins to dry. It will come off easily now, but it won't come off at all if it dries. Good! I like the way you have lightened some of your colors and darkened others. That makes a better contrast.

Ways to Display. While the children are still painting their boxes, ask if anyone has an idea about how they could be displayed. Yes, you could just lay them on a shelf or counter, but then you would have to turn them over to see all the sides. Can you think of some other way so that every side could be seen. That's a good idea! You could hang a string through one corner and suspend the box as a mobile. That would be a particularly good way of showing the smaller boxes. Several of them might even be used together to make one mobile. What can you do with the great big ones? Someone may suggest nailing a rod to a wooden base. The rod could then be inserted through diagonal corners of the box. Or one corner of a large box could be rested in a heavy jar or other container. You may want to use a variety of display techniques, but see that each box is exhibited.

Everybody knows it's impossible to make a three-dimensional painting—but there they are! And aren't they great!

MAKE IT EASY—FOR YOURSELF!

1. If polymer is not available, use the tempera paint without it. The finished boxes will have the typically dull finish of tempera paint. If you want, you could put a clear, glossy varnish on them to give a shiny and waterproof finish.

2. Have some easel brushes available for painting extra large surfaces.
3. Don't spread the paint too much. Apply it rather heavily so that it will cover any advertising or designs that may be on the box. If polymer is not used with the tempera paint, you may have to add a tiny bit of liquid soap to the paint to make it adhere to shiny surfaces of the box.
4. Polymer will not change the color of the paint. It dries clear and shiny.
5. Cover all work areas with newspaper to protect them from the polymer. If any of it spills, wipe it up immediately with a damp sponge. While it is wet it is no problem, but once it is dry it is waterproof.
6. Plastic squeeze bottles make ideal paint dispensers. Paint in them remains moist and usable from one art lesson to the next.
7. Dip brushes into water before putting them into the polymer. Keep them in water *all the time* they are not in use. Wash them *thoroughly* several times when the work is completed. Keep them in water until they are thoroughly clean. Remember, polymer is an adhesive—it will glue the bristles together if any of it remains in the brushes.
8. Polymer on your hands reacts much as glue does. It will not wash off. Rinse your hands in warm water and then rub them together or peel off the film of polymer. Soap is not necessary.

Let It Drip!

Watercolor Paintings *(Suggested for Grades 4 through 6)*

Objectives

1. To introduce watercolor in a way which guarantees success.
2. To experiment with new materials.
3. To use line as an important part of design.
4. To learn to blend watercolor.

Materials

9" x 12" white drawing paper	containers of water
rubber cement	facial tissue
boxes of watercolors	newspaper
large watercolor wash brushes	

Does a drip, drip, drip bother you? You just have to get up and turn it off? Well, don't this time—let it drip! It won't bother you a bit.

Have you ever used rubber cement? Yes, I'm sure many of you have. It is a kind of glue, isn't it? But this time we're not going to glue anything with it—we're going to paint with it. Yes, that's right—we're going to paint with it!

Let your class gather around you at a large table where you have all the materials you will need. I said we're going to paint with the rubber cement, so of course we'll need some paint too—watercolor this time. But let's forget that for a minute while we see what we can do with the rubber cement.

Drip Rubber Cement. Rubber cement usually comes in small jars with a brush attached to the cover. Remove the cover and let the glue drip back into the jar. See, it is a rather heavy glue. Dip it in the jar again and then lift it out. I don't want big puddles of glue, so I'll let the big blob of glue drop off. Then I'll quickly hold the brush over my white paper.

Move your hand slowly above the paper so that the rubber cement dribbles onto the paper in uneven lines. There isn't any more dripping from the brush, so I'll dip it again. I must remember, though, to let the big blob fall back into the jar before I let more lines drip onto my paper. Be sure to hold the jar above the white paper so that the rubber cement will drip onto the paper rather than onto everything else.

Continue to move the dripping glue while it drops in long sweeping lines, short or long curves, wiggly lines, horizontal lines, diagonal lines, vertical lines—even dots.

There, I think that is enough, don't you? If I put on too many lines, they would run together and just make puddles. No, they don't show well on white paper, but they will become very important when the painting is finished. Let's leave it to dry a bit while we think about the watercolor.

If watercolors are a new material for your class, talk about them a bit. They look easy to use, but did you know that they are harder to manage than other kinds of paints? Yes, if you've ever tried them, you know that!

Prepare Watercolors. Most watercolors come in dry form like these, so the first thing you have to do is add ____? Of course, you have to add water—a big drop or two on each color you will use. I'll add water to each color because I don't know yet which ones I'll use. There, that will soften the paint so that it will work better.

We're going to use very wet paint and paint rapidly with it. There won't be anything realistic in the paintings—just lovely colors that blend together. Which color would you like to have me use first? Let one child choose a color.

Paint Rapidly. All right, blue (or whatever color is chosen) will be a fine color. I'll need lots of it, so I'll dip my brush into the water and get as much as possible on it. I won't even wipe off any of it—if the water drips a bit, it won't do any harm. Then go quickly into the blue paint, moving back and forth until the brush is loaded with it.

Sweep the brushful of blue paint across the paper that has the lines of rubber cement on it. Pay no attention to the lines that were dripped on—go right over them. I'll need more paint in a hurry before this begins to dry. Load the brush with water and then blue paint again—then sweep back and forth on the paper. Repeat this three or four times until approximately half the paper is covered with uneven areas of blue paint.

Another Color. There are still parts of the paper that haven't been painted, so let's choose another color to put there. Yes, green (or anything else) will be fine, but I must hurry. I'll wash the brush as quickly as possible and then go into the green paint with a big brushful of water.

Continue painting as you did before, this time filling the unpainted areas. Overlap the colors only slightly—just enough to let the wet edges blend together. Fill all the areas or leave a small part for a third color.

The colors blended nicely, didn't they? But I had to work fast to finish before any of the paint dried. Now we'll have to wait until every bit of the paint is dry before we can finish the picture. Oh, no—it isn't finished yet. The painting is all done, but we have to get off all that rubber cement before the picture is finished. Why did I put it on if I have to take it all off? Well, that's a good question, but I can't show you until the paint is dry. In the meantime let's see about cleaning up the paints.

Clear Away Paint Supplies. Wash the brush in the container of water. Yes, the water does look dirty, but it is all right. Wipe the extra water on the brush back into the container. Then lay the brush—handle and all—flat on a crumpled piece of facial tissue which you hold in your other hand. Pull the brush across the tissue, turning it slightly as you do so. See what has happened. The dirty water has been absorbed by the tissue. Hold up the brush and show how nicely pointed the bristles are. If puddles of water and paint have spilled over into the paint box, wipe them up with the same tissue. You won't be able to get it completely clean—no artist's paints ever are. Now I'll empty the dirty water—we'll have one person empty all the cans of water—and immediately wipe the container dry with the facial tissue. Yes, the tissue is very dirty by now; but see how clean it has made everything else.

The paint on my picture still isn't completely dry, so we'll just leave it while you make your pictures. Then I'll finish mine while you wait for yours to dry.

Share Rubber Cement. Give each child a piece of white paper and distribute your supply of rubber cement so that there will be a container of it for each group of children. As one child in the group finishes with it, he will give it to the next child. Walk about the room to assist wherever you are needed. When the last child in each group finishes with the rubber cement, he should screw on the cover and put the jar in a designated place.

Now for the painting. No, no! Don't touch your fingers to any of the lines of rubber cement! Leave them just as they are. As soon as you have your container of water and box of paints, put a big drop or two of water on each color that you are going to use. Yes, only two or three colors are enough. Which color are you going to use first?

Fine—get as much of it as you can on your brush and spread it quickly over areas of your paper. Oh, you'll have to work much faster than that or the paint will dry around the edges. Then the colors wouldn't blend. That's the way to do it! Paint in areas rather than just making wiggly lines.

Don't you think that is enough of one color? Certainly! Go right on to the second color just as quickly as you can. Oops—wash the brush before you put it into another color. Good! You are painting so rapidly that the edges are blending nicely. You've just about finished, haven't you?

Remind the children to wash their brushes and wipe them across the piece of facial tissue. Keep them completely flat so that the brush will be nicely pointed. Just once across the tissue is enough. Then wipe up any extra water or paint that is spilled in the box.

Let one child collect the water from the containers on each child's desk. An easy way to do it is for him to go to each desk and empty the container of water into a pail or large can he has with him. Remember to wipe out your container as soon as it has been emptied. Have one child collect each of the materials.

Now you'll have to wait until your picture is dry before you can finish it. But my painting has dried while you were making yours, so let me show you what to do next.

Removes Easily. Have your class gather around the table again. If you have ever used rubber cement before, you know that one of the nice things about it is that it is easy to remove any extra cement. That's right. All you have to do is rub your fingers over it and it pulls off into little rubbery rolls. Well, *all* of this rubber cement is extra now—so I have to rub it all off. Rub the ends of your fingers over one area of rubber cement. See—it comes right off. But look! The paper underneath it is completely white—no paint on it at all.

There will be exclamations of surprise and delight. Continue to rub over other lines of rubber cement to expose more and more lines of white paper. The rubber cement just covered up the paper so that we could make lovely patterns of white lines.

Must Wait. It's too bad you can't finish your picture right now, but it will be worth waiting for, won't it! It won't make any difference how long the painting is left with the rubber cement on it. When you rub over it, the cement will roll right off. But the paint must be completely dry or you will rub wet paint over the lines—and that would spoil the white design.

After the paintings have dried and the children have rubbed off all the rubber cement, have them give titles to their pictures. A good picture deserves a good title, you know.

When all the paintings are on display there will be drips, drips, drips all over the place! But you won't hear them, so they won't bother you. You'll see them—and love them. So let it drip!

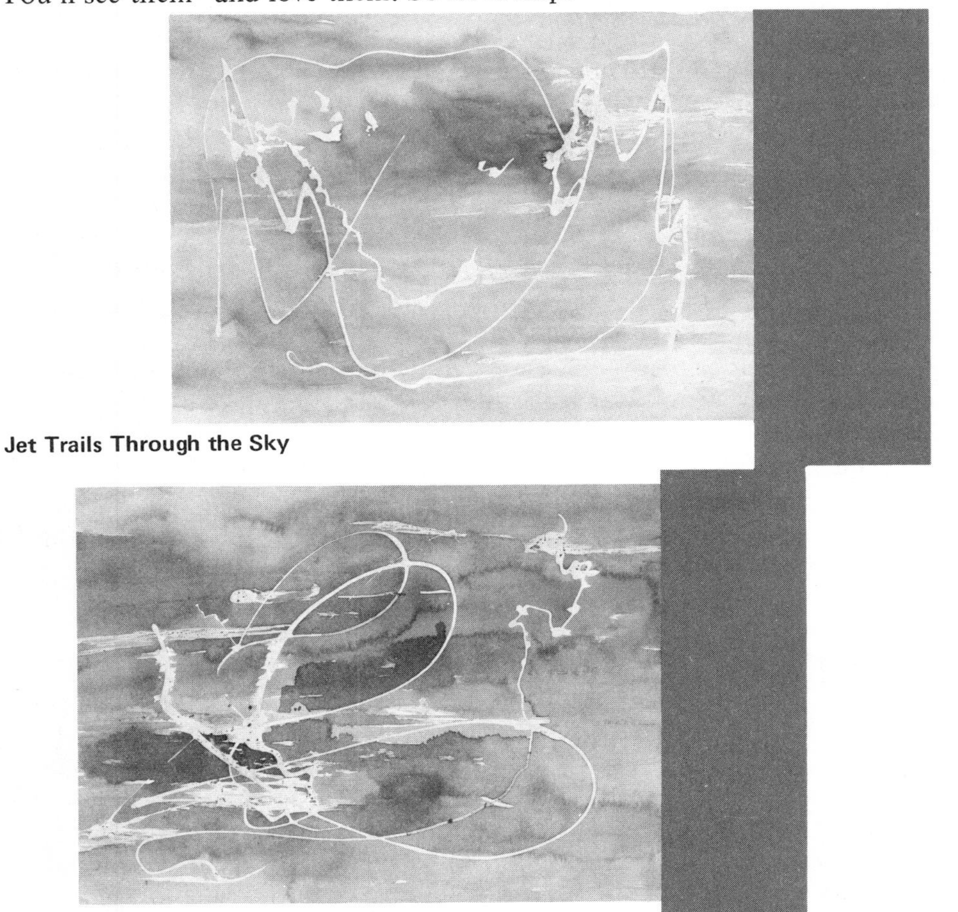

Jet Trails Through the Sky

Sailfish in the Sea

MAKE IT EASY—FOR YOURSELF!

1. Cover all work areas with newspaper.
2. Have each child put his name on the back of his paper with pencil before he begins his work.

3. Several children can share one jar of rubber cement. One for every four or five children is fine.
4. Stand to do both the dripping of rubber cement and the watercolor painting. It will permit greater freedom of action and better control.
5. Don't give out any watercolor supplies until all work with the rubber cement is finished. This will allow time for it to dry partially before painting over it—which will keep the brushes in better condition.
6. Once the children begin work with the watercolors, urge them to work rapidly. Know ahead of time what you are going to do, and then work as quickly as possible—with no stops between each action.

A Crossword Picture

Painting on Tissue Paper *(Suggested for Grades 4 through 6)*

Objectives

1. To use a combination of familiar materials in a new way.
2. To experiment with a picture that is both realistic and non-objective.
3. To develop an awareness of harmonious space relationships.

Materials

12" x 18" manila drawing paper
white tissue paper
rulers, pencils
watercolors, brushes, water containers
black felt-tipped markers—permanent type
newspaper
masking tape

You've seen crossword puzzles; you've probably even done them. But did you ever see a crossword picture? Well, let's make some.

If you ask your class what a crossword puzzle is, everyone will be sure to know. They see them in the daily paper, in special books, probably even in their workbooks at school.

But most crossword puzzles look so much alike. The squares are all the same size, the color is all the same. They're fun to do, but they don't look attractive at all! Let's make a crossword picture—one that's fun to make and will look good when it is finished.

You Need Spaces. The first things you need for a crossword puzzle are the spaces to put letters. So the first things you need for a crossword picture are ______? Of course—spaces to put pictures. Have your class gathered around you so that they can see how you begin.

You'll need a large space for an important picture, so we'll put in that space first. Would the middle be a good place for it? Well, no, not really. It's not a good idea to put anything exactly in the middle because then the spaces around it all look alike and so they aren't interesting. It would be better to put the large space a little to one side—like that. Draw a straight line down one side of the manila paper, slightly off center. Add other lines—top, bottom, and one side—to change it into a large rectangle. We'll even put in that top line and bottom line to make the spaces above and below the large rectangle different sizes, too.

That's a good beginning! We already have several spaces that are different sizes. But a crossword picture should have more spaces than that, so we will break up some of these areas into more spaces. Should any of them be the same size as others? No, let's try to have each one different—some big, some small, some middle size.

Continue to draw straight lines—only verticals and horizontals—until there is a well-balanced and pleasing arrangement. Let children suggest where the various lines should be placed, but guide their thinking so that the final result will be a good design. It should include one large rectangle and several others of various sizes, including some that are quite small.

Put in the Important Picture. Now, those are much more interesting spaces then you ever saw on a crossword puzzle, aren't they? Yes, it does look like a picture already, but we're not going to call it finished yet. Remember that we said the big space was going to be for an important picture? Well, let's put it in now. What will it be? It can be any one thing you want it to be: a man, a boat, a cat, a tree, a guitar, a duck—anything you like. We will make this one a flower, and then you can decide what you would like your own special object to be.

We started our picture on manila paper with pencil lines, but our finished picture won't have any pencil lines on it—and it won't even be on this paper. This was just to help us get started. Our crossword picture is going to be done on white tissue paper. Lay a piece of tissue paper over the manila paper on which you have the rectangular shapes. The paper will probably be slightly smaller than your 12" x 18" manila paper, so move it about until you find the space arrangement you like best. There, that looks good, so I'll put a speck of tape across each corner to hold it right where I have it now. See—the pencil lines show through the tissue paper, so I won't have to draw any of them on this paper. Instead I can use a black felt-tipped marker to draw right on top of them onto the tissue paper. Now that they are in their right places it is easy to put them on the tissue paper.

Let's make that flower that I said was going in the big space on my picture. It is a tall, thin space, so my flower will be ______? Tall and thin, I will draw it to fit the space. Use a black felt-tipped pen to draw the picture. Begin near the top and draw a large but simple blossom. Next it needs a stem—a slightly curved one will be more graceful than a straight one. It can come almost to the bottom of the space. There's still space enough for a long, thin leaf. Decide where it will look the best, and draw it.

Other Pictures. That's only one picture in our crossword picture. We need to put more pictures in some of the other spaces. They should be pictures that will look as though they belong with this flower. What are some things you think of as belonging with flowers? Various things will be suggested: sun, rain, bugs, butterflies, bees. Draw several of them in different spaces where they will help balance the larger flower. A sun might go in one rectangle. Draw a round sun and make the rays around it fit the space it is in. You might decide to draw a whole row of tiny bugs in a long, narrow rectangle. That's enough—don't make too many things, because there is still more to do to the picture.

So far our whole crossword picture is in the same color. That's easy to change; we'll paint it with watercolors. Usually when you paint with watercolor you use lots of water, but this time you will use very little of it. Can you think of any reason why? Yes, most of the spaces are small, but there is an even better reason. It is something about the paper. You are right! The paper is so thin that the water—and paint—would go right through it if you used much water. Besides that, the paint would glue the tissue paper to the manila paper underneath and it might tear when you took it off. But all that is easy to prevent—just use very little water.

Decide on Colors. Demonstrate the painting part of the picture. Let one child decide what color the flower will be. Red? That will be a good color. Put a tiny bit of water and red paint on your brush and paint each petal inside the black lines. It is really very easy because the black lines are like a fence and help your brush to stay in the right place. Try not to let it go on the other side of the fence!

While there is red paint on the brush, wouldn't it be a good idea to paint another red—or pink—area somewhere else? All right, let's do that. Yes, all—or at least most—of the areas are going to be painted with different colors. That will make a good-looking crossword picture! Let someone suggest a good place for red. Be sure it is away from the flower you have just finished. Then let another child suggest another area for red—away from the one you have just done so that it will look good and so that there will not be any danger of the color crossing the "fences" and blurring with a wet color. Does it have to be the same kind of red each time? No, no, of course not. It might have less paint to look lighter, or it might have just a speck of another color in it so as to change it slightly. Let different children suggest places for various reds until there is enough of that color and another one is needed.

Then choose another color and decide several places where that would look good. Paint just one or two of the areas so that the children will see the effect of the change of color. Yes, you could use another color—perhaps two or three more. Yes, some areas could be left unpainted. Then they would be white areas, and you would have to plan their arrangement just as carefully as you did the red ones and the other colors. Yes, you could paint right over the lines of the sun—and the bugs, too. But let's get those pictures drawn first.

Get the Children Started. Give each child a piece of 12" x 18" manila paper, and remind him to make a large rectangle first—off center. Then divide the rest of the paper into other rectangles of various sizes. Be sure those lines are all vertical or horizontal—don't let any of them slant. Don't worry if you put a line in the wrong place. It is easy enough to change it, and it won't ever show on your good paper. It won't even get on the tissue paper, will it! Good! That's a fine beginning. Just another line or two and you will be ready for your tissue paper. Don't put in too many spaces. That would be hard to paint and it would be crowded, too. Take out some lines if you need to.

As you walk about the room give each child a tiny piece of tape and a piece of tissue paper. When you are sure they are doing a good job of space arrangement, give them black markers.

No, don't use the rulers with the felt markers. They might smudge, and besides, you don't need them. You have a straight line underneath. That's right! Make the marker move along quickly, otherwise it might blur a little where you stop it. The lines look better on the tissue paper, don't they! Be sure to make that big important thing fit the large space you saved for it. Then think of something you can put in one or two other spaces. Be sure they are things that belong together.

The marker drawing will be done quickly, so have the watercolor materials available where children can get them as they are ready for them. Remember to use very little water so that it won't soak through. If you see a little puddle of paint, spread it out right away before it can soak through. Remind children to use the same color several times on different parts of their pictures before they change to another color. Compliment them on their careful work and encourage them to think and plan.

Almost as if by magic the pictures will begin to take form. Children will be eager to remove the tape from the corners so that they can see their completed pictures. They will be surprised and delighted when they do. Once the tissue paper pictures are away from the manila papers, they will sparkle and come to life. They will be unique and absolutely fascinating. What else would you expect of a crossword picture!

MAKE IT EASY—FOR YOURSELF!

1 Use pencils and rulers to make the various size rectangles on the

The Lone Flower

The Beach

manila paper. Make as many changes as necessary for a pleasing arrangement; the lines won't be on the completed picture. Then put the pencils and rulers out of the way.

2. If a full sheet of tissue paper is cut into quarters, each piece will be slightly smaller than the 12" x 18" manila paper. Move the tissue paper over the manila paper until the most satisfactory arrangement of lines is found.
3. Half an inch of masking tape is plenty for each child. It can be divided into four parts—one to put across each corner. You want only enough tape to hold the tissue paper in place while working on it. It may tear the tissue paper when it is removed, so use as small a piece as possible.
4. Use very little water and paint. It spreads easily on the tissue paper. A little paint goes far. If it puddles, smooth it off immediately.
5. A piece of wax paper may be inserted between the tissue and manila papers before painting if you wish. This will make sure the two don't stick together.
6. Keep the caps tightly on the felt-tipped markers all the time they are not in use. They dry rapidly and a marker is useless once it dries.
7. Work quickly and lightly with the marker. Press only hard enough to make a smooth line. If you press too hard—or work too slowly—it may blur slightly on the tissue paper.
8. You may want to plan two lessons for the work—one to plan and use the black markers, and another for the watercolor painting.

On the Spot

Watercolor Painting *(Suggested for Grades 4 through 6)*

Objectives

1. To provide experience with watercolor.
2. To increase ability to plan a well-designed landscape painting.
3. To experiment with various watercolor techniques to obtain a desired effect.
4. To learn to blend colors for a more effective painting.

Materials

photographic slides, projector, screen
12" x 18" white drawing paper
watercolors
large brushes
containers of water
newspaper
facial tissue

Have you ever been lucky enough to be on the spot at just the right time so that you were able to take a beautiful picture? Sure you have—lots of times! Probably you have boxes full of lovely slides that prove you were on the spot. Why not get them out and let them be the basis of an art lesson!

Choosing a Scene. Ask the children if they have ever seen an artist painting outdoors. Probably most of them have. Why do you suppose an artist takes all his materials outside to paint? Yes, he wants to make a picture of what is outdoors, and he can do it better if he is right on the spot and can see what it is that he is painting.

Pretend you are an artist and want to paint a landscape. It would be fun to really go into the woods or to the city or the seaport, or to any place at all to paint. But we are going to so many places today that we will have to go by pictures instead of by car or boat or plane.

Start your trip by using the projector to show a slide. Perhaps it is a seaport where there is a large ship at the pier. Wouldn't it be nice to be able to paint a picture like this! But probably you wouldn't want it to look exactly like this. Is there too much in this picture? Is there something you would leave out if you were an artist painting a picture on the spot? Perhaps people in the picture detract from the ship. Well, leave them out of your picture. A camera can't change anything, but you can.

The next picture you show may have been taken along the California coast. Tall palm trees rise high above the rim of sandy beach and blue water. Lovely, isn't it! Most of the lines are vertical. But look more closely. If you were going to paint that scene—if you were on the spot—what would you change? Yes, you might want to leave out the road and the automobiles. You might want to leave out a few of the palm trees. You would arrange the rest of the palm trees to create vertical lines that were placed in a pleasing arrangement. That would make your picture look better than the camera picture, wouldn't it?

Now let's go to the rolling hills of New England and see the rippling stream winding its way through the trees on either side of it. Looks like a cool place to be on a hot day, doesn't it? But if you were really there, would you change anything in your painting? Of course you would! You couldn't possibly paint every one of those rocks, so you would put in just a few of them to give the feeling of the place and to make your eye move along the stream. There must be hundreds of trees, so you would decide which ones would look best in your picture. You might even move some of them so that they were in just the right places. A camera can't do that, can it!

Show other pictures—perhaps a field of partly mowed grain. See how the repetition of bales left in the field creates a rhythm. You would want to have that in your painting, wouldn't you? But perhaps you would like to move the mowing equipment so that it isn't right in the middle of your picture. It would look better a little to one side. The picture has mostly horizontal lines, doesn't it? The hills, the mowed field, the rows of bales.

Discussing the Slides. Show several more slides and take time to talk about each one. Let children point out those parts which they would want to include in their painting if they were right on the spot. Let them suggest those things which they could eliminate in order to simplify their pictures. A camera must show everything exactly the way it is, but an artist can change things.

As you look at each picture, talk about the colors. Notice the contrast between light and dark—usually a sudden change. When you paint your pictures, be sure you have something dark touching something light. An artist has to plan for that. Notice, too, the kinds of colors in the pictures. Are they all clear, bright colors just as they are in a paint box? No, no—not at all! See how light the sky is—you would have to add lots of water to make it look that way, wouldn't you? Are the leaves on those trees just one kind of bright green? Of course not! They are many shades of green, so you would have to add other colors to the green when you painted them. Sometimes you would put some yellow on the brush with the green; sometimes you would use blue on the brush with the green; sometimes you might even add a speck of black.

Painting Techniques. Talk about various painting techniques: more than one color on the brush at a time so that the colors blend unevenly on the paper; the brush with so little paint on it that it is almost dry and skips over the paper without painting all of it; painting on wet paper to make the clouds in the sky soft and indefinite on the edges.

Do any of the things in the pictures look as though they had a line drawn around them and then were filled in with color? No, nothing looks like that, so you won't paint anything that way. Sometimes you will lay the brush flat to paint a wide area and sometimes you will use just the point of the brush to paint a thin line. But you will never draw an outline with the brush and then fill in the space.

Preparing to Paint. Well, that's enough talking about pictures; now let's paint them. Pretend you are an artist right on the spot of a lovely picture. Pick out the important parts and arrange them to look good. Have something close to you. Perhaps it will go from the top to the bottom of your paper. Then there will be something in the distance—something much smaller to show that it is far away from you.

Decide what you need to paint first. It is a good idea to begin with the lightest part of your picture first and work toward the darkest part. That way you can sometimes paint right over the top of something else without having it show. Should it be on wet paper or dry paper? What colors will you use? Will there be more than one color on the brush at a time? You are really building a picture, so plan it carefully.

What will you paint? Well, you will each have to decide that for yourself. Perhaps it will be some place you have been and know very well. You may have especially liked one of the spots we visited today. Or you may want to make up an entirely new place. Just think of your paper as the picture you would see if you focused your camera and looked through it. But, remember, the camera would have to show every detail of the scene. It can't think and choose, but you can, so plan your picture.

Have all the necessary watercolor materials ready. You will need large white paper (at least 12" x 18"), a box of colors, paint brush, container of water, and newspaper for each child.

Thinking and Painting. Plan your picture so you will know just where to paint each part of it. Then begin to paint loosely and freely. Remember, no outlining–no drawing with paint. Just put the color on quickly and don't worry about it. Oh, I didn't say don't think about it! You have to do lots of thinking to arrange all the parts of your picture. That's what a camera can't do, isn't it! If you plan a good arrangement and blend your colors, you will have a pleasing picture. So hold the brush loosely, blend the colors, paint rapidly, and think–think–think.

Children need constant reassuring and reminding while they are painting with watercolor. So walk about the room complimenting one here about his beautifully blended colors, another one there about the pleasing grouping of objects. Urge one to make something larger to fill more space, urge another to overlap some part of his picture so it won't be just spots. Suggest that one child spread the paint more rapidly but that another relax and wait for an area to dry before he paints something touching it. Wet areas that touch run together, you know.

Put the finished pictures in a safe place to dry while painting materials are cleared away. When you come back to those paintings, you'll be surprised that they look so good. Don't expect perfection; watercolor is a difficult material to handle and it takes lots of practice to be an expert. But you have been striving mainly for a well-planned picture, so a compliment for a child's success in this effort will help him to be more successful in other ways the next time.

Let each child show his painting and tell about it if he wishes. You have to be right on the spot with a camera, but with a paint brush–well, you're always right on the spot, aren't you? These paintings prove it!

MAKE IT EASY–FOR YOURSELF!

1. You may want to spend all of one art lesson just looking and talking–and paint another day.
2. Cover all painting areas with newspaper.

Crashing Waters

In the City

3. Have the watercolor materials ready before the beginning of the lesson. You will need watercolor boxes, large watercolor brushes (wash brushes, if possible), individual water containers, white drawing paper, and facial tissue for wiping out boxes and water containers.

4. No pencils! Paint without sketching. After the children have learned to handle the paints freely, you may want to permit them to sketch the essential parts of their pictures with a light color paint. This permits better planning, of course, but to allow it at this time could easily result in detailed drawings that are filled with paint.
5. Encourage children to plan their pictures mentally. Changes can be made, of course, but the planning is the most important part of this lesson. A good plan is a good beginning.
6. Keep the pictures simple. Plan pleasing spaces rather than being concerned with details.
7. Encourage the children to stand while painting. It permits more freedom of motion. Hold the brush near the end of the handle to make it easier to use the brush lightly and loosely.
8. Clean up the easy way. Each child should wash his brush in his own container of water (even if it appears dirty) and then wipe it on his facial tissue. This draws out the dirty water. Empty the water containers in the sink or collect the water in a pail. Wipe the container at once with a tissue, and it will not need to be washed. Let each child fold his newspaper with the tissue inside. Select four children and have each child collect one of the supplies—boxes, brushes, water containers, newspapers.

2
Construction Paper

The Tall and the Short of It

Exaggerated People *(Suggested for all Grades 2 through 6)*

Objectives

1. To demonstrate that exaggeration may make a picture more interesting.
2. To encourage children to make pictures of people even though they are not completely realistic.
3. To use cut paper to create a fun picture.

Materials

18" x 24" white drawing paper, cut 9" x 24"
15" x 12" white drawing paper
9"x 12" and 12" x 18" colored construction paper
newspaper
paste
paste brushes

Overweight

Have you ever been so pleased with yourself that you felt nine feet tall? Or so embarrassed that you wanted to shrink out of sight? Probably so! Let's make some pictures which will show the tall and the short of it.

Imagining Ourselves Different. Ask your class if they remember the story of *Alice in Wonderland*. Help them recall the dream in which Alice would suddenly become very small when she needed to go through a short doorway, or would suddenly grow very tall when she needed to reach a high table.

Alice drank strange liquids or ate mysterious cookies and mushrooms to make herself grow tall or short, but we're just going to use our imaginations. Let's pretend we're made of rubber so that we can be stretched tall or pushed close together. So be a magician and change yourself to a rubber person.

Good! Is everyone a rubber person now? Well, if you are, pretend someone stretches you taller—and taller—and taller. Will you still be as fat as you are now when you are stretched way up there in the air? No, of course not! When the rubber "you" is stretched taller and taller, you have to get thinner and thinner, don't you? What would happen if you were squeezed down lower and lower? Certainly! The more you were squeezed down the shorter and wider you would get.

Show the class two pieces of paper—one a tall, thin one and one a short, fat one. Would you rather be a tall, thin person who fits this paper, or would you rather be a short, fat person who fits this paper? You may make whichever person you want, but remember, he must be stretched to fit the paper, or he must be pushed down to fit the paper.

Talk for a while about what the different parts of the body will look like. The head won't look like your head, will it? If it is a tall you, the head will have to be tall—and thin, too. It will be a tall, narrow oval. If it is a short you, the head will be a short—and wide—oval. Would the neck be different, too? Of course it would! It would be very long and narrow—or it would be very short and wide. What would the rest of the person be like? Why, either stretched or pushed together. A tall person would have a long, narrow body and long, long thin legs; even the feet would be short and pulled up tall. The body of a short person would be pushed down wide and short. The legs—and even the feet—would be very wide.

Making Exaggerations. Let the children talk and ask questions about their rubber people until they are in the mood for some real exaggeration. Then let them choose a tall paper or a short paper. While they choose colored paper to use to make their people, give each child a pair of scissors so that he can go to work immediately.

Some children are timid about exaggerating, about going to extremes, so you will have to continue to encourage them. Yes, that's going to be a short person—but also such a tiny person. Your paper is wide, so make your person short and wide, too. That's a fine head he has for a stretched-out person! It's so long and narrow. If it was turned the other way—so that it was short and wide—it would be a good head for your person, wouldn't it? That looks like the body for just an ordinary person. Doesn't your person need a tall, skinny body to fit the rest of him? Is your person getting too tall to fit on the short paper? Could you make part of it shorter and fatter? Just pretend she is rubber and you could push her down and out!

When the children have begun to let themselves go and are really making exaggerated people, give each one some paste so that he can complete his picture.

They are certainly the tallest people—and the shortest people—anyone ever saw. Even Alice in Wonderland couldn't have changed any more than your people have. You'll want to display them where everyone will enjoy them.

MAKE IT EASY—FOR YOURSELF!

1. For the tall people cut 18" x 24" white drawing paper in half so that it is 9" x 24". Cut paper about 15" x 12" for the short people, so that they will be wider than they are tall.

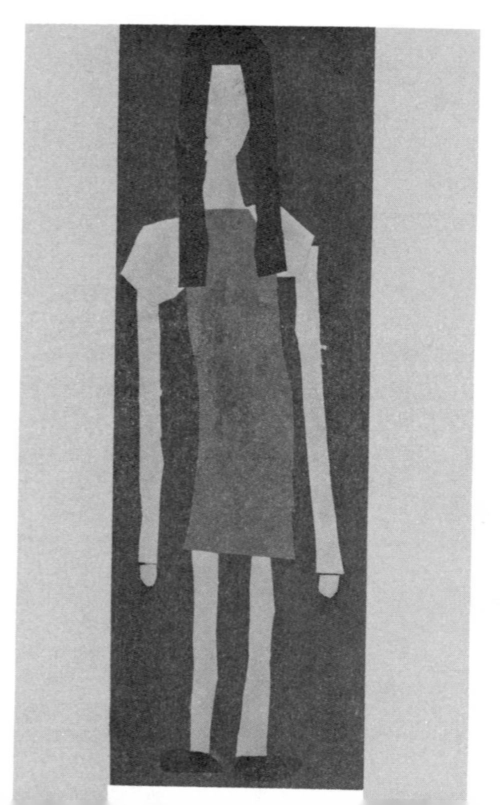

Extra Tall

2. Have a wide variety of 9" x 12" and 12" x 18" colored construction paper from which children may choose. Have a group at a time select two or three beginning colors. This way everyone will be able to begin his picture quickly, and then return for additional supplies as they are needed. Encourage children to share paper with their neighbors when they need only a little bit of a color.
3. No pencils! See a shape—then cut it without drawing.
4. Give each child half a page of newspaper to paste on so as to keep his picture clean. It can be folded in half so as to take less space on the desk, and when a clean area is needed it can be folded in reverse.
5. If paste brushes are not available, a satisfactory paste applicator can be made by folding a scrap of paper several times until it is a quarter- to a half-inch wide. Then bend it in the middle to give it added strength.
6. Let the children show their pictures at the end of the lesson before they are arranged in a display. Talk about the exaggeration that they show.
7. Before you display the pictures, trim them on the papercutter so that the pictures fit the background they are on. A short picture will look even shorter if extra paper at the top or bottom is cut off. If extra paper on the sides is trimmed off, a tall picture will look even taller.

A Little Shadow

Shadow Pictures *(Suggested for Grades 1 through 6)*

Objectives

1. To observe how light changes the shape of a shadow.
2. To experiment with changing the outline of a single object.
3. To observe the effect of light and shadow on a color.
4. To create a rhythmic and balanced picture by repeating a single motif.

Materials

6" x 9" oaktag
6" or 12" applicator sticks
tape
12" x 18" colored construction paper
pencils or crayons
scissors
paste and paste brushes
newspaper

I have a little shadow that goes in and out with me;
And what can be the use of him is more than I can see.

—Robert Louis Stevenson

Have you ever walked beneath a street light at night and discovered something new about yourself? Yes, you had a shadow that went right along with you. Did it always look just the same—just like you?

Shadows Change. Talk for a while about how shadows change. Sometimes they are in back of you and sometimes in front, depending upon where the light is. They can move from side to side, but they can do other things, too. They can even change shapes! Sometimes they are fatter than you are, and sometimes they are thinner. Sometimes they are taller than you are, and sometimes they are shorter.

Color of a Shadow. What color is a shadow? The children will almost certainly say that shadows are always black. Are you sure? Well, let's find out. Hold a piece of paper so that it casts a shadow on a light blue piece of paper. Is the shadow really black? No. It is blue—a darker blue, but still blue. Hold the paper so that it casts a shadow on a light green piece of paper. Is it black this time? No, not at all. It is ______? Right! It is green, but a darker green. Repeat the experiment several times, each time letting the shadow fall on a different colored piece of paper. Note that the shadow is always the same color as the rest of the paper, but it is a darker shade. The shadow just makes the paper—or whatever it touches—darker.

Instead of using a plain piece of paper to make shadows, let's change the paper into a picture of something real. What would you like to make? Yes, it could be a dog—or any kind of animal. Certainly, you could make a flower, a bird, a truck, an airplane, or anything else.

Make the Object. Cut out a simple object from a piece of 6" x 9" oaktag. Make it a fish, a butterfly, a person, or whatever you would like. Hold it so that it casts a shadow on a piece of paper. It would be easier to see the shadow if my hand didn't get in the way, wouldn't it? Well, that is easy to fix. We'll just make a handle for it.

Place a 6" or 12" applicator stick on the object so that it extends from the center out one side. Attach it to the oaktag with a couple of pieces of masking tape. There, that makes a fine handle.

Make Shadows. Let several children take turns holding the object so that it casts shadows on a piece of paper. That's right—turn the object so that the shadows change. See, you can make the shadows thinner or fatter than the shape you are holding. They can even be different lengths. But

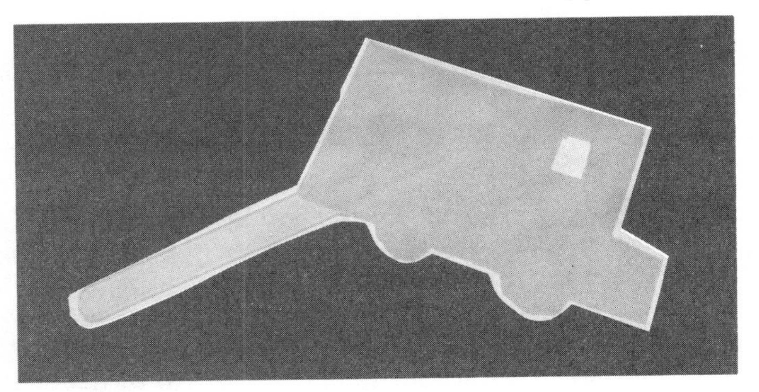

Truck

the color of the shadow is always the same—darker than the piece of paper.

Each time you make a new shadow the old one disappears. Perhaps we can do something about that, too. Take a piece of dark-colored paper and make shadows on it. With a pencil or crayon, draw a line around each shadow. Oh, you have to hold the shape very still while you draw so that the shadows don't change. Let several children outline shadows as they or other children hold the object. Try to make each shadow-shape different.

You didn't know one object could look so many ways, did you? But there they are, all these different shapes from this one thing.

Arrange Shadows. Could you make a picture with all of these? Certainly! All you have to do is cut them out and arrange them on another paper. You could move the shadows around until they looked just right, and then you could paste them to the background.

What color paper would you use for the background? Any color? Are you sure? No, of course, the background couldn't be just any color. It would have to be the ______? Right! The same color as the shadows, but a lighter shade. If you had red shadows you would put them on light red or pink paper. If you had dark purple shadows you would use a light purple paper for the background. That's right! Shadows are always the same color, but they are a darker shade of the color they are on.

Give each child a piece of oaktag and a pair of scissors. Think about your picture before you cut anything. Make it as large as you can on that size paper.

While the children are cutting their shapes, you will have time to give each child an applicator stick and a piece of tape. This will give you a chance to see what each child is doing as you walk about the room. Encourage the child who is hesitant, slow down the one who is working too rapidly, and assist in any way you are needed.

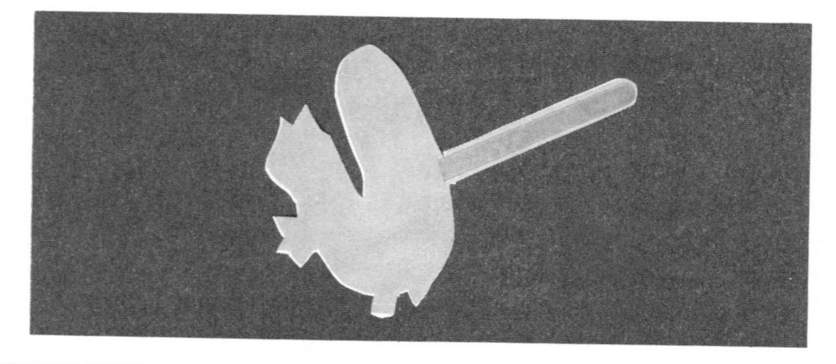

Squirrel

Find a Sunny Place. After a child has completed his object and has attached the handle, let him choose a dark-colored piece of paper for his shadows. Then have him find a sunny place in the room where he can work.

That's the way to do it! First, make the shadow look just like the object. Draw around it as carefully as you can. Then change the shadow so that it looks different from the one you have just made. See how many different kinds you can make. Have you tried tipping the object so that it casts a long skinny shadow? No, you can't let the shadows overlap because you are going to cut out each shadow separately. Oh, cut the shadows carefully. The edge of the cut-out shadow should be just as smooth as the edge of the object that made the shadow.

Plan Arrangement. Encourage each child to rearrange his cut-out shadows until they create a pleasing and rhythmic picture. Of course, the background they are put on will be a lighter shade of the same color as the shadows. Shadows are always a darker shade of the color they are on.

Yes, some of the shadows may go off the edge of the paper. Then, when your picture is finished, you can cut off the extra parts. But if you do that, remember to balance the picture by having something off all the edges. Good! Having your shadows move in different directions looks fine. It helps your eyes move easily from place to place, doesn't it! Are all the heavy or big parts of your picture on the same side? That makes that part of the picture too heavy. Yes, move them about until they balance better.

As soon as a child has a pleasing arrangement, let him paste each shadow to the background. Before long the room will be filled with shadows—lovely shadows, all kinds of shadows.

You all have little shadows that go in and out with you;
They change their shapes and colors—
and they help make pictures, too.

MAKE IT EASY—FOR YOURSELF!

1. You may want to read the poem "My Shadow" by Robert Louis Stevenson.
2. Have a variety of colored 12" x 18" paper, but be sure to have light and dark shades of each color: a light shade for the background and a darker shade of the same color for the shadow.
3. You may like to go outdoors to draw the shadows. Return to the classroom to cut out the shadows and arrange them on the background.
4. Have each child put his oaktag scraps in the wastebasket before he gets his colored shadow paper. This will give him more work space at his desk and will make the final cleanup easier.

5. As the children cut out the shadows, walk about the room collecting their scraps of paper. Hold a piece of 12" x 18" paper as a tray and let each child pile his flat pieces of paper on top of it. This will give each child more work space and will make the cleanup easier.
6. Give each child 3 or 4 inches of masking tape. Attach it to the side of the desk so that it will hang free and not fold over on itself or become attached to scraps of paper. This will be enough to cut in two for attaching the applicator stick to the object.
7. If applicator sticks are not available, have each child bring in a tree branch about 8 to 10 inches long.
8. Teach children to do all their pasting on a piece of newspaper to keep their work areas and their pictures clean.

Day Dreams

When-I-Grow-Up Pictures *(Suggested for Kindergarten through Grade 4)*

Objectives

1. To provide an opportunity for a child to express a personal desire.
2. To help a child express a complete idea in visual form.
3. To stress the idea of making the most important thing the biggest.
4. To encourage children to put people in their pictures.

Materials

12" x 18" white or manila drawing paper
9" x 12" colored construction paper
scissors
paste and paste brushes
newspaper

Everyone likes to daydream! Maybe it's just a little dream about buying a new pair of shoes you saw displayed in a store window—or maybe it's a giant dream about exploring on the moon. But whatever it is, it's a wonderful way of living in the future. Only good things happen in daydreams.

Do you ever daydream? Of course you do! Everyone does! What are some of the things you daydream about? You will get a variety of answers. One child may daydream about a party she is going to after school; another child will daydream about playing baseball. Others will daydream about exploring space, flying a jet, or being a dancer or truck driver or mountain climber—or anything else that young minds can imagine.

Good Daydreams. Most daydreams will have two things in common: they will be happening in the future and they will be about something the child wants to do. Those are good daydreams! Daydreams are always good, aren't they?

Suggest to the children that they daydream about what they would like to be when they grow up. You want to be a baseball player. Would you enjoy playing in a big stadium with thousands of people watching? You want to be an explorer and discover all kinds of new things about space. Would you be all alone or would another explorer be with you? You wouldn't look the way you do now. What kind of clothes would you wear?

Talk for a few minutes more about other things the children would like to do when they grow up. Each time, make comments and ask questions which will focus the child's thinking on something visual. What will you be wearing? Who will be with you? Will the airplane look like the kind we see now? How will it be different? Where will you be?

I am an electrician repairing the wires. The door of my truck is open.

Concentrate on Action. Concentrate, too, on the action involved in the daydream. Nurses are busy people. What will you do when you are a nurse? Do truck drivers do anything besides just sit in the truck and drive? Oh, yes, sometimes they do other things. Perhaps you can show that. Have you ever watched a waitress carry a huge tray filled with dishes? She carries it above her shoulders, doesn't she?

Be sure you give many children a chance to talk. Encourage the quiet child to express an opinion. Many ideas described will help children visualize their own personal daydreams.

Let groups of children take turns selecting paper from an assortment of 9" x 12" colored construction paper. A pair of scissors will be the only other thing they will need immediately. Later you may give them pieces of 12" x 18" white or manila drawing paper for the background of their pictures.

As you walk about the room, remind them to make themselves first. You are the important part of this daydream–you as a circus performer or mountain climber, a fireman or engineer, a dancer or pilot. So make yourself big and important. Show us what you will be doing. There will still be plenty of space for other people or things around you. Oh, you are so small! You are no bigger than a bug! Perhaps you can make that one of the other less important people in your daydream. Make another "you" much bigger. Good! I think I can tell what you will be doing when you are a doctor. I will want to see that again when you have more done. What do you think you will see on the moon when you explore it?

Tell About Pictures. Children will be eager to show their pictures, so have a quick showing at the end of the lesson. Let each child have an opportunity to tell something about his picture–the title, perhaps, or some added information that the picture doesn't show. Encourage the rest of the class to comment about the unusual things, the unique way a child has found to express an idea, the pleasing arrangements. Be sure the discussion is always constructive so that each child feels the value of his work.

Plan to display each picture. If they can not all be exhibited at the same time, arrange one area that is easy for you to change often. But be sure that within a short time all the pictures have been put on display. The child needs to know that you value his work. This will give him more confidence in himself and will be an incentive for even more effort another time.

Daydreams are fun–whether you are thinking about them, making them, or looking at them! The ones on display will be wonderful ones, and they will prove that only good things happen in daydreams.

MAKE IT EASY–FOR YOURSELF!

1. Have the 9" x 12" colored construction paper arranged in two areas of the room, and assign half the class to each area. This will speed up the beginning of the lesson and prevent crowding at either area during the lesson. Let groups of children select only two or three beginning colors so that everyone will be able to get started quickly. Let them return for

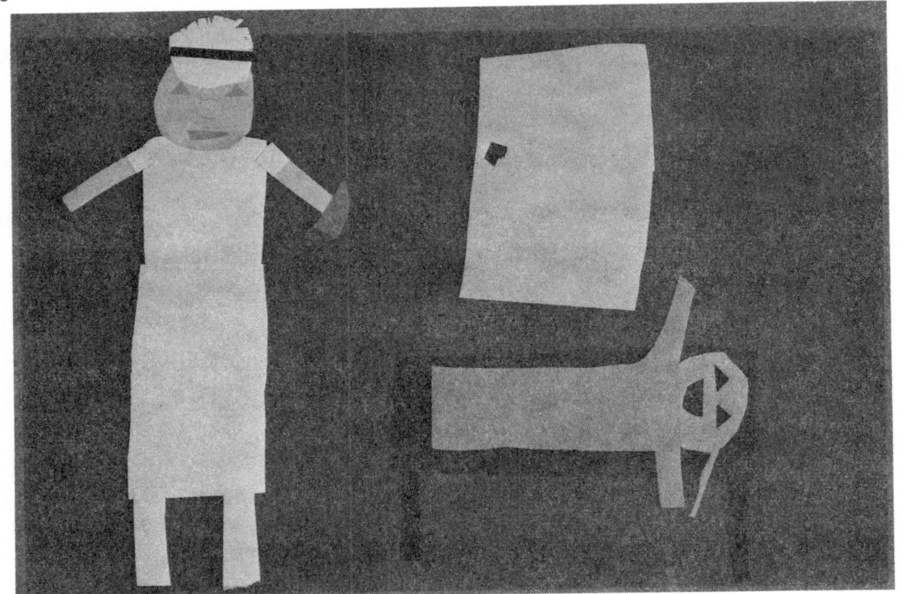

I will be a nurse.

more colors as needed, or let them exchange small pieces with their neighbors.

2. It is a good plan to keep a box of large scraps of colored paper which can be used when a full sheet is not needed. Just spread them out on a table or counter during the lesson and return them to the box when supplies are put away.
3. Do not give out paste too soon. If children have it at the beginning of the lesson, they are apt to paste each thing as soon as it is cut. Instead, encourage them to move things about until the most satisfactory arrangement is made. When things are pasted too soon, little thinking is done. You can distribute paste during the course of the lesson by giving each child a little of it on a scrap of paper.
4. If paste brushes are not available, a satisfactory paste applicator can be made by folding a scrap of paper several times until it is a narrow strip (a quarter- to a half-inch wide). Then bend it lengthwise in the middle to give it added strength. Try to keep children's fingers out of the paste. Sticky fingers are a handicap to good work. Children who are used to working this way may be satisfied to continue to use their fingers, but encourage them to use a brush or paper applicator instead.
5. Give each child a half-sheet of newspaper for his pasting. The paper may be folded in half to take less work space; and, when a clean area is needed, the paper can be folded in reverse.
6. Several times during the course of the lesson, walk about the room and collect the scraps of paper that are to be thrown away. Keep them flat and it will be easy for each child to add them to the pile you have. This

will give the children more work space on their desks and make the final cleanup easier.

7. Clean up the easy way. As soon as a child finishes his picture, have him put his scissors in a designated place; put extra paste, if any, back in the jar; put paste brushes (if used) on the sink counter to be cleaned later; lay all scraps of paper on the newspaper and put them all in the wastebasket.

Wiggle, Wobble, Slide

Cut Paper Pictures *(Suggested for Grades 2 through 6)*

Objectives

1. To use a familiar material in a creative way.
2. To discover ways of making things move in a picture.
3. To experiment with paper to express a meaningful idea.

Materials

9" x 12" and 12" x 18" white and colored construction paper	newspaper
paste and paste brushes	scissors

Pictures aren't real things so they can't move. Of course not! But wait a minute! Did you see one wiggle . . . and wobble . . . and slide?

Have you ever made a picture with an animal in it? Sure you have! Maybe you made a horse running—except he was stuck to the paper and couldn't run at all! Or perhaps you made a picture of yourself taking your pet dog for a walk. But both of you were stuck to the paper and neither one of you could move! Have you ever made a picture with something in it that really did move right across the picture?

Move on the Ground. What are some ways that real things move? Yes, they can walk or run—or jump or crawl or hop—just the way you do when you move about. Animals and people—things that live on land—move about that way, don't they? I can think of some other things you would find on land, but they don't walk or hop or skip—or even crawl—the way you do. Right! An automobile moves about. You might want to have an automobile move in your picture. Other similar things will be suggested: bicycles, motorcycles, roller skates, baby carriages, trucks, buses, trains.

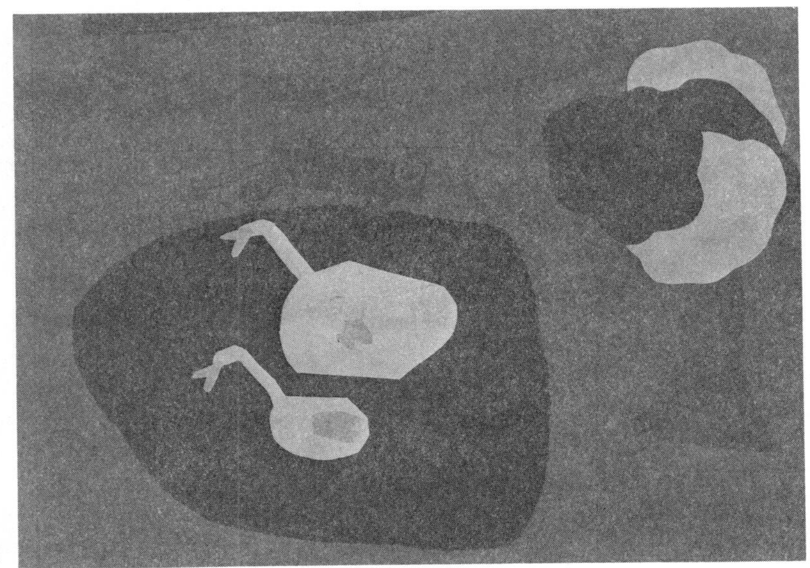

Duck Pond

This diagram was used with the illustration.

In the Air. Well, no, a helicopter doesn't move about much on the ground, but it does move about in the air. What are some other things that fly through the air? Yes—airplanes, gliders, rockets. What living things fly? Birds, butterflies, bugs, bats, flies, mosquitoes.

Through the Water. Those are all things that move about in the air or on the ground, but some things move about in the______. Of course! There are things that move through the water. What? Fish, turtles, frogs, tadpoles, lobsters, crabs. Ships, canoes, rafts, submarines, sailboats. Yes! Even people. People can walk on the ground and they can swim in the water.

In More Than One Place. Talk for a minute more about things that can live in either water or on the ground. People, turtles, frogs, ducks. Have the children think of things that can move about on the ground and fly through the air. Birds, bugs, ants, airplanes. Are there things that can fly and also swim? Ducks, seagulls, seaplanes.

Encourage children to think and to take part in the discussion. Try to get them to think of original ideas. Have them suggest other things that might be in their pictures. Could you show that the turtle lives both on land and in the water? Stress the idea of motion in the picture.

Remind the class again that the pictures they make this time will have something in them that really moves—from one part to another part. How can you do that? Someone will probably suggest pasting only part of the object to the paper so that the rest of it is loose and wiggles. Yes, that would be fine for a flower that sways in the breeze—or to show that the leaves really do move when the wind blows. But if you paste any part of your object, it won't be able to move across the paper.

How They Can Move. Can you think of some other way of making a part of your picture move? How could you make a bird fly from there to there? As you talk, draw a line across the blackboard. Or how could you make a fish swim from there to there? Draw another line on the blackboard that curves once or twice. That's right—no part of the thing that is going to move can be pasted to the paper. As you move your hand back and forth across the lines someone will probably see that you are giving them a clue. Yes! You could cut that line in your paper instead of just having it drawn on. Suppose it was a line through the sky. How could you make a bird fly across it? Certainly! All you would have to do would be paste a strip of paper on the back of your bird, insert it through the cut line, and you could move him easily along the line. The strip you pasted on the back would be a handle for you to hold as you moved your bird. *"Duck Pond"* uses this technique.

Suppose you want to make something like a car that will move in a straight line all the way from one side of your picture to the other. What will happen if you cut such a long line? Right! Your picture will fall apart. Encourage the children to think of another way they can make a part of their pictures move. What do you have at home that can slide back and forth in a straight line and never fall off that straight line? What about something like a curtain? You can paste a flat loop—like a curtain ring—on the back of the thing you want to move across your picture. Then take a long strip of paper—this would act like a curtain rod—thread it through the ring, and paste each end to your picture. Now you can move your car—or man, or whatever you want to make—back and forth on your picture, without even cutting the background! Be sure to have the children make the "curtain rod" the same color as the background so that it will not be noticed. *"Motorcycle Ride"* uses this technique.

More Than One. This will probably be a new idea to the children, and they will have lots of ideas—and questions, too! Certainly you can have more than one thing that moves in your picture. But be sure you don't cut so many lines—or such long ones—that your picture falls apart. If you want to make a very long line, make a "curtain rod." Yes, you could have just one thing that moves across a line and something else that just wiggles in one place. Yes, you may make the background first if you like, or you may want to make the thing that moves first. Do it whichever way you like.

Give each child a pair of scissors, and let groups of children take turns selecting beginning materials. This will get them started quickly. Later you can give them paste, paste brushes, and newspaper.

Hm-m. Looks like something is going to dive from the sky right down into the water. I wonder if it is going to be a seagull. That's a fine turtle. Have you decided where he is going to be—and where he will move? Oh, but your automobile is so tiny no one will see it! Could you paste it somewhere in the distance—where it would look small—and make a large, more important car to move down the street? Of course things can overlap in your picture. As your horse runs he may overlap other horses as he moves. Is he going to win the race? Looks as though your rocket is moving through space. It must be on its way to the moon!

Motorcycle Ride

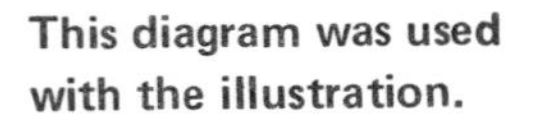

This diagram was used with the illustration.

Time to Experiment. Continue to help children as you move about the room. Question, comment, and suggest. Compliment one child for his original idea, help a second one to solve some problem of movement, encourage another to express his own idea. It will be a time of experimentation, so show a new idea to the class as it develops. It will encourage other children to be original, and at the same time it will recognize that particular child.

It will be a busy time as each child concentrates on his own picture. Finally it will be time to show all the pictures to the class. Each child will want to demonstrate how parts of his picture move. You may even have to hold a picture while the child uses both hands to show how two things can move at the same time.

Usually you want children to keep their hands off other children's work, but this time it will be important that they touch the pictures and move them. So display all the pictures within easy reach. One day the turtle is on a rock; the next day he has slid into the water. One day the bird is sitting on the tree branch; the next day he is flying through the sky. One day you are walking your dog in front of your house; the next day you are both way down in the next block. It's fun to change a picture—to make something in it wiggle or wobble or slide!

MAKE IT EASY—FOR YOURSELF!

1. Have several colors of 12" x 18" construction paper for the backgrounds and a variety of colored 9" x 12" construction paper for the rest of the pictures. Let each child select a background color and a couple of smaller pieces. When they need additional colors, urge them to share leftover pieces with other children—or, if necessary, return to the supply area.
2. Don't be in a hurry to give out paste. See that children have a good start first. This will encourage them to move the parts about and rearrange them before pasting them in place. This gives you time to assist and make suggestions.
3. To keep his picture and his work area clean, give each child half a newspaper page to do his pasting on. The newspaper may be folded in half to take less space on the desk; then, when a clean area is needed, it can be folded in reverse.
4. Encourage children to keep their fingers out of the paste. If paste brushes are not available, a satisfactory paste applicator can be made by folding a scrap of paper several times until it is a narrow strip. Then bend it lengthwise in the middle to give it added strength.
5. If too long a line is cut through the background, it may tend to spread apart when the picture is picked up. This can be corrected by pasting a

paper bridge across the back to hold the two parts together or by using the "curtain rod" technique.

6. If the movable parts tend to fall out of the picture, they need a longer piece of paper pasted on the back of them. Or paste a strip of paper pointed upward and another one pointed downward. This will hold the movable part firmly on the cut line, but will permit it to move easily.

It Was in the Paper

Collage with a Theme *(Suggested for Grades 3 through 6)*

Objectives

1. To experiment with collage as a form of art.
2. To become aware of the possibility of using realistic and abstract forms in the same picture.
3. To develop the ability to organize a rhythmic and balanced picture.

Materials

newspaper
12" x 18" white and colored construction paper
scissors
paste and paste brushes

Just because it was in the paper doesn't mean it has to stay there. Put it in your picture instead.

Let's play a word game for a few minutes. I will name one thing and you name three other things that seem to belong with it. For example, if I say "automobile," you might say ______? There will be such suggestions as *tire, stop sign, people, gasoline, garage.* Good! Let's try it again. "House": chairs, stove, people, curtains, lamp, fireplace. "Tree": birds, leaves, bugs, branches, swing, squirrels.

Keep Them a Secret. Then ask each child to think of something else—and to think of three other things that he associates with it. No, don't tell anyone what they are. Keep them your secret to put in your picture.

Have your class gather around you at a table. Let's see—I think I'll make a picture using the tree we talked about. This picture will be a collage—a picture made by pasting different kinds of things together.

Some of the things will be real and some will be just shapes and colors. First, let's choose a background paper to paste the parts of the collage to. Then we'll begin with a big picture of a tree cut from newspaper. Yes, newspaper is often used in a collage. Cut a tree that is about half as large as the piece of 12" x 18" paper that will be the background. Lay the tree on the paper.

Pleasing Arrangement. Should the tree be placed in the center of the picture, like that? No, it will make a much more pleasing space arrangement if it is a little off center so that both sides of it are not the same. Yes, it will be a good idea to make a vertical picture because the tree is taller than it is wide.

While we are talking about pleasing space arrangements, let's do something else to make the background space more interesting. Ask one child to select another color of construction paper that will make a good contrast with the background paper. Fine! A bright color makes a pleasing contrast with the dark paper.

This color is to help make the background more pleasing, so it will have to be cut into smaller pieces. Should both pieces be the same size? No, of course not! It will be more pleasing to have a variety of sizes. That is what will make the collage interesting. Cut one paper into a long piece about twelve inches long and five inches wide. There—that's a large one, so I'll make the other piece smaller—shorter and a little narrower, too.

Make a pleasing color and space arrangement with the two pieces of paper on top of the background color. Then lay the newspaper tree on top of them so that it overlaps part of each piece.

Three Other Things. That looks good so far, but there are three other things that belong in the picture—three things you think of with a tree. This is a summertime tree with all the branches covered, so perhaps it would be a good idea to show a branch as one of the three things. All right—if you would like, we will also include some leaves and a bird.

As you talk, cut a branch which divides into several smaller branches from a piece of the construction paper you have. There will be plenty of paper left from the pieces you used to cut the background shapes. Lay the branch on a part of the background where there is a contrasting color. See—it helps to move that color over to this part of the picture.

Now for a few leaves. Choose at least one new color for some of them. Find an empty area and group them together.

Complete Arrangement. Where would be a good place for a bird? Yes, he might go on the branch. Yes, he could be cut to fit that small empty space—or he might overlap the tree. Well, if this were your picture you would have to decide where you thought he would look best, and then you would have to decide what color to use. And then, last of all, after you were satisfied with your arrangement you would paste everything in place.

Select Materials. Let groups of children take turns selecting two colors of construction paper while you give out scissors and a piece of newspaper.

Yes, cut the newspaper picture first—the part of your picture that tells what the collage is about. Then plan the background areas of your picture. Those colors will make good contrasts in your collage. That's an excellent newspaper frog. I wonder what three things you will put with it. Don't you think that airplane is much too small to be the most important part of the collage? Yes, make a larger one—a much larger one! Oh, but you can cut smoother lines than that! Good! Fish, waves, and sun go fine with your tall, graceful sailboat. Certainly it's all right to have the sun another color besides yellow. This isn't a realistic picture. But haven't you ever seen the sun when it didn't look yellow? What would happen if you turned your small horse in the other direction? Yes, that is better, isn't it! Now he looks as though he is running into your collage instead of out of it—and so your eye goes into your collage too, instead of out of it. You are ready to paste your collage, aren't you?

Feel Successful. Continue to help each child as you walk about the room. Some children will need only an appreciative comment from you. Others will require more attention. Compliment, encourage, assist in whatever way is needed to make each child feel successful.

When all the collages are finished, have a quick showing. Let each child tell whatever he would like about his picture. Use the occasion to point out unusual ideas and particularly good ways of arranging them. Make the sharing period a part of the teaching time.

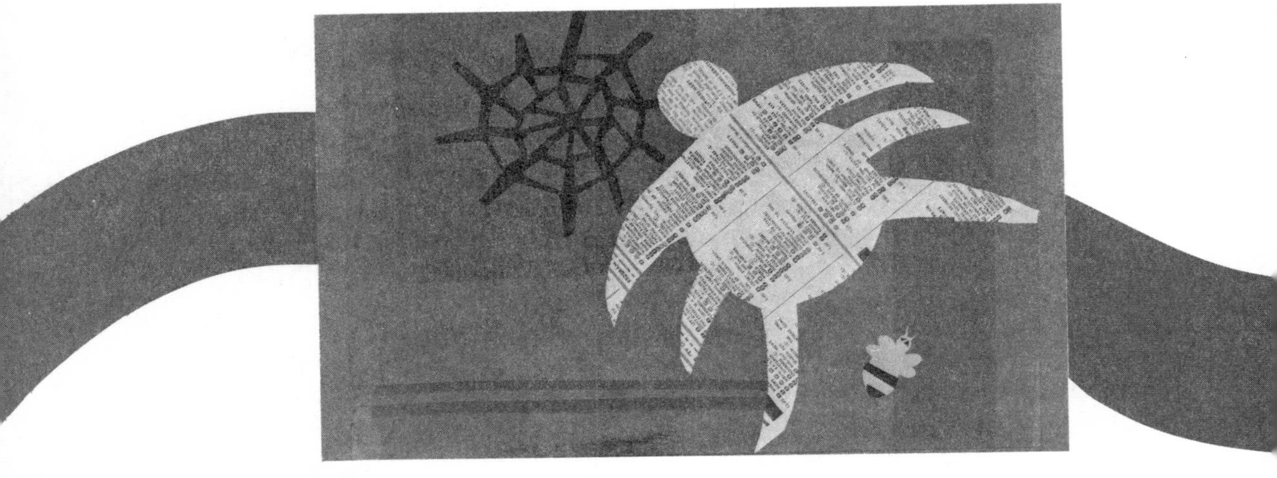

Come into My Web

Oceans Are for Everything

There will be newspaper in every picture, but you won't want to read any of them. You'll be too busy looking at and enjoying each collage.

MAKE IT EASY–FOR YOURSELF!

1. The classified ad section of the newspaper is particularly good for this lesson. It creates the effect of a textured material. You may want to substitute wallpaper–or have some to use in addition to newspaper.
2. No pencils! Encourage children to think of and to visualize their objects and then to cut them without any previous drawing. Pencils result in tight, rigid pictures with distracting lines on them.
3. If additional colors are needed for small parts, let children share their colored paper with one another.
4. Don't give out paste too soon. Encourage the children to arrange and rearrange their pictures before they paste them. If they have paste at the beginning of the lesson they will paste each part as soon as it is cut.
5. If paste brushes are not available, satisfactory paste applicators may be made by folding a scrap of paper several times until it is about a half-inch wide. Then bend it in half to give it added strength.
6. Always teach children to do their pasting on a piece of newspaper in order to keep their pictures and their work areas clean. A half-page of newspaper can be folded in half so that it takes little space, and, when a clean surface is needed, it can be reverse folded.
7. Encourage children to give titles to their pictures. An original title often can make an excellent picture out of what had been only an ordinary one.

A Purple Elephant?

Cut Paper Animals (*Suggested for Grades 1 through 4*)

Elephant

Objectives

1. To encourage children to think of the characteristics that make a particular animal recognizable.
2. To demonstrate the value of both realism and non-realism in the same picture.
3. To introduce a simple way of creating a three-dimensional mural.

Materials

colored construction paper
newspaper
paste and paste brushes
scissors
tape
6" applicator sticks
Styrofoam

Don't look now—but there's a purple elephant in back of you!

Have you ever seen a green giraffe? No? Well, have you ever seen a purple elephant? No? Are you sure? Have you ever seen a polka-dotted camel? A plaid monkey? A striped bear? Well, you're going to see all of those things today, because we're going to make them!

Recognize Animals. Talk for a while about what makes different animals recognizable. How would you know it was an elephant even though it was purple? Certainly! The long trunk and big ears would tell you. What kind of a tail does an elephant have? Right! Just a little one—hardly any at all. What makes a camel look like a camel? Of course! It has a big hump on its back—or sometimes two humps. You would recognize him even if he were red with black polka dots, wouldn't you!

What other animals would you find in a zoo? Fish? They have to live in water. Let's just make animals that can live on land. Talk about the characteristics of the animals that are mentioned: lion, zebra, seal, rhino, kangaroo, turtle, monkey.

Perhaps you can think of another animal you might find in a zoo. Think of how you could recognize him, even if he was a strange color—or perhaps striped or checked or polka-dotted or plaid—or even flowered.

No Realistic Colors. Show the children the colored paper that is available. No, there isn't any tan or gray or brown. They would be too much like the real colors of those animals. This time make them strange colors with strange designs on them.

Let groups of children take turns selecting one or two colors of paper to begin. Give them scissors and have them begin their animals right away. Yes, you can cut your animal all in one piece if you like, or you may want to make each part separately and paste them together. Do it whatever way will be easiest for you. Certainly, you may have more than two colors! You may need three or four or five colors. Look around to see who has the color you need, and ask that person if you may share his paper.

As the children work, walk about the room helping wherever you are needed. Encourage the child who is slow to start. What animal do you know a lot about? Can you close your eyes and see a camel—or a giraffe—or a monkey? Compliment the child who is original. Good! That looks just like a hippopotamus even if it is green. What are you going to add to it to make it a strange hippopotamus? Oh, I can tell what that is easily enough! The big mane around his head says that he is a lion even though he has yellow spots on his purple body. Help the child who is having trouble visualizing details. Does the trunk of an elephant stick out in a straight line, or does it grow from his head? Right! It starts the same size as his head, then grows narrower and longer. And it goes all the way to the ground. Yes, make it longer and wider at the head.

At the same time that you are walking about the room to help, give each child a little paste on a scrap of paper, a paste brush, and a piece of newspaper to do his pasting on.

Not Finished Yet. When the first animal has been finished, ask the class to stop work. Show the finished animal to the rest of the class. But it isn't finished yet. Oh, yes, it looks finished, but it can't stand up by itself—and an animal isn't much good if it can't stand. But we'll fix that. We'll give him a bone to make him strong. You couldn't stand either if you didn't have any bones! Take a 6" applicator stick and place it in back of one leg so that almost an inch of the stick extends below the foot. If any of the stick extends beyond the top of the animal, break it off. Then place one piece of tape over the stick near the top and another piece near the bottom.

There, that will make a bone through the animal so that he can stand up straight. Now we'll put him in the zoo. Push the stick down into the sheet of Styrofoam so that the animal's foot rests on the surface of the Styrofoam. When your animals are finished, you may bring them to the zoo and find a good place for them. Put the larger animals near the back and the smaller ones near the front so that all of them will show.

While the children continue their work, give each one a stick and a piece of tape about two inches long. Attach the tape to each desk so that it will remain in usable condition.

Hippo

Fill the Zoo. Gradually the zoo will be filled with more and more animals until all of them are there. Then take time to look at each one. Let the class gather around the display. Have one child find an animal that he is sure he can identify even though it may be orange with black zig-zag lines. Ask who made it. Is he right–is it a camel? Good! Let someone else identify another animal, and so on until each one has been named. The child who made each animal will be proud as it is identified–and there will be little doubt about most of them.

Of course there's a purple elephant–with yellow stripes! Why not? There's a red camel, too, and there's a blue monkey, and a polka-dotted hippopotamus, and a plaid bear.

MAKE IT EASY–FOR YOURSELF!

1. Construction paper cut to 6" x 9" will be large enough for these animals. Provide only bright colors and black. Eliminate any browns or grays in order to encourage children to use non-realistic colors.

Lion

2. No pencils! Think of the shape and then cut it without any preliminary drawing.
3. If paste brushes are not available, a satisfactory paste applicator can be made by folding a scrap of paper several times until it is a narrow strip. Then bend it lengthwise in the middle to give it added strength.
4. Teach children to do their pasting on a piece of newspaper to keep the pictures and their work areas clean.
5. Larger animals may require two sticks to hold the legs in place. Taller animals may need two sticks overlapped and extending into the long neck. Or 12" applicator sticks may be used.
6. Styrofoam that is 18" x 24" x 1" makes the best base. If this is not available, several smaller pieces can be used. Or small mounds of non-hardening clay can be substituted to hold the sticks upright.

The Zoo

Three-Dimensional Animals *(Suggested for Grades 2 through 6)*

Objectives

1. To use paper as a three-dimensional medium.
2. To experiment with ways of making paper three-dimensional.
3. To stimulate imagination and inventiveness.

Materials

9" x 12" white and colored construction paper
scissors
paste and paste brushes
newspaper

Remember when you used to go to the zoo? It was a favorite place, wasn't it? It would be fun to go there again, but if that is impossible, then bring the zoo to your classroom.

Ask the children in your class how many of them have ever been to a zoo. Well, if you haven't been to a real zoo, you may have seen one on television. Or certainly you have seen pictures of the animals at a zoo. Which is your favorite?

Favorites. There will be all kinds of answers. Elephants and giraffes are always favorites. But then, too, so are bears and monkeys. Almost every animal will appeal to some child. Talk for a few minutes about the appearance of each animal—the long legs and long neck of the giraffe; the squirrel's bushy tail; the camel's hump—or even two of them; the elephant's long trunk that he can swing over his head; the kangeroo's strong hind legs.

It would be nice to be able to go to a zoo to see all those animals, but as long as we can't do that, let's bring the animals here and make our own zoo. There's just one problem; all the animals have to be able to stand up by themselves. No, they won't be pictures; they will be three-dimensional animals.

What You Can Do with Paper. What can you do to a flat piece of paper to make it three-dimensional so that it can stand up by itself? Yes, you can curve it and fasten the two ends together to make a cylinder. See, now the paper is made into a shape that has thickness; it is three-dimensional. What else could you do to change the two-dimensional paper into a three-dimensional shape? Continue to get children to suggest ways of changing the paper. It can be done in three basic ways: curving, folding, crumpling. Get the children to think of as many variations of these as they can. Yes, you can run the paper over the blade of a pair of scissors. That will curl the paper. Or perhaps you would rather curl it around a pencil. Did you ever try cutting a line into the center of a paper and then overlapping the edges? That mounds the paper up into a hill.

Talk about the many ways of folding paper: into hinges; into box-like shapes; into reverse pleats; folding two strips of paper over and over each other into a spring-like object. Even crumpling can be done in different ways. The crumpled paper can be left as a ball, or it can be opened again into an almost flat, bumpy paper.

Porcupine

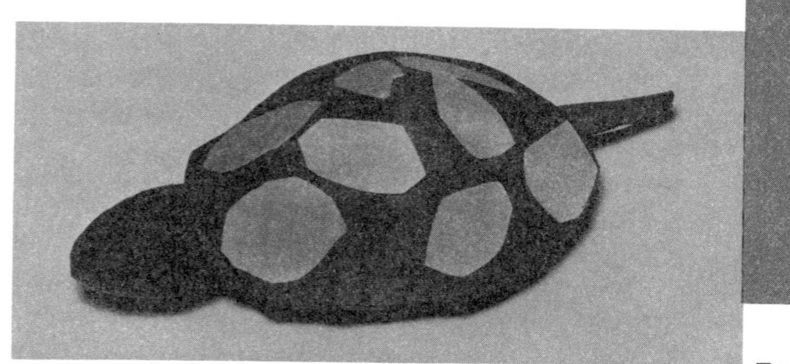

Turtle

Strong Enough to Stand. When you make your animal you may even be able to think of a new way of changing a flat piece of paper into a three-dimensional shape. Decide what kind of an animal you would like to make, and then choose your paper. No, the animal you make doesn't have to be the color the real animal would be. He has to be strong enough to stand, but he may be any color you like. You may have a red elephant, if you like.

Do you think you may be making the body too large? A huge piece of paper will be weaker than a smaller one, you know. No, you don't want it too tiny, either! Let the feel of the paper tell you how big is just right. That could be the body of almost any animal, couldn't it? I will have to come back to see it again before I can tell what it is going to be. Oops! Isn't one leg longer than the others? An animal with one long leg would have a hard time standing, wouldn't he! Yes, he would do just what that one does! Good! I know exactly what he is going to be.

Continue to encourage children to experiment, and compliment them when they do something original. Assist a child who has some special problem and question another child to help him think more creatively.

Make a Zoo. Have a table or counter space where the finished animals can be displayed. As each child finishes his animal, let him include it in the zoo. When all the animals are on display, have the children gather around them. Call attention to the different ways several similar animals have been made. Perhaps there will be three or four elephants, but each one will be made differently. The body of one may be a cylinder, another a crumpled ball, another a folded piece of paper. Observe the one-of-a-kind animals: the porcupine with pointed quills over its body; the mouse with tiny ears and long tail. Notice the inventiveness of some children: the turtle whose head pulls under its shell when you pull out the tail; the monkey whose coiled tail lets him hang from your finger.

Who needs to go to the zoo! Why, there's one right in the room!

MAKE IT EASY—FOR YOURSELF!

1. No pencils! No preliminary drawing. Don't add any details with pencil or crayon. If the parts are too small to cut from paper, they are too small to show.
2. If the children do not know the meaning of three-dimensional, explain it. Flat paper has two directions (or dimensions): width and length. A three-dimensional object is like a pile of papers: it has another direction—depth or thickness.
3. The animal must be balanced and sturdy enough to stand alone.
4. Let groups of children take turns selecting only one or two papers. This will get everyone started quickly. Then let anyone return to the supply area whenever he needs more paper. Small pieces may be shared with nearby children who have the needed colors.
5. Each child should have a little bit of paste on a piece of scrap paper. He will also need a piece of newspaper to do his pasting on. This will keep his work area clean and result in better work.
6. You may find it useful to also have available a stapler and a roll of masking tape to help with unusual problems.
7. If paste brushes are not available, satisfactory paste applicators may be made by folding scraps of paper several times until they are narrow strips. Then bend them in the middle to give them added strength.
8. Make the final cleanup easy. Have each child pile all his scraps of paper *flat* on his newspaper. Collect them by piling one on another as you walk about the room—or let several children collect them. Collect the scissors, and the cleanup will be finished.

Make It Strong

Strip Sculptures *(Suggested for Grades 3 through 6)*

Objectives

1. To use a two-dimensional material to create a three-dimensional picture.
2. To provide opportunity to experiment with changing the form of a material.
3. To "build" a picture by adding parts to it.

Materials

12" x 18" white and colored construction paper
scissors
paste and paste brushes
newspaper

Yes, spinach may help make you strong. Vitamins may help, too. But they won't do a bit of good for a piece of paper. What can you do to make it strong?

Three-Dimensional Things. Have your class gather around you at a large table or desk. Hold up a narrow strip of paper about an inch wide and eighteen inches long. It is weak, isn't it! It just flops over; it won't stand up straight by itself. Can you think of any way of making this strip stronger so it will stay up straight? Someone will probably suggest pasting a piece of cardboard to it. Yes, that would certainly be strong, but you would have to use something besides a strip of paper to do it. Try to think of some ways of making just strips of paper stronger without having to use anything else.

Someone will almost certainly say to paste two strips together. Yes, that might help some, but see, when I hold two pieces together they still bend over. Is there some way you could make this strip of paper three-dimensional? Three-dimensional things are usually stronger than two-dimensional things.

Several children will have ideas, so hand the strip to one of them. He may fold it through the middle the length of the strip. Well, hold it up and let's see if it is strong. Good! It stays up straight all by itself. You have made it stronger. Another child may fold it one or more times in the other direction. Yes, that keeps its shape better, so you have made it stronger in a different way. Lay the square or triangle or zigzag—or whatever the shape is—flat on the table. See, it will stand up on its side now. It wouldn't do that before.

What else can you do with paper to change its shape besides folding it? Remember—it has to stay a strip. No shapes can be cut from it. This will remind children that they can curl it. Of course—you can round it as well as keep it in straight lines. Let someone bring the two ends together to make a circle. That could stand up tall on the table, or it could lie on its side. Either way it will be strong enough to keep its shape and to stand by itself.

Create a Real Object. Explain to the class that they are going to use strips to create a real object that is strong enough—and steady enough—to support itself. Oh, no, you won't paste it to a base to support it. If you make a person, he must stand on his own feet. If you make a truck, the wheels must hold it steady. If you make a dog, he may be sitting down or standing—but if he is lying down he isn't very strong. He might even be dead. So don't make something that has to lie down. Yes, you can cut the strips any length or width you want, but everything must be a strip when you use it.

Let the children take turns selecting several beginning strips of paper. Give each child a pair of scissors, a bit of paste, a paste brush, and a small piece of newspaper to use for pasting. Encourage them to make the base of their objects first—out of strips, that is. Be sure that the feet or the wheels or whatever your object will stand on are large enough and strong enough to support the rest of the object.

Yes, your objects may be any sizes you would like them to be. But which do you think will be stronger—a great big object made of strips or a

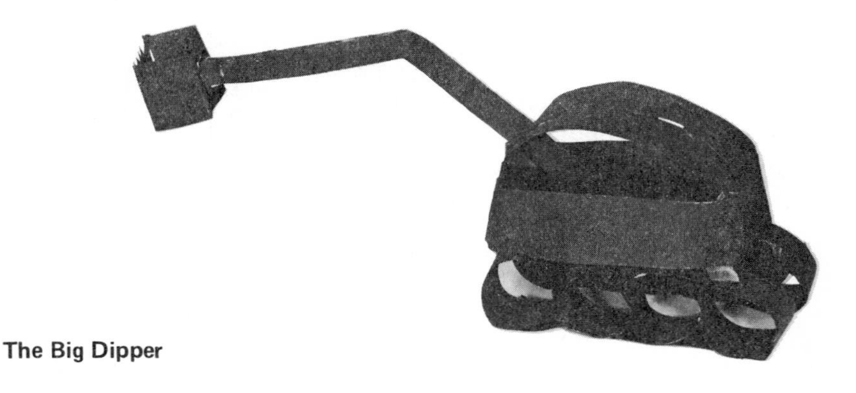

The Big Dipper

rather small object made of strips? Yes, probably the smaller one. Make a large circle from a whole strip of paper and another one from only half a strip. Show children the two circles. They will see that the large one wiggles more and is less stable than the small one.

That's a good way to make a caterpillar. He can bend and move the way a real one does. Oops, your animal is top heavy. He falls right over on his head. Can you add anything in front to help hold him in place? Yes, larger paws–and perhaps a smaller head–might help to balance him. Can you add anything to the sides of your objects so that they will be wider than just the width of one strip? A wide object will be stronger and steadier than a narrow one. That's a fine idea! No one else thought of making playground equipment. Your swing really moves, too, doesn't it!

Making strong, self-supporting objects out of just strips of paper is more difficult than it first appears, but most children enjoy the challenge. Some of them will need only time and materials to create some unusual three-dimensional objects. Others will need almost constant encouragement and reassurance.

All at once you will have a collection of things that range from rabbits to rockets, caterpillars to heavy earth-moving machinery, robots to anything young minds can imagine. Each will have been made from weak strips of paper. But paper doesn't have to stay weak, does it! There are many ways to make it strong.

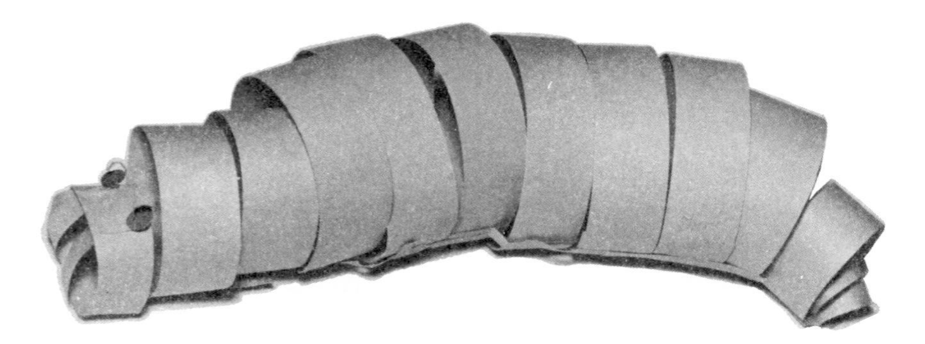

The Wiggler

MAKE IT EASY–FOR YOURSELF!

1. Cut white and colored 12" x 18" construction paper into strips of two or three widths–from a half-inch to about an inch and a half. Leave some of the paper uncut so that children may cut their own strips if they want slightly wider ones. It will help them get started, however, if they have some pre-cut strips in the beginning.
2. Let children return for more strips when they need them.
3. Give each child a small amount of paste on a scrap of paper.

4. Give each child a small piece of newspaper—a quarter of a page is enough—on which to do his pasting.
5. If paste brushes are not available, a satisfactory applicator may be made by folding a scrap of paper several times until it is a narrow strip. Then bend it in the middle to give it added strength.
6. Have a sharing experience at the end of the lesson. Comment about the many methods children have used to make their objects sturdy. Make sure the value of each child's work is appreciated (even if it topples over!) so that he has a sense of worth and accomplishment.

Walk In!

Three-Dimensional Mural *(Suggested for all elementary grades)*

Objectives

1. To provide the opportunity for children to plan and work on a cooperative project.
2. To introduce the concept of distance in a picture.
3. To demonstrate the importance of overlapping in a picture.

Materials

9" x 12" white and colored construction paper
scissors
6" or 12" applicator sticks

At the Airport

paste and paste brushes
newspaper
masking tape
18" x 24" x 1" sheet of Styrofoam

The sign on the office door told you to walk in. The unsuspecting fly was invited to walk into the spider's parlor. Well, there won't be any sign or any invitation, but you'll walk in—right into the picture.

Have you ever made a mural? Probably lots of times! Perhaps you painted them or maybe you used cut paper—or even crayon or chalk. In any case, it was a big picture that all the children worked on. Later it was hung on the bulletin board or even in the hallway where everyone could see it. That's the way it is with most murals—but this one will be different.

Stand Things in It. Explain that the mural the children are going to make this time will be a three-dimensional mural. Can the parts be pasted flat against a big piece of paper, then? No—in fact, there won't even be a big piece of paper for the background. Show the class the long piece of Styrofoam. That will be the background, but in this case nothing will be laid against it—instead things will be stuck into it so that they will stand up from it. Tear off a scrap of colored paper and tape an applicator stick to the back of it. You can imagine that this is a person or a giraffe or a tree—or anything else that might be a part of the mural. See, I have left about an inch of the stick below my object so that I can push it down into the Styrofoam—like that.

What Will It Be? But we haven't said what the mural is going to be about—and, of course, we have to decide that so everyone will make part of one picture. What kind of a mural would you like to make?

There will be all kinds of suggestions for the mural. The time of year may suggest a spring mural; dinosaurs are a favorite subject with many children, so that may be another suggestion. Sports, school activities, space programs, the airport, almost any subject may be used as a mural theme. Talk a bit about each idea as it is suggested. Yes, someone could be planting seeds. Of course! A garden has to be watered and weeded, so other people could be doing that. Would there be other things in the mural, too? Houses, trees, pets, cars, birds? Where did the dinosaurs live? Do you know what the different kinds of dinosaurs looked like? Would you like to limit the mural to spring and summer sports—or do you want to include any kind of sport? Certainly, you could include roller skating and bicycle riding. They are sports—and lots of fun, too!

Finally, let the class vote and decide which one of the suggestions will be used for the mural. Talk about that particular idea in more detail. You may even want to plan who is going to make specific things that will be needed. Only one or two of some things can be used in the mural, so be sure that no more than that will be made, as you will want every child's work to go into the finished picture. There will be other things in the mural that can be used in any quantity. It won't matter how many flowers are in the garden; how many spectators watch the launching of a space craft; how many dinosaurs roam the forest; how many people are riding bicycles or jumping rope.

Begin Work. Let groups of children take turns selecting the colored paper they will need to begin their first things for the mural. Give them the other materials they will need immediately: scissors, paste, paste brushes, and newspaper. As you walk about the room during the lesson, you can give them an applicator stick and a piece of tape.

Help each child to do his best work. Each part will be important to the whole mural. Make your flower or dinosaur or airplane as detailed and as interesting as you can. Encourage children to make only one thing for the picture but to make it a valuable contribution. Of course, those who work rapidly and well—or those who have a simple object to make—should be allowed to continue work and make a second part for the mural. This will allow the slower children to work at their own pace without pressure to make more and more.

Near and Far. When six or eight children have finished, let them gather around you at a table. Have each child determine a good place for his contribution and push the stick into the Styrofoam. They will probably want to put the big things in the back and the tiny things in the front—"so they can be seen." Point out that this is the wrong way to arrange them. Look out the window or down the hall and notice that things in the distance appear to be smaller than similar things nearby. Gradually help children understand that objects appear to be smaller the farther removed they are from us. So the biggest houses must be closer in the mural and the smaller ones must be put ______? Farther away! Right! The little trees that you have made must belong in the ______? Distance! and the taller, bigger trees should be placed ______? Right! Closer to you.

Working in the Garden

As more children finish their objects, let them bring them to the mural which already has some parts in it. Explain the near and far (large and small) arrangement to them. Then let the child decide the best spot for his contribution. When a poor choice is made, guide the child's thinking until a better choice is made. Praise the child who makes an especially good selection. As the space gets smaller you can talk about how things overlap: the shrubbery that is planted in front of the house; the park swings partly in front of the slides; the baseball batter in front of the catcher.

Some changes will need to be made in the arrangement as more objects are added. Move them about until every child's work is included and until the mural is complete. Most murals are just flat pictures, but this one is different—this one invites you to walk right in!

MAKE IT EASY—FOR YOURSELF!

1. Cut 9" x 12" construction paper in half to make 6" x 9" pieces. The smaller size is better for this technique.
2. If Styrofoam is not available, use small mounds of non-hardening clay to hold the applicator sticks. Place the clay with objects on a large piece of paper.
3. The Styrofoam may be cut in half to 9" x 24" if a long area is needed. Place the two halves end to end to make a mural 9" x 48" long. Fasten the two halves together by inserting applicator sticks through the inch-thick ends to act as pins. If the sticks are broken, the sharp ends will be easier to force into the Styrofoam.
4. No pencils! Cut all parts without preliminary drawing. Do not add pencil or crayon lines.
5. Stick the end of a piece of tape about six inches long to the edge of each child's desk. This will keep his supply of tape free from the other materials on his desk so that it remains in good condition.
6. Be sure the children press the tape close to both sides of the applicator sticks so that the paper objects won't slip.
7. Let the children return to the supply area for more materials as they are needed. Encourage them to get paper from a neighbor when only a tiny bit of a color is needed.
8. If you do not have paste brushes, a satisfactory paste applicator may be made by folding a scrap of paper several times until it is a narrow strip. Then bend the strip in the middle to give it extra strength.

3 Chalk and Charcoal

In the Mood!

Mood Sounds *(Suggested for all elementary grades)*

Objectives

1. To become more aware of the relationship between the sense of hearing and the sense of sight.
2. To provide opportunity for interpreting mood sounds in visual form.
3. To experiment with color and line to create a mood.
4. To use two similar materials in different ways.

Materials

12" x 18" white or manila paper
colored chalk
charcoal
newspaper

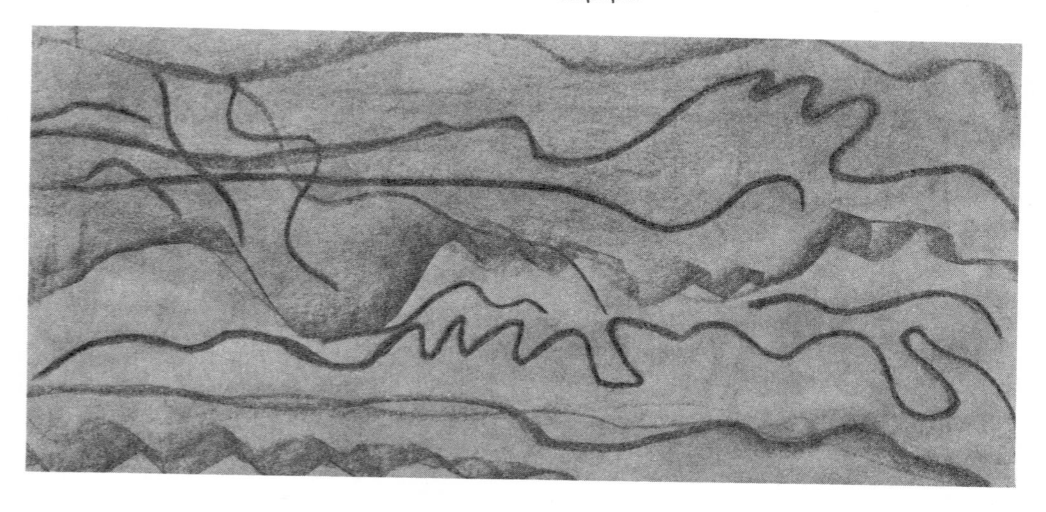

Light and Pleasant

Have you ever found it difficult to get an easy job done? You just weren't in the mood! That won't be any problem this time; we're going to create our own moods.

You've heard loud booming noises, and sounds so quiet you had to listen for them. But have you ever heard a happy sound? Yes, when you hear someone laughing you know they are happy. But what is there about the sound that is happy? Could you use your hands to show what the sound is like? At first the children may be hesitant. But encourage them by motioning with your own hands. Our hands help us say what we mean, you know. We talk with our hands all the time.

Experiment with Hands. Would a happy, laughing sound be a straight line? No, that doesn't seem right, does it? As the children begin to experiment with their hands, someone will begin to make circular motions. Good! That begins to look like it! Big, round motions look like a laugh—and the louder the laugh, the bigger the motion!

Would you draw all sounds in round motions? Suppose you had quiet, restful music on the record-player while you were having dinner. What kind of lines are quiet and restful? Try it with your hands again. Yes, they are flat lines. When you are quiet and resting—sleeping, perhaps—you lie flat. Flat lines are quiet, peaceful lines. Move your hand back and forth in slow, horizontal lines.

What would an irritating sound look like? Irritating sounds don't have to be big, do they? Sometimes just a little sound can be very irritating. Run a piece of chalk against the blackboard so that it squeaks and screeches. How irritating! But it's only a little sound and probably couldn't be heard outside this room. The little sounds were ______? Sharp!

Talk about scary sounds—gay sounds—weird sounds—mournful sounds. What kinds of lines do each of them make? Some of them may be continuous sounds, some may be separate sounds. Some may be long lines, some may be short lines.

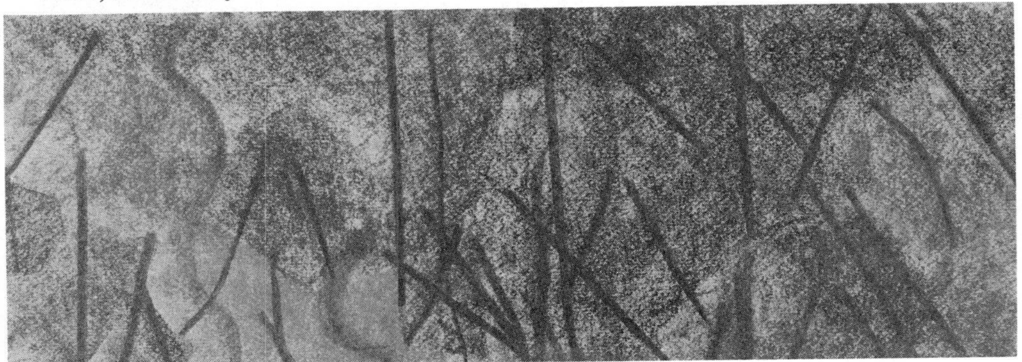

Loud Clashing

Color of Sounds. If we are going to make a picture of sounds we have to use more than lines. Every picture must have color. Some colors are happy, some sad, some noisy, some quiet.

Gay colors would make happy sounds, wouldn't they? Dark, dull colors would be ______? Right! Sad, unhappy sounds. If you wanted to show that a sound was soft, you would use soft, quiet colors—light colors. Talk about combinations of colors that are weird–or scary–or gay–or whatever mood you want to be in.

Fills All the Space. Explain that the color will really be like sound: it will go everywhere. Color will fill all the paper, just as sound fills all the space. Lay the colored chalk–several colors of it–on its side and rub so that it fills all the paper. Later the children will make the lines of the sound with charcoal.

Give out necessary materials: newspaper, 12" x 18" white or manila drawing paper, colored chalk–and later a piece of charcoal. As children work, encourage them to exaggerate. If it is a scary sound, make the colors very scary. If it is an irritating sound, make the colors very irritating–not just a little annoying! If it is a restful sound, make those colors really light and peaceful. If you want to make the sound even quieter, rub the colors gently with a piece of facial tissue. Fill the whole paper with color. Make it go everywhere, just as sound goes everywhere.

Add Charcoal Lines. Now let's put in those lines that will help the colors show the sounds even better. Are they straight sounds or rolling sounds or pointed sounds or jagged sounds? Are they little sounds or big ones? Continue to ask questions that will keep the children thinking in terms of sound and line.

It will be a noisy room–not with people, but with pictures! There will be all kinds of sounds that show that the children really have gotten in the mood!

MAKE IT EASY–FOR YOURSELF!

1. Cover all desks with newspaper to protect the surface from chalk dust; it's easier than having to wash the desks. When the pictures are finished, have each child write on the back of his picture the kind of mood that is represented. Do that before the newspaper is removed so the chalk will not make an impression on the desk.
2. If sets of colored chalk are available, give each child his own box. Otherwise, let children take turns selecting desired colors from one central supply.
3. Sticks of chalk–and charcoal–are easier to handle if new pieces are broken in half. The shorter length is easier to use and is less likely to shatter into tiny pieces.
4. Some chalk dust will collect on top of the papers. Show children how they can drop it off the picture onto the newspaper rather than blowing it off.
5. Collect the chalk as soon as children begin to use charcoal. This will get an unnecessary material off their desks, thereby giving them more work space. It will also prevent the chalk from being knocked onto the

floor—where it would undoubtedly be broken and cause a cleanup problem.

6. If charcoal is not available, use black chalk in its place.
7. Teach children to hold charcoal under the hand and between the fingertips, rather than the way they hold pencils. Use the charcoal lightly—for better motion and rhythm—and then darken it to look more effective.
8. You may want to spray the pictures lightly with a fixative, if they are to be displayed where children may rub against them.

Put Your Eyes to Work

Chalk and Charcoal *(Suggested for Grades 4 through 6)*

Objectives

1. To use a combination of similar materials in the same picture.
2. To use similar materials with different techniques.
3. To train the eye to be more observant.
4. To learn to group things in an interesting way by overlapping.
5. To create a pleasing still life.

Materials

still life objects:
rag doll, stuffed toy, ukulele, sheet music, can of oil, funnel, fruit, wood, hammer—any assortment of objects

12" x 18" or 18" x 24" white drawing paper
colored chalk
charcoal
newspaper

You're always telling the children in your class to use their imaginations. That's fine, but they have eyes, too. Have you ever told them to put their eyes to work?

Still Life Arrangements. Gather together a wide range of objects from which you can make several still life arrangements. Include things which would be more likely to appeal to the girls and things which would be more likely to appeal to the boys. Spread them out on a table where everyone can see them. Point out the variety of objects—the rag doll and stuffed toy dog, the ukulele and the piece of sheet music, the can of motor oil and the funnel, the apples and oranges and other artificial fruit, the box of cake mix and the bowl and measuring cup, the scrap wood and hammer and nails, and whatever else you decide to include.

Explain to your class that they are going to draw these things. Oh, no, not all of them! You will draw just the ones you want to draw. But first you will choose which ones they will be, and then you will arrange them together so that you can draw them all in the same picture.

Some of the children may know that such an arrangement is called a still life. Choose someone to select several objects and make an arrangement of them—a still life. Good! That would make an interesting picture. Would someone like to make another still life of different objects? Comment about the pleasing arrangement—or suggest a minor change that will make the grouping more attractive. Mention the variety of sizes of the objects in the still life, the way they overlap each other so that they seem to belong together rather than remain isolated objects. Talk about lines that lead your eye into the arrangement. They will help people to see your picture, won't they?

Colored Chalk. Explain to the children how their still life pictures will be made. First of all, they will be made with colored chalk. That can be done quickly. Choose some simple object—an oil can, a bottle, an apple—to demonstrate. Lay a piece of colored chalk on its side on a paper, and with a few quick motions create the general shape of the object. Don't try to make it exactly like the object you are drawing—just similar enough so that you can recognize it. Later you can make it even more like the real object, but don't worry about that now.

There, that was easy to do, wasn't it! If you want to, you can make the chalk look softer and smoother by rubbing it lightly with a piece of facial tissue. Wrap a piece of tissue around your index finger and rub the chalk slightly. See how this changes it! Choose another color chalk and quickly make another shape by laying the chalk on its side and rubbing. Be sure one shape seems to overlap the other as though it were a real still life arrangement. Smooth the color with the tissue.

That's enough to recognize the two things that have been drawn, but there is a way of making them look even more real. How could that be done? Several suggestions may be made. Certainly someone will say something about lines. Well, there aren't any lines there yet—just areas of soft color—but lines would help it to be more real. So let's add some lines.

Charcoal. With a piece of charcoal quickly sketch the lines of the vase or apple or box or whatever you have colored. You will probably find it easier to sketch lightly at first. It will be easy enough to darken the lines later. Look carefully at the object you are drawing, for now is the time to

Teddy All Dressed Up

Yum-m-m!

make it look as real as you can. Put in as many details as you think are important.

Should just a line be drawn around the area of colored chalk? Of course not! The colored chalk was just so we could recognize the object, but now we want it to look real. So look very carefully before you draw. That looks more like the real objects, doesn't it, and the bits of color outside the lines don't matter at all, do they?

Keep Arrangements Simple. Several children will want to use the same objects for their still life drawings, so let some of them get together to choose and arrange their materials. Urge them to keep their arrangements simple. Simple but well-planned pictures usually look the best, you know. Set up the arrangements in different parts of the room so that each group of children may cluster near their still life to make their own pictures of it. Each picture in the group will be slightly different—even though they are drawing the same materials—because each child will see it from a slightly different angle.

Walk about the room encouraging children to do more looking than drawing. Which is the tallest object in your arrangement? How much taller is it than the shortest object? . . . Do those sides really curve out, or do they curve in? Which way did you make them? . . . Does the bottom of the can really look like a straight line, or does it seem to curve?

Questions and Comments. Continually ask questions and make comments that will help the children to see and to put what they see on their papers. Remember, though, that it isn't important to have the chalk drawing exactly right. If someone makes a shape curve in the wrong direction but sees his mistake, it can still be corrected when the charcoal lines are drawn. So don't be in a hurry about giving out the charcoal. Even after all the colored shapes have been finished, urge each child to examine his work carefully and compare it to his still life arrangement. Changes can be made with the charcoal but each child must be aware of the changes he needs to make.

Look, look, look before you draw with charcoal. Remember the places you were going to change. Sketch lightly first, and then you can darken the lines later.

You will be proud of all the finished pictures. It is easy to make a picture with our imaginations. But it is harder to make a picture when our eyes have to work, too.

MAKE IT EASY—FOR YOURSELF!

1. Cover all work areas with newspaper. Chalk washes off desks, but it is a waste of time to have to do unnecessary cleaning.
2. Use at least 12" x 18" white drawing paper. Even larger paper—18" x 24"—will be better.
3. If boxes of colored chalk are available, let each child have his own set. Otherwise let children take turns selecting several colors from a general supply source.
4. Use the chalk flat on the side to create areas of color rather than lines. If you are using new sets of chalk have the children break each stick in

half before using any of them. A half a piece of chalk is easier to handle than a whole piece, and it is less likely to break into tiny, unusable pieces.

5. Don't give out the charcoal at the beginning of the lesson. It is better to wait until each child has made a good beginning with the chalk. Encourage each child to see where he will make changes in shape before he uses his charcoal.
6. Be sure children darken all charcoal lines. The sharp contrast between the pale colors and the dark black lines gives character and interest to the drawing.
7. As each child finishes his work, have him put his chalk and charcoal in designated places. Fold all the sides of the newspaper toward the center so that no chalk gets on the desks or floor. Then put the folded newspaper in the wastebasket.

The Circus Is in Town!

Sketch with Charcoal *(Suggested for Grades 3 through 6)*

Objectives

1. To capitalize on seasonal interests as motivation for an art lesson.
2. To experiment with using chalk in a new way.
3. To develop the ability to sketch loosely and freely.

Materials

18" x 24" white drawing paper
charcoal
colored chalk

What wonderful news to hear! The circus is in town!

When I say the word *circus*, what do you think of?

Sure, you do! You think of clowns and elephants, but there are so many more things to see and to do when you go to a circus. Let's have everyone in the room think of something different. Go around the class quickly to see if each child can instantly name something about a circus.

Don't stop for those who are slow or who repeat something that has already been mentioned, but come back later and give them a second chance. It will be a fun game and will encourage individual thinking.

Many Things. Balloons, lions in a cage, clown juggling plates, elephant standing on a barrel, Ferris wheel, fat lady, thin man, sword swallower, ice cream cones, cotton candy, hot dogs, peanuts, bag of hot popcorn, tiger jumping through a ring of fire, bareback rider, dancing horses, acrobats, tightrope walkers, trapeze artists, bear riding a bicycle, red and yellow tent, crowd of spectators, drummer leading the parade, acrobatic dogs, zebra, giraffes, lion tamer, seals balancing a ball—the list goes on and on, and offers more than enough suggestions for everyone.

We're going to make pictures which will have some of these things in them, but you will have to choose which ones you want to make. Let's see how we can do it. Have your class gather around you while you demonstrate.

Side of Chalk. A big paper like this should have something big put on it first. It doesn't *have* to be something big like an elephant or the tent—but it can be, if that's what you decide to make the biggest thing in your picture.

I'm going to choose some little things—some balloons—and make them big. Let's see—balloons that are sold at a circus should be bright colors, shouldn't they? I'll make them red and orange and green. Lay the red chalk (half a stick or less) flat on the paper, and rub a large circle on the white paper with the side of the chalk. Did you notice that I didn't put it right in the middle of the picture? It will look better if it is not exactly in the center.

Circus Time

I'm going to make a bunch of balloons to be sold, so I'll make another circle of color. Lay the orange chalk flat and rub it into a circular area. I'm not even going to try to make it a perfect circle. The color is just to make it look pretty and to remind me that these are going to become balloons later. Add several more areas of color to represent other balloons that are together.

What else would you like in this picture? A lion? All right, let's choose a couple of colors for this lion. Remember, he doesn't have to be the color of a real lion. Pink and purple will be fine. A lion has a big ruff of long fur around his head, so I'll make that first with purple chalk. As you talk, lay the chalk flat on the paper and rub a scalloped circle with a hole in the middle. We'll leave that for his face.

Now for a pink body—just a big oval shape is enough as though he were sitting looking at us—and a long line made with the chalk flat. And he needs a bushy part at the end of his tail—and, oh, yes, a pink face. He doesn't look much like a lion yet, does he; but the size and color and shape remind me that one is going to be right there.

It is a good idea to use colors over again, so I think I'll use the orange chalk for the top of a tent over here. I'll make the sides purple so I can use some of that color again. Are there more empty spaces where other circus things could be put? Certainly! Lots of them. But let's pretend they are all filled in so that we can see what to do next.

Let's pretend there is a red seal over there with a green and orange ball. No, I'm not going to take time to put it in the picture. You imagine it is there. It could be quite a large one, couldn't it? And there would still be space close to it for a little cage. Yes, there might be an acrobat in this big space and perhaps a little monkey over here.

Fill the Background. Those chalk areas tell me what belongs there, but there is still some white paper around each thing. White paper is too quiet for a noisy circus, but that is easy to fix. There isn't any yellow on this picture, so I'll lay a piece of yellow chalk flat and fill in all the white places. Looks better already, doesn't it?

No, no! It isn't finished. Remember, I said those colored shapes I put on were just to *remind* me they were to be balloons, a tent, and a lion—and all the other things that we are going to pretend are there.

Sketch with Charcoal. Now let's make them come to life. We'll use the charcoal for that and sketch on top of the colored areas. As you talk, begin to sketch the tent. Don't try to draw a continuous line, but sketch each part with a free, quick motion. Sketch one side of the tent top. Swing the charcoal down in a rounded, sweeping line. Do the same thing for the other side of the top. Let's add a bit of tent pole sticking out of the top—just a line, like that. Make each scalloped line around the edge of the top a separate line—sketched rapidly and smoothly with a rhythmic motion.

Call the attention of the class to the fact that the charcoal lines don't all connect. Some may overlap slightly; others don't quite touch. They don't quite fit on the color that is in the background, either. They're not supposed to. The color, we said, was just to *remind* us that a tent belonged there—and the charcoal lines are to show it more clearly.

Sketch the balloons. Make two or three sweeping motions to complete each circle. Add a string to each one and slant the string lines so that they all come together at the end. The charcoal lines don't match the colored circles completely, aren't perfectly round, and are broken and overlap in several places—but that's all right. We can see that one important thing in the circus is a bunch of balloons.

Finish the lion by sketching lines around him. He needs a face, too, so do that with charcoal. Yes, we could add some other details with the charcoal. Certainly! Some lines—like that—on his tail help us to know that it has some long, bushy hair at the end of it. Add other touches to the balloons to make them look three-dimensional, a pennant to the top of the tent pole, or some other details.

Darken the Charcoal. When you sketch, you draw loosely and rapidly and lightly. But the charcoal lines don't have to stay light. When you have finished a light sketch, go back over the lines to darken them. Hold the charcoal close to the end you are drawing with and press *hard* on it. Don't worry about the tiny bits of charcoal that break off. They can be blown right off your paper, and they won't do any harm.

The Acrobat

Materials. When the children have returned to their own work areas, give each one a large white paper and a box of colored chalk. Have two children share a box, or, if sets of chalk are not available, have a bulk supply so the children can choose what they need.

Would it be a good idea to choose your background color first? Then you could put that piece of chalk to one side for later and not use it for any of your circus things. Make something big first—but don't put it right in the middle. Looks as though it is going to be an upside down tumbler. That is an excellent beginning! Will that be the weight that the circus strong man picks up?

It wouldn't be a circus, you know, without lots of performing animals, so put several in your picture. Yes, clowns, too! Ferris wheels are fun, aren't they? Don't worry about it not being quite the right shape. That will be changed when you sketch over the chalk.

As you walk about the room, give each child a piece of charcoal—half a stick or less.

Yes, as soon as you fill in the background, you will be ready to sketch each of the objects you have indicated with chalk areas. Good! I'm glad you remembered to hold the charcoal close to the end. Oh, sketch faster than that! You don't want your things to look stiff. That's right! Make one motion and lift the charcoal off the paper.

I see some wonderful things appearing. All at once they begin to look great, don't they! Yes, I'm sure you can darken the charcoal line more than that. That's a fine idea. If there is still too plain an area—an empty space in the background—draw something with charcoal right on top of the background color.

Assistance. As you walk about the room, continue to assist each child in any way he needs. It may be just a word of praise or recognition; it may be encouragement to give the hesitant child confidence; it may be a question, an answer, or a bit of advice to help each child do his best work.

The finished pictures will be delightful, and each child will be anxious to show his to the rest of the class—and then to see it on display with all the others. The circus *has* come to town—right into your classroom!

MAKE IT EASY—FOR YOURSELF!

1. No pencils! No preliminary drawing—it would spoil the free effect you are trying to achieve.
2. A chalk stick broken in half is easier to handle and gives better results than a whole stick. You do not spoil the chalk by breaking it in

half—you improve it, and double your supply. Half a stick is less likely to break into tiny pieces that have to be thrown away. The same is true of the charcoal.

3. Paper will absorb only a limited amount of chalk, so avoid pressing too hard with it. Excess chalk will remain as dust on the paper and can be blown away gently. Too much excess chalk should be shaken off into the wastebasket.
4. Emphasize that the chalk areas are only for the approximate shape. The charcoal lines need not—and should not—match them exactly.
5. *Sketching* implies rapid, loose motions. Encourage the children to lift their charcoal off the paper between each motion. This promotes freedom of motion by loosening their hand muscles, and it avoids drawing in a rigid, continuous line.
6. Sketch lightly to achieve maximum freedom of motion. Later, press on the charcoal to darken the lines. Bits of charcoal will break off as you darken the lines. This is normal. Excessive breakage can be prevented by holding the charcoal close to the drawing end.
7. If the finished pictures are to be displayed where fingers or clothing can rub against them, spray them with a light coat of fixative. Hair spray makes a fine substitute if regular fixative is not available.

Not Really

Outdoor Sketching *(Suggested for Grades 4 through 6)*

Objectives

1. To learn that a picture may have real things in it without being entirely realistic.
2. To experiment with abstracting by simplification and exaggeration.
3. To provide opportunity for improving skill in sketching.
4. To increase ability to select or eliminate parts of a real scene in order to plan an abstract picture.

Materials

cardboard at least 12" x 18"
charcoal
12" x 18" white drawing paper

House Among Trees

It's a lovely day. Do you *want* to stay indoors? Not really! Well, then, let's go outside.

If you suggest to your class that they go outdoors for an art lesson, they will be enthusiastic. So let's take advantage of a delightful spring day and go outside to draw. We'll draw a landscape. But, does the landscape have to look just the way we see it? No, not really.

Abstract Art. Before you go outside remind your class of some abstract art they have seen. Or if abstract art is new to them, tell them that sometimes artists draw pictures of real things and real places but they don't look entirely realistic. Artists have many ways of abstracting a picture. Two ways they do it are by simplifying the picture and by exaggerating part of it.

Have your class stand at the windows so they can see the landscape outside. Let's pretend we are outside and ready to draw a picture. What is the first thing an artist would do? Well—before he did anything else he would have to decide just what he wanted to draw. Would he try to draw everything he sees? Oh, no! That would be impossible—and besides, abstract artists like to simplify things. So the first thing he would do would be to decide on just a few things to put in his picture.

Ask the children to suggest some part of what they see that would make an interesting picture. It might be a building, a group of trees, a bridge, an automobile. Yes, any of those would make an interesting abstract picture.

Simplify and Exaggerate. Suppose you were going to abstract that tree. How could you do it? Yes, you would simplify it–you would leave out some of the tiny, unimportant parts. But how else could you simplify it? Talk about kinds of lines. Which are the simplest–the plainest–kind of lines? Certainly! Straight lines are the simplest you can get. So if you straightened out some of the curving, twisting lines of the tree, you would have simplified the tree. Pretend the tree is made of clay or rubber. Then you would be able to smooth out some of the rough parts and straighten some of the wiggly lines.

But an artist likes to exaggerate some parts, too. How could you do that? Perhaps some important branch on the tree forms a rounding line. Well, just exaggerate it–make it more rounding and extend it farther. Make it thicker and smoother.

Plan how a building might be abstracted. Which lines could be left out? Are there any lines that could be straightened? Which lines could be extended? It would be the same building but it would look different.

Give each child a piece of 12" x 18" white drawing paper that has been taped to a slightly larger piece of cardboard. Also, give each child a piece of charcoal. Now let's go outside!

Find an Interesting Picture. Remind children to look in all directions to find an interesting picture. Don't try to include too much. Your abstract picture will look much better if you don't try to include too many things in it. Pick out only one thing or a group of things that you can make so large that they will fill your whole paper. Plan the size of it so that it will take up all of your paper. Yes, it would be a good idea to draw it quite realistically first. Oh, don't put in every detail. It would be silly, wouldn't it, to put in something you knew you were going to take right out again. But put the main things in just as you see them. Draw them lightly so that you can abstract right over them.

Good! That will fill your paper nicely without having to add other things. Use your charcoal lightly. Then you will be able to change things and later you can darken whatever you want to. Don't worry about the background yet. Sometimes abstract artists don't put in a background, or they may make it very unimportant. Just think about the big, important part of your picture.

Begin to Abstract It. As a child begins to get a rather realistic drawing, encourage him to begin to abstract it. Do you have some curved lines that you could straighten? Yes, even that curved line for the little hill could be straightened. How can you straighten a curved line? Easy! Just pretend your charcoal is taking a walk around that line, but decides to take a shortcut across part of it. Oh, it can't take much of a shortcut, or there wouldn't be a hill any longer. Perhaps about three straight lines would keep it a hill—but a simple hill with only straight lines. Fine! That was a good part to exaggerate. The line was already long and straight, so all you had to do was extend it and make it even longer. Good! That was a good way to exaggerate the aerial—by extending the horizontal line on one side. Sometimes artists emphasize an unimportant part by making it much larger than usual.

Return to the Classroom. When everyone has some part of his picture abstracted, have the children return to the classroom. It will be easier to see the pictures there and to complete the final touches. Have each child remove his drawing from the cardboard, and have the cardboard collected so that it is out of the way.

Walk about the room encouraging a child here to extend some line—perhaps right off the paper; another child to simplify—to straighten—some wiggly, fussy lines. Compliment, encourage, and suggest until each child has a pleasing picture. It should be abstract but still realistic enough to be recognized.

Finish the Pictures. Now let's finish the pictures. No, they're not finished until you have darkened the important lines of the picture. Show the children that by pressing on the charcoal they can make lines very black. Should all the lines be dark? No, of course not! Darken only those that are important, the ones that you want to be sharp and clear. Other lines can stay light. That will give a pleasing contrast just as when you use dark and light colors. Oh, don't worry if little bits of charcoal break off. That always happens when you press on it. Hold the charcoal stick close to the end near your paper so that big pieces won't break off. Oh, press hard! Make the lines dark.

Don't worry too much about the background. If the main part of your picture is big and important there is very little background space. Perhaps you will want to indicate some trees or a hill or buildings in some of the space, but keep the lines light. They are not important so don't let them show too much.

Finally the last picture will be finished and you will want to have a quick showing. Talk about the ways they have been abstracted. Notice pictures of the same place that have been abstracted so that they look very different from each other. Then plan to have an exhibit of each child's work. You'll be delighted with every one of them. Do the sketches look just like the things we saw outside? Not really!

MAKE IT EASY—FOR YOURSELF!

1. It will help to show some pictures of abstract art. Some modern artists

you might like to use as examples are Feininger, Marin, Schmidt-Rottluff, Braque.

Trees

2. Have the cardboard—used in place of drawing boards—slightly larger than the drawing paper. If only 12" x 18" cardboard is available, cut the white drawing paper to be slightly smaller. Tape it to the cardboard.
3. Small pieces of charcoal are easier to handle than whole sticks, so if you have new pieces, break them in half or in thirds. This does not spoil them—it makes them more usable and less likely to break into tiny pieces too small to use.
4. When you first go outside, keep your class around you while you define the limits they are to stay within. Make the area large enough to provide a variety of subject matter and to give each child a work area to himself. (Every artist likes to work alone, you know.) But limit the area so that it is small enough for you to supervise and so that you can move quickly from one child to another.
5. When you return to the classroom, give each child a piece of newspaper to work on to protect his desk from the charcoal. Charcoal washes off, but it is a waste of time and most teachers will prefer not to have to do it.
6. Protect clothing from charcoal by having children roll their sleeves above the elbows so that they won't rub across the pictures. It will protect the pictures, too.
7. Older children may want to use charcoal erasers to remove unwanted lines or smudges. Charcoal erasers are kneaded erasers, so show the children that as parts begin to pull away from the eraser they can be pushed back into it. If a point is needed on the eraser to get into a small area, a bit of the eraser can be squeezed into a protruding point. Don't overuse the erasers.

8. Remove excess charcoal bits and dust by dropping them on the newspaper. Don't push them off with your hand as this would smudge the charcoal.
9. You may want to spray the finished pictures with a light coating of fixative. This will prevent them from being smudged if they are to be displayed in an area where children might rub against them.

4 Collages

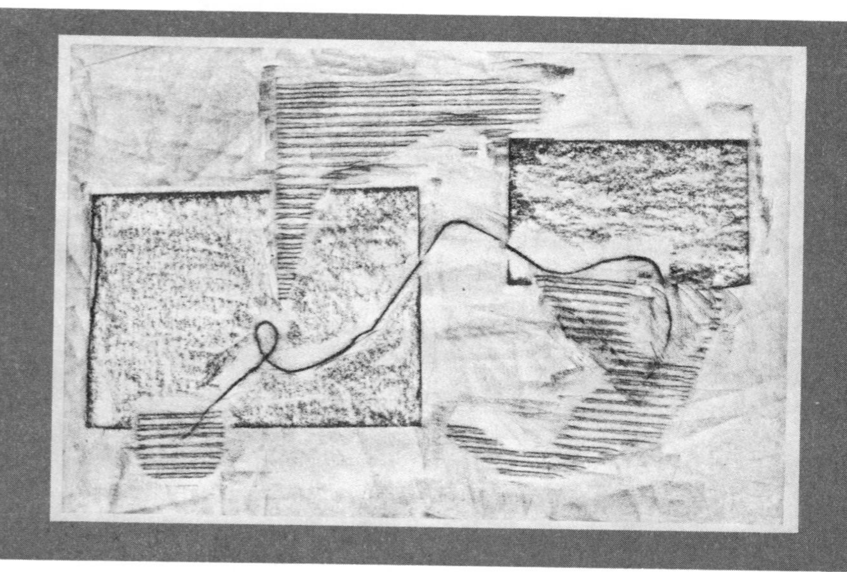

Millions of Colors

Color Collage *(Suggested for all elementary grades)*

Objectives

1. To realize that there are endless varieties of a single color.
2. To use one color to create a collage.
3. To experiment with overlapping to create a pleasing arrangement.
4. To learn that bright and dark colors advance and light colors recede.

Materials

assorted materials in a variety of colors:
 paper, fabric, yarn, buttons, corrugated
 paper, sandpaper, felt
9" x 12" or 12" x 18" colored
 construction paper
paste and paste brushes
glue
newspaper

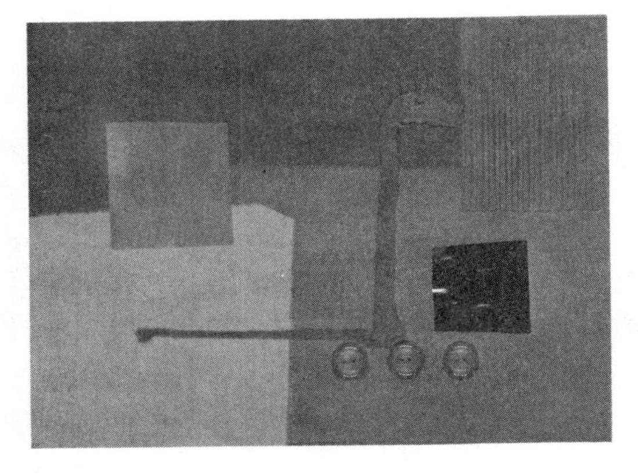

The Scooter

If someone asked you to name all the colors, you would probably start off with red, yellow, blue, green ——. But your list would soon end. Suppose someone told you there are millions of colors.

Name All the Colors. Ask your class to name all the colors they can think of—you write them on the blackboard. Someone will surely start off with red, yellow, blue, green, orange, purple, brown, black. Write them that way across the board. That's a good beginning, but is that all? Someone will probably say white. Yes, include that. Don't argue the point of whether or not black and white are colors. But aren't there other colors? Pink? Of course! It is really a light ______? Red—so we'll put it under the word red.

This will open a whole new series of words, depending, of course, on the age and experience of the children in your class. Some words you or your class may suggest are maroon, scarlet, gold, navy, gray, tan, magenta, cerise, turquoise. Each time a new word is suggested, write it under its general color category.

But aren't there other colors? Oh, yes, there are! There are more and more and more—forever! Let's take gray, for example. Gray could be lighter and lighter until it is almost white. Or it could be darker and darker until it is almost ______? Black, right. That could happen with every color, couldn't it? How else can colors be changed so that they look different? Right! Red, for example, could have just a speck of yellow in it. That would make it different. Or it could have more and more yellow in it until it is orange and then more and more until it is almost plain yellow again. Yes, you can also change red by adding a speck of blue—or any color—and then adding more and more of it. How many colors could you finally make? Millions of colors!

We're not going to have millions of colors to use today, but we are going to have lots of them. Have boxes of different kinds of materials: cloth, yarn, paper, buttons, odds and ends of any kind. Look, here is a piece of blue cloth, but so is this—and this—and this. But they are all different kinds of blue, aren't they? Let two or three children select several other blue items. Put them all together in one area.

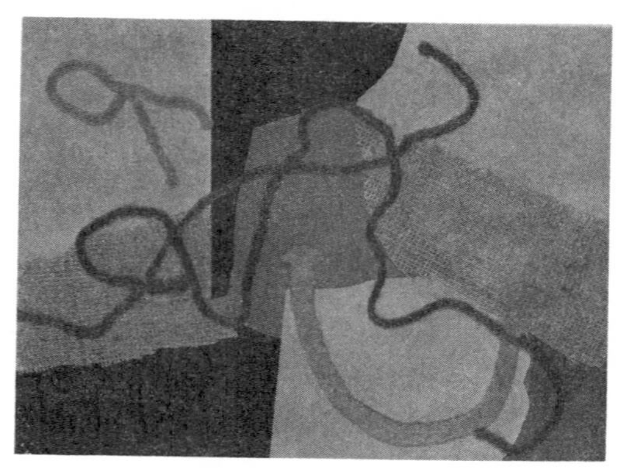

The Enchanted Jumble

Arrange the Colors. The colors—the many kinds of one color, really—look good, don't they? But could you arrange them so that they would look still better? Let one or two children begin moving them about to make a more pleasing arrangement. Yes, if you overlap some of the pieces, that looks good, doesn't it? Good, I'm glad you covered that empty space where the table showed. That didn't look good in the picture. Could you change something so all the big pieces wouldn't be on one side? Yes, it would balance better if some of the big pieces were in different parts of the arrangement. Do some of the blues seem more important than others, even though they are not big pieces? You are right! Bright colors seem to stand out and say, "Look at me!" Which kinds of blue are quiet and stay off away from you? Right! Light blue does that. Bright colors–and dark colors–seem to come toward you, and light colors–or dull colors–seem to go away from you.

That's a very good design. The only trouble is that it won't be able to stay there–or we can't pick it up to move it somewhere else. But that is easy to change; we'll each make a color picture and paste it onto a paper. It will be called a collage–a picture pasted together.

Explain that each person's collage will be made of just one color–but many varieties of that color. Of course, you may use any of the materials, as long as they are of the same color. Then you will move them about on a piece of paper until they look just right. Finally you will paste them to the piece of paper so that you have a color collage.

Let groups of children take turns selecting materials, and give each child a pair of scissors. That will be all he needs for a beginning. Oops, one color, remember. Your collage will be red or green or black–or whatever *one* color you want it to be. It's a good idea to arrange the big things first. Then you can overlap them with some smaller pieces. Move them about until they balance. Remember that bright and dark colors come forward and call attention to themselves more than light or dull colors. Light and dark colors together make a pleasing contrast. Good! That group of small shapes balances that large shape nicely, doesn't it?

The room will be a busy place as children select more and more materials until each of their color collages is complete. There may be only a few variations of color on each collage, but when they are all put on display they will clearly say–millions of colors!

MAKE IT EASY–FOR YOURSELF!

1. Have a wide assortment of materials and colors. Include construction paper, corrugated paper, cardboard, various kinds of cloth (burlap, percale, textured materials, wool) felt, yarn, string, buttons, coated wire, tongue depressors, sandpaper.
2. Use either 9" x 12" or 12" x 18" colored construction paper for the base of the collage. If each child chooses the same color of paper he uses for the rest of his collage, he may let some of the background paper serve as one of the color variations in his picture.
3. To get the work started quickly, have each child select only a few of the larger pieces for his collage first. Then permit the children to return to the supply area for more materials whenever they need them. Extra

supplies should be returned whenever they are not needed so that other children can use them.

4. Don't give out pasting supplies too soon. If children have paste at the beginning of the lesson, they are apt to use it immediately instead of moving their parts about until they have a pleasing, well-balanced and rhythmic design.
5. Give each child a half page of newspaper to do his pasting on. It is not necessary to cover the desk with newspaper—the small piece is just to use to keep the picture clean. Fold it to take less space on the desk, and it can be folded in reverse when more clean area is needed.
6. Give each child a small amount of paste on a small piece of scrap paper. Leave the extra supply of paste where the children can get more if they need it. Have glue available for such things as buttons and wire.
7. If paste brushes are not available, a satisfactory paste applicator can be made by folding a scrap of paper several times until it is a quarter- to a half-inch wide. Then bend it in the middle to give it added strength.
8. Display the finished collages individually by mounting them on separate backings, or even make a group collage by arranging all the collages of one color together to create one large red collage, one large yellow collage, one large blue collage, one large collage of each color.
9. Make a chart of the new color words.

Getting the Feel of It

Texture Collage *(Suggested for all elementary grades)*

Objectives

1. To experiment with texture as an important element of art.
2. To create a single impression with a variety of materials.
3. To provide an opportunity for selecting materials to satisfy a particular need.
4. To discover that materials have value in themselves without being transformed into something realistic.

Materials

12" x 18" white and colored construction paper

smooth materials: plastic, aluminum foil, linoleum, satin,

paste and paste brushes
glue
newspaper
soft materials: cotton batting, felt, flannel, yarn, fur, facial tissue
hard materials: tongue depressors, buttons, wood, shells, wire, pebbles, metals
metallic foil
rough materials: corrugated cardboard, twigs, sandpaper, coarse twine, wire screening

We can look at a thing, but it doesn't always tell us what we want to know. Sometimes we have to handle it—try getting the feel of it—before we really understand it. Some pictures are that way, too.

Variety of Materials. Spread out on a large table a wide variety of materials. Include all kinds of things—from regular construction paper to pieces of chicken wire; from cotton batting to dry twigs; from velvet to sandpaper; from tiny shells to foam rubber; from one extreme to the other. Have your class gather around the table.

That's a strange variety of things, isn't it? Look them over carefully and then decide on one that particularly appeals to you. The first person you ask to select one piece of material will probably pick one of the more unusual ones, perhaps a piece of velvet. That's a good one to start with, but I wonder why you chose it.

Perhaps the child will tell you it was the color he liked. But there is a piece of construction paper the same color. Why didn't you choose it instead of the velvet? The child may not know why. Was it because the velvet looked so much softer than the piece of paper that it was more inviting? Probably so! Let another child feel it. It is delightfully soft. Well, let's put it over here to one side.

The Thunderstorm

Ask another child what material appeals to him. Again, it will probably be one of the more unusual materials, perhaps a piece of corrugated cardboard. It may be a pretty color, but no different from the color of other regular paper, so there must be another reason for choosing it. Yes, the little "hills" on it make it look interesting and feel______? Yes, it feels rough and bumpy! That feels very different from the velvet, so let's put it in a different place—over there.

Texture. Use the term *texture.* Explain that the texture of a thing is the feel of the surface of it. Use *feel* and *texture* interchangeably. Let another child choose an appealing material. It may look interesting—like a piece of chicken wire—but it also feels interesting. Run your hand over it. The chicken wire feels rough (or hard), so put it with that kind of material. The linoleum feels smooth (or hard), so put it with other material that feels smooth (or hard). The cotton batting is soft, soft, soft. Put it with the other soft things. Let each child have a turn selecting, getting the feel of it, and putting it with other things that have a similar feel. Something may have two feels—rough and hard, for example. Put it with either group, and if there is a second piece of the same thing put it with the other suitable group of the same texture.

The Feel of Color. Talk for just a minute about color. Do some colors "feel" different from other colors? Oh, the paper may feel the same—it may be the same texture—but do the looks of the colors make you think of different textures? Light colors make you think of soft things, right! So if you are going to make a collage that has a soft texture, you will want to put it on a color that makes you think of soft things. It might be light blue or pink or light purple—or any other light color. Bright colors make you think of ______? Good! Of rough things or perhaps hard things. Dull colors make you think of ______? Right, smooth textures. Dark things remind you of ______? Hard things, of course.

So decide what kind of texture your collage will have, and then choose a color that "feels" the same way. Let the children take turns choosing a piece of colored paper and several items all of which are the same texture.

Cover a Large Area First. Begin with a big piece of material of some kind so that it will cover a large area at one time. If it is a piece of smooth cloth, make it a big piece. If it is rough corrugated cardboard, leave it large. Fill a big area first, and then you can add other things on top of the large areas. You can overlap with the smaller things.

Good! There is no doubt but what you are going to have a soft collage. All of your materials feel soft. What will happen if you begin with a few shells first? Well, you will have trouble because you are beginning with the little things instead of something large. Save the shells—the little things—

until last, and then you can find a place on top of something else for them. You have all the rough things—except that tongue depressor. Tongue depressors are smooth. They wouldn't be much good if they were rough, would they! Can you think of some way of making it rough? Of course, you could! You could break it so that it had rough, jagged edges.

Continue to comment about selection and arrangement of materials. Encourage those children who are hesitant and unsure of themselves. Compliment a child who is original.

The Feel of Shapes. Begin to talk about the edges of materials. Does a rough piece of corrugated cardboard look rougher if the edges are smooth and rounding or if they are torn or even cut in sharp points? Of course it does! Rough or sharp edges help to make the material look even rougher. Well, if you wanted a thing to look smooth, then, you would keep the edges ______? Smooth! Are soft lines straight or rounded lines? Yes, they are rounded lines. So hard lines must be ______? Straight, right! Try to make the shapes you cut "feel" the same as the texture you are using.

Do the edges of your collages all have to be even with the edges of your pieces of colored paper? Oh, not at all! They can be straight and smooth if you are making a hard collage, but they don't have to be the same hard and smooth lines that they are now. If you are making a rough collage, shouldn't the outside shape of the collage be rough, too? So make the outside shape rough by tearing it—or rough by cutting pointed or jagged lines. A smooth or soft collage should have smooth or soft curving edges. What do you do with the extra colored paper? Why, you cut it off—or tear it off!

That's right—you might cover up all your colored paper so that it doesn't show at all. It doesn't have to show. But it might show if it adds to the texture, perhaps on a smooth collage. Or if you used chicken wire on a rough collage, the paper—a rough color—might show under the wire. You think about your collage and what you want the texture to look and feel like.

Attach the Parts. As the plan of each collage begins to develop and fits with the texture, give each child a little paste on a scrap paper—or a tube of glue if he is using materials other than paper, cloth, yarn, string, and other such supplies. Glue will be necessary for wood, wire, buttons, leather, and other similar materials. Each child should also have a small piece of newspaper to do his pasting on or to keep the glue from getting on his desk. Remind the children not to remove all the parts of their collage before pasting them. Just remove and paste (or glue) one thing at a time and return it immediately so that the arrangement will not be disrupted.

Continue to walk about the room assisting in any way you can. Help every child to feel successful.

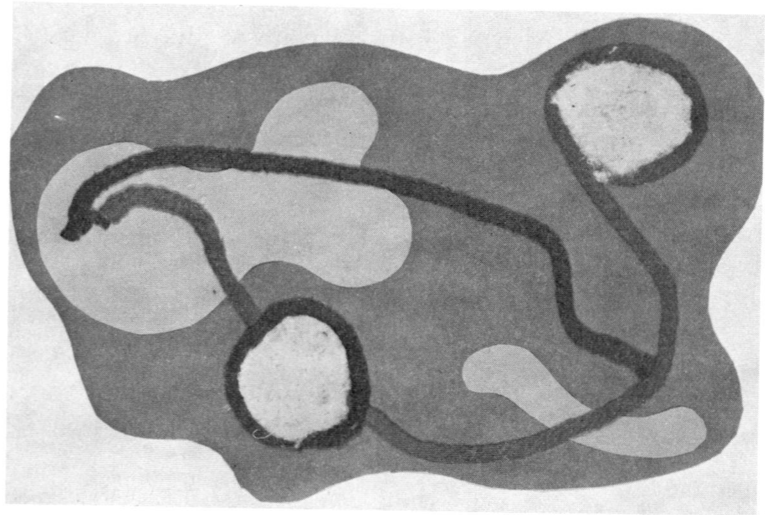

Mr. Softy

Pleased with Themselves. When you see the work after it has been completed, you will be proud of your class—and they will be pleased with themselves. They did get the feel of it, and their collages prove it! You will want to make a display, perhaps one section for each texture. Or you may want it to be a puzzle—but one that's easy to solve! Mix the textures on the display. Have some cards that say: soft, hard, smooth, rough. When visitors come to the room, invite them to label one of the collages with the right texture. Each child will be pleased as his picture is correctly identified. See, other people get the feel of it, too!

MAKE IT EASY—FOR YOURSELF!

1. Have as much variety in the textured articles as you can. Try to get some of the more unusual materials: fur, sand, spun glass, bark. Also, include large pieces of cloth, cotton batting, felt, sandpaper, corrugated cardboard, so that there will be large pieces for the backgrounds of the collages. Have several of each kind of material. Have enough articles so that each child will be able to have several large things and several small ones.
2. Begin the collages with the large items and work toward the small ones. Overlap the parts and group small things together to help your eye move easily from one place to another.
3. Choose a suitable color for the background in case some of it shows on the finished collage: hard—dark or bright; soft—light; rough—bright; smooth—light or dull.
4. Don't use the whole background paper and so finish with a 12" x 18" rectangular collage. Make the outside shape fit the feel of the collage: rounding for soft or smooth; straight for smooth or hard; uneven or jagged for rough.

5. Have a pair of wire clips available to cut wire or pipe cleaners. Do not use scissors even though they will cut these materials. The wire damages the blades of the scissors. Most pliers have a wire-cutting edge.
6. If children do not know the term collage, explain it to them. It is a French word meaning *pasting.* So a collage is a picture made by pasting the parts together.

Different, But the Same

Collages *(Suggested for Grades 3 through 6)*

Objectives

1. To introduce collage as an art form.
2. To experiment with texture as an important element of design.
3. To create unity through the variation of a single motif.

Materials

9" x 12" and 12" x 18" white and colored construction paper
newspaper
scissors
paste and paste brushes
assorted materials: printed cloth, wallpaper, sandpaper, cork, corrugated cardboard, fabric

A fish is a **fish** is a *fish*. They are all different, but the same. A bug is a **bug** is a *bug*. They are all different, but the same.

Does every flower look alike? Of course not! That's a silly question, isn't it! Well, how about bugs—do they all look alike? No, there are all kinds of them. All kinds of sizes and shapes and colors. But you can tell they are bugs, even though they are all different. What other things can you think of that come in a variety of shapes and colors and sizes? Certainly! If you go fishing—and are lucky enough to catch any fish—they are probably all different sizes, even if they are all the same kind of fish. Maybe some are so small you have to throw them back into the water again. The ones you take home with you are certainly different sizes and shapes and colors from the fish you have in an aquarium—or the ones you might buy at the store to eat.

Variety of Ideas. Continue to talk for a few minutes about other things the children suggest. There will be such wide varieties as toads and trees, snails and sailboats—as well as the usual birds, butterflies, trucks, and rockets. Encourage children to describe differences in size and shape. Add your own comments to theirs.

Explain to the class that they will make collages. Each collage will have just one kind of thing in it. It may be frogs or fish or turtles or trees or rabbits or anything you would like. But whatever you make will come in a variety of shapes and sizes. There will be one other way they will be different, too . . . you will make them from a variety of materials.

Color and Texture. Show them the assortment of materials you have: 9" x 12" white and colored construction paper, newspaper, wallpaper, cardboard, cork, sandpaper, corrugated cardboard, fabric. Talk about the colors: light and dark colors, bright and dull colors. Different colors for your butterflies or frogs will make them look different. But there is another way these materials are different. They ______? Right! They feel different. Let a child touch the cloth and then the sandpaper. Have another child run his fingers over the sandpaper and then the corrugated cardboard. They don't feel the same, do they? They don't even look as though they feel the same. They have a different *texture.*

Raiding Ants

If "texture" is a new word to the class, comment about it further. It is how a surface feels (or even looks) as you touch it. You may want to let the children close their eyes and touch an item. Can you identify it just by the texture? Then comment about the materials that look more textured than they feel. Yes, the light and dark areas of the newspaper appear to give it a texture. Right! So do the patterns on the fabric.

Do you have an idea for your collage? Remember, it will be just one kind of thing, but it will come in a variety of shapes, sizes, colors, and textures.

Choose Materials. Let groups of children take turns selecting a background paper and two or three kinds of materials. Choose colors that will

Boats Galore

look well together and select more than one texture. Choose the materials that you want to be most important in your collage, and cut big sailboats or birds or whatever you are going to make from them. Then you can cut little ones from the leftover pieces. You will need more than two or three kinds of material in your collage, so where will you get them? Certainly! You may share them with other children, or if no one has what you want, you may return to the supply area for them.

Good! That is a big one! Make another big one out of another material, and be sure it is a different shape. That will make an excellent beginning. Oh, that is a fine bee, but he is such a little one! Make a giant bee— as though he were under a huge magnifying glass. Of course you can make them bigger than real bees. You aren't making real bees; you are making a picture of them—a bee collage. You have two giant fish right together. Do you think you could find a better place for one of them? That's much better! Are you going to use another texture? Certainly, you may get whatever you need. If there is no one who can share his with you, get it from the supply table. That's a fine idea! No one else thought of making ants! I like the way you have grouped those tiny bugs together. They look much better that way than if each one were in a different part of the collage. Aren't you going to overlap some of your trees? Overlapping helps your eyes to move easily from one part of the collage to another. Oh, yes, that looks much better, and now you have space to add more trees. Of course, you may begin to paste them to the background as soon as you have just the right arrangement.

Continue to walk about the room assisting each child in any way he needs. A compliment may be enough for one child, a question or a comment for another. You may have to spend more time with others. Some children need almost constant approval in order to gain confidence in themselves.

Feeling of Success. When all the collages have been finished and all the supplies put away, have a quick showing. Let several children at a time show their work to the rest of the class. You may want to see all the birds at one time and all the fish together, or you may want to see a variety of subjects at one time. Comment about those that have a number of different textures in one collage. Compliment the children who chose an unusual subject. Encourage the child who has shown more imagination than usual, the one who has done a neater job than he ordinarily does. Ask various children to select a collage with a wide variety of sizes, another with a good color combination, another that lets your eye move easily from place to place. Try to mention something good about each child's work: a unique idea, a good choice of color or material, maybe just one little spot that looks good. Help children to see how a slight change could have made an improvement, but find something you can compliment so that each child will end the lesson with a feeling of success and a willingness to try again.

When you display all the collages in your classroom, you will have a wide assortment of things. Each flower on the collage will be different, but every one will be a flower. Each turtle will be different, but every one will be a turtle. In each collage every item will be different, but all will be the same.

MAKE IT EASY—FOR YOURSELF!

1. No pencils! Children will do much better if they are taught not to do any preliminary drawing with a pencil. Teach them to think and then to cut.
2. Have each child take only two or three materials at first. This will let every child get started quickly and will give them all a better choice of materials. Encourage them to share leftover supplies with other children. If necessary, let them return to the supply area for additional materials.
3. Encourage children to repeat the same materials in different parts of the collage. This will help to add rhythm and balance to the picture.
4. It is a good idea to have an extra set of scissors that are used only to cut cloth. Scissors that are used for cutting paper soon become dull and are almost useless with cloth. Mark the cloth scissors in some way and teach children never to use them for anything else.
5. Don't give out paste too soon. You want to encourage children to move and rearrange parts of their collages until the right effect is created. If they have paste in the beginning, they will tend to paste each item as they cut it.
6. If paste brushes are not available, have children make paste applicators. Fold a scrap of paper until it is a narrow strip, then bend it lengthwise in the center to give it added strength.

7. If any nonporous materials (such as aluminum foil) are used, you will need to have glue available. Paste is fine for any kind of paper or cloth.
8. Encourage children to give titles to their collages. A good title can make an excellent picture out of an otherwise ordinary one.

Get an Extra

Collage and Rubbing *(Suggested for all elementary grades)*

Objectives

1. To introduce texture as an important element of design.
2. To experiment with a variety of materials.
3. To introduce collage as a form of art.
4. To introduce texture-rubbing as a form of art.

Materials

12" x 18" white or colored construction paper
textured materials: corrugated cardboard, sandpaper, string, yarn, burlap
Other materials: cardboard, wallpaper
scissors
paste and paste brushes
newspaper

Whenever there is something important, you are told to get an extra. There's a sale at the store, and you are advised to get an extra of whatever the item may be. A special event happens, and the newsboy tells you to get an "Extra" (a special, extra issue of the paper which covers the event) and "read all about it!"

Usually, when you make a picture, you try only to make it look good. But did you ever try to make a picture that you could feel?

When you ask that question, the response you get will depend upon the age of the children and their previous experiences. The older children may have made texture collages or used textured materials, and so they will remember that they felt those materials. It will probably be a new idea to the youngest children.

The Feel of Materials. Spread out the materials they will use on a large table and let them gather around it. Talk about the corrugated paper. The ridges on it make it look rough, don't they? Feel it–run your fingers lightly over it. Does it feel rough, too? Certainly it does! If you use corrugated cardboard in a picture, you could feel it as well as see it.

Is there another material that also looks rough? Yes, the sandpaper. Does it feel rough, too? Try it. Close your eyes and touch the piece of string. Do your fingers bump as they go over it? Feel any of the other rough materials that you may have.

Feel the colored construction paper. Does that feel rough? Well, the edge does; but the rest of it is smooth, isn't it? The colors are good to look at but not good to feel in a picture. Feel the wallpaper. Does that feel rough? No. But it is pretty, and it will look good in a picture—even though you can't feel it.

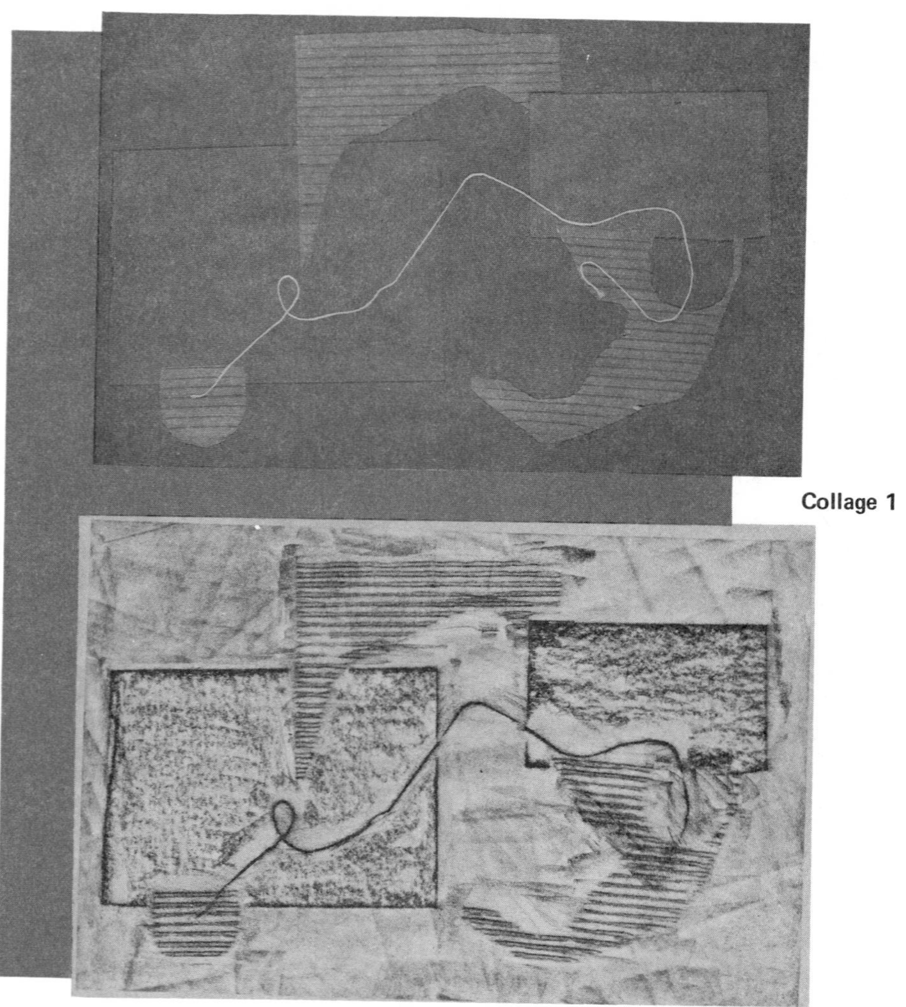

Collage 1

Make an Arrangement. Begin to arrange some of the materials on a piece of colored construction paper. Include some that have a definite texture and some that are merely pleasing colors and shapes. Does it look good to have all the textured materials together and all the plain ones together? No. It would look better to have some of the materials we can feel in different parts of the picture. That will help to balance the picture.

Talk about colors that make pleasing contrasts—dark and light, dull and bright. Repeat the same colors in different parts of the picture, just as textures are repeated and moved about in the picture. Overlap some of the plain materials.

What could you do with the string or yarn? It is a line instead of a shape like the other materials, so let's use it as a line and let it help to move our eyes from one part of the picture to another. See, you can put it where it will repeat some line that is already in the picture—or you can make it move from one part of the collage to another part, like that.

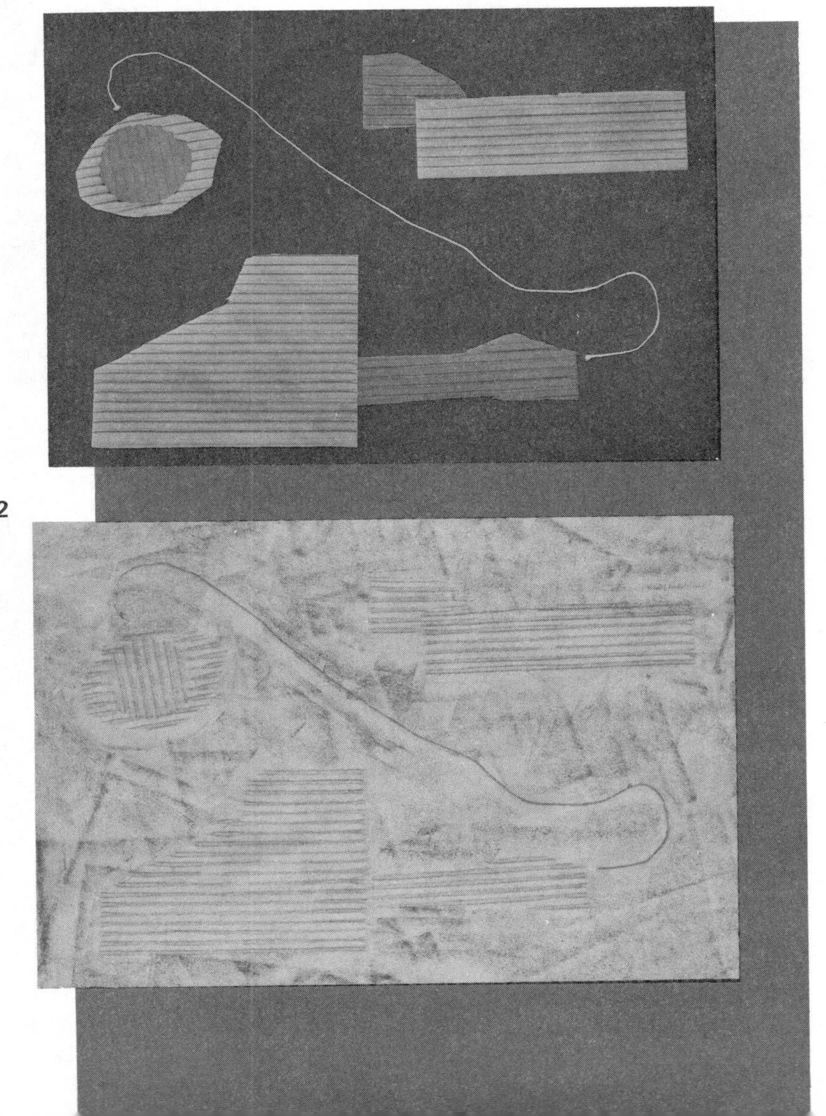

Collage 2

Choose Beginning Materials. Let groups of children take turns selecting several beginning materials from the table. Choose a large piece of colored paper for the background; choose a color that will look good with the materials you have chosen.

That's the way to begin! Start with a large shape first while you have plenty of space for it. Do overlapping textures feel good? It would be hard to paste them that way, wouldn't it? Move them about until they look just right. Good! The same material repeated in another place helps your eyes move easily from place to place. Do you have a part of your collage which looks crowded? Yes, if you left out one or two pieces, it might look better. Yes, the string does look better when it makes a simpler line. When your arrangement is just the way you want it, paste it to the background.

Before long, each of the collages will be finished. As you walk about the room, show several of the pictures to the rest of the class. Comment about the repetition of texture and color. Call attention to particularly pleasing arrangements. See how the string is used to bring the parts together—how your eyes follow the lines from one place to another.

Another Picture. They look good, don't they? Some parts of them would even *feel* good if we touched them. But let's prove that they have an interesting texture. Let's make another picture just like this one, only without any sandpaper—or any corrugated cardboard—or any of the materials we have already used. How can we do that?

Let your class gather around you again. Take a completed collage and lay a piece of plain white paper over it. Let several children rub their hands over it. Can you feel the picture under it? Sure you can! But you can't see it. So let's make a picture of what you can feel.

Rub with Crayon. Choose a crayon and remove the paper wrapper from it. Lay the crayon flat on its side and rub it back and forth over part of the white paper which is lying on the collage. Extend the crayon rubbing slightly beyond the edges of one of the shapes on the collage. See—there it is! The crayon has shown us what we could feel underneath the paper. Let's use the same crayon on another part of the paper. Where else would this color look good?

Repeat Color. Let one child suggest an area. Rub the side of the crayon over that area until the shape that is underneath appears on the paper. It may be an important textured area, such as corrugated paper—or it may be a plain piece of cardboard, so that only its outline will show.

Ask another child to select a second color crayon—one that will blend with the first, or one that will make a pleasing contrast. Rub another area or two until the outlines or textures of the material beneath appear on the paper. Complete the rubbing with one of the two crayons or with a third, if you like.

Compare the Pictures. Now let's look at the two pictures together. Lay them side by side so that you can compare them. They are different, but they are both good to look at, aren't they? One you can feel with your fingers, and the other one you have to feel with your eyes. The shapes and the arrangements are the same, yet the pictures are different—made with different materials.

When the children have returned to their desks, let them continue to finish their collages and then to make rubbings of them. Each child will want to show both his pictures, so have a quick display of all of them. Then plan a longer exhibit of them, including at least one by each child.

It isn't every day that you make such special pictures—a collage and a rubbing! But then, it isn't every day that you make one picture and then get an extra.

MAKE IT EASY—FOR YOURSELF!

1. Explain the meaning of *collage*. It is a French word meaning a *pasting*. Usually a variety of materials are included.
2. Have a good assortment of textured and plain materials so that each child will have a choice.
3. Don't give paste to the children right away. Encourage them to experiment and rearrange before they finally paste the pictures. When you see they have a good beginning, give each of them some paste on a scrap of paper. A tongue depressor makes a fine tool for dispensing the paste.
4. Teach the children to do their pasting on a newspaper in order to keep their pictures and work areas clean.
5. If paste brushes are not available, a satisfactory paste applicator can be made by folding a scrap of paper until it is a narrow strip and then bending it in the middle for added strength.
6. If you keep a scrap box of crayons, they are fine for this lesson. If children use their regular crayons, have them remove the top half of the wrappers.
7. Have the children clear away all extra materials before they begin their rubbings. This will give them additional work space and make the final cleanup easier.
8. Hold the collage and covering paper steady while making the rubbing. If either of them moves, there will be a distracting double image—just as when a camera moves while the picture is being taken.
9. Encourage children to give their pictures appropriate titles. A picture is often improved by a good creative title.
10. Divide the lesson into two parts for young children. Make the collage in one lesson and the rubbing in the next.

5 Mobiles and Constructions

What's in a Shape?

Strip Sculpture *(Suggested for Grades 3 through 6)*

Objectives

1. To use a two-dimensional material to create a three-dimensional picture.
2. To provide an opportunity to experiment in changing the form of a material.
3. To build a picture by adding parts to it.

Materials

12" x 18" white and colored construction paper
scissors
paste and paste brushes
newspaper
string

Fish Story

"That's just a circle," you say. But wait a minute! It may be the eye of a wise old owl, or the head of a mouse, or the wheel of an automobile, or even part of a person. What's in a shape–any shape? Why, anything you want!

If I told you this strip of paper is the head of a rabbit, would you be surprised? Well, it might be! No, it doesn't look like it right now, but couldn't you change it some way? No, we're not going to cut pictures of things out of these strips–they are too narrow for that. Can you think of any other way of changing these strips?

Add Parts. Someone will certainly think of bringing the two ends together to make a circle. Yes, a circle reminds us of many things. What would you add to this circle if you wanted it to become the head of a rabbit? Probably the first thing children will suggest will be ears. Make two ears by creasing two more strips in the middle, bending back each end, and attaching them to the circle. Cut the strips first so that they are the right length for two long rabbit ears.

What else do you need to make this into a rabbit? Continue to add a body and a round tail. Yes, you might want to add paws, too. Perhaps you could think of some way that you could make the paws and the tail form a steady base so that the paper rabbit could sit without falling.

Other children may think the rabbit needs eyes and a mouth. Fine! How could you add them to the circle? The eyes might be so big they touched both sides of the head. Then it would be easy to add eyes, wouldn't it? And perhaps they would help you add a nose and mouth, too.

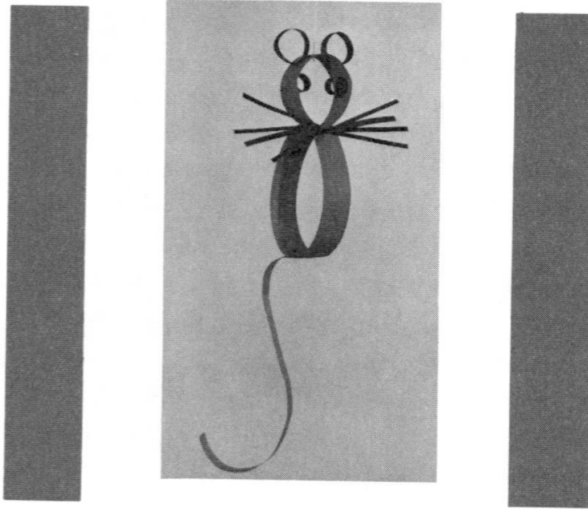

Mr. Mouse

Strips Only. Do you want to have just one big shape for his body? Perhaps it would be stronger if there were something inside that shape to help support it. It has to be done with strips, remember—no other shapes. Encourage the children to be original and to think of different ways it could be done: more circles could be fastened inside the larger one until the whole area is filled; other strips could be fastened at the top and bottom of the large circle to enclose it in a cage-like structure. Perhaps you can think of other ways, too.

Standing or Mobiles. Let each child have several strips of paper. Give each of them a little paste and a paste brush. Encourage them to experiment. If you know just what you want to make, you may begin right away. But if you're not sure, just make several shapes and try putting them together. Perhaps they will give you an idea. Yes, you may make them any size you would like. They may be giants when you finish them, or they may be tiny objects. You decide which you would like yours to be.

Yes, you make them strong enough to stand by themselves, or, if you would rather, you may make mobiles out of them. Then you would have to be sure that the parts were carefully attached to each other so that they wouldn't come apart when they were hung. They have to be strong either way.

Good! No one else thought of making an alligator. He will look better standing than hanging as a mobile, won't he? But your butterfly must surely be a mobile—right? That's a good way of making a poodle! All the tiny circles fastened together make him look as though he has curly fur. Could you give your pig a curly tail? Perhaps you could roll it around a pencil—or run it across the blade of a pair of scissors—like that. Good. Your sailboat had to start with a different kind of shape for the sail, didn't it!

Encouragement and Reassurance. Some children will only need time and materials to make their three-dimensional objects. Others will need almost constant encouragement and reassurance. These are important ingredients for them, and they look to you to supply them. Occasionally you will need to lend a hand to hold a shape in place or to help to balance a stubborn object. After all, there are times when everyone could use a third hand!

Don't be discouraged when nothing seems to be happening at first. It takes time and patience to change those strips of paper into three-dimensional fish or poodles, sailboats or bicycles—or whatever else they will eventually become. Suddenly you'll have a roomful of tigers and turtles, birds and butterflies, rockets and racers. You'll never wonder again about what's in a shape. You'll know—it can be anything!

MAKE IT EASY—FOR YOURSELF!

1. Cut some paper into strips of various widths—from about 2" to as narrow as 1/2". Let a group of children at a time choose several of these. It will help them plan their own three-dimensional objects if they have these pre-cut strips at the beginning. Later they can cut more of whatever size they need.
2. Have an assortment of white and colored 12" x 18" construction paper from which the children may select the colors they want to use.
3. Give each child a small amount of paste on a scrap of paper.
4. If paste brushes are not available, a satisfactory applicator may be made by folding a scrap of paper until it is a narrow strip and then bending it in the middle to give it added strength.

5. Give each child a small piece of newspaper—a quarter of a page is enough—to do his pasting on. When a clean area is needed, either fold the newspaper or get another piece.
6. Have some thin string to attach the mobiles so that they can be displayed immediately. (Be sure the paste is entirely dry first so that it won't come apart.) Have an area ready where the other objects may be displayed.
7. Have a sharing experience at the end of the lesson. Make sure the value of each child's work is appreciated so that he has a sense of worth and accomplishment.

Cat and Mouse

Mobiles *(Suggested for Grades 3 through 6)*

Objectives

1. To choose from a variety of materials for a specific purpose.
2. To experiment with materials by changing them from two- to three-dimensional.
3. To learn to balance objects of different weights.
4. To provide an opportunity for working cooperatively.

Materials

white and colored construction paper
paste and paste brushes
glue
scissors
newspaper
assorted materials: wire, pipe cleaners, cloth, string, cotton batting, buttons, roving
heavy wire, thin doweling, or small tree branches for mobile frames

"Want to play 'Cat and Mouse'?"

Ask your class to play a word game with you. You will say one word and they will reply with another that tells what the first would be pursuing. For example, if you say "cat" they will reply with "mouse." Ready?

"Bird . . . " "Worm!" Right—the bird would be after the worm.

"Spider . . . " "Fly!" Right—the spider would try to catch the fly. Now you think of two things that belong together.

Many Ideas. There will be all kinds of things suggested: an elephant and a peanut; a rabbit and a carrot; a fish and a worm; a bee and a flower; a rocket and the moon; a butterfly and a flower; a dog and a bone. Those are all fine ideas! Perhaps you will be able to think of two other things that belong together—one thing that will be after another.

One Thing After Another. Tell the class that they are going to make mobiles—a cat-and-mouse type of mobile where one thing is after a second thing. It might be your elephant trying to reach that peanut, or it might be your fish after the worm—or whatever you decide to make.

Show the class the variety of materials that are available. Explain that some part of each mobile must be three-dimensional. Yes, a part of it may be flat—two-dimensional—but something must be three-dimensional—it must have height, width, and depth. Yes, all of it may be three-dimensional if you like. No, don't worry about size. Make each part any size you like; just make it look good. The peanut would probably have to be larger than a real one, but the elephant might not be much larger than the peanut he is after. You will decide how big you want each part to be—and what you want to be three-dimensional.

Welcome!

Choose Partners. Two children will work together to make one mobile. Remind the class that when they work with someone else they should choose someone who works much the way they do—someone whose work they like. Remember, you will have to reach decisions together, so choose someone you will work with well. Let a few children at a time select working partners.

Partners will need a few minutes to talk things over and decide what they will put in their mobiles. There will probably be all kinds of questions, so you will be busy, too. Yes, the rabbit and carrot was your idea, so you may make that. But that idea belongs to you, so no one else should use it. Certainly, you may make a mouse and a piece of Swiss cheese. That is a fine idea and it will belong to just you. No, you won't have to make both things the same size or weight. Just make two separate things first, and we will take care of balancing them later. Yes, you may both work on each part—or you may each make one of the two parts of the mobile. You decide that.

Some pairs of children will agree quickly on a subject and go to work immediately. Others will be undecided and need some encouragement or suggestions from you. Move quickly about the room, asking a question to get one pair of children thinking, offering a suggestion to another pair, helping wherever you are needed.

Oh, I can tell already that is going to be a rocket! Will it be on its way to the moon? So far everything you have made is flat. What are you going to make that's three-dimensional? Yes, that will be fine. You want a needle and thread? I'm sure I can find some for you. That's an excellent way of making a spider web. Do you think it should be a little larger?

Comment about Work. It will take time for children to discuss and plan and then make the two parts of their mobiles, so don't rush them. As parts of different mobiles are completed, show them to the rest of the class. Comment about something that is unusual, something that is three-dimensional, something particularly well made, something with a good choice of materials. Give the children who made them a sense of pride in their work, and encourage the other children to be creative.

When the two parts of one mobile have been finished, have the class stop and look at them. Hold the two parts up at one time. Should both parts hang from string the same length so that they are right next to each other—this way? Or would it look better if they hung at slightly different lengths—this way? Yes, they do look better when one is just a little lower than the other one.

How to Balance. One part is very heavy and the other part is very light. How will you be able to balance them on the same mobile? No, the length of the string won't make any difference. That's right! It's how near to the center or to the ends of the stick or wire you place them. Show the class the choice of materials for the frame of the mobile—the part from which the two things will hang.

Like a Seesaw. Remind the children of how it was when they played on a seesaw. Were you able to balance with a much bigger person than you? Yes, perhaps you were on one end of the seesaw and your mother was on the other side. She was heavier than you were, so did she sit at the end of the board, or did she have to sit nearer the center? That's right! The heavier person sat closer to the center, and the lighter person sat nearer the end.

Well, couldn't you do the same thing with your mobile? Tie a string to the center of the frame of the mobile so one partner can hold it while the other partner balances the two parts. Then tie a string to each part. Tie a loose knot at the other end of the string and fasten it to the frame of the mobile. Move the heavier part closer and closer to the center and the lighter one nearer and nearer to the end until the two parts balance each other.

Of course you can balance them! You just have to keep trying. That is almost balanced now. See how one side dips slightly? Move the heavier one just a bit more toward the center. See, that does it! But your two parts are almost exactly the same weight, so they will be almost the same distance from each end. Just see where they will look the best.

Before long, one mobile after another will be completed, and you will be busy hanging them all. Gradually your classroom will take on a new and unusual appearance. There may be a cat and mouse overhead. Or there may be a mouse after a piece of cheese, or a bug ready to land on a flower, or a spaceship headed for the moon, or . . . .

Dinnertime

MAKE IT EASY—FOR YOURSELF!

1. The objects on the mobiles should be relatively small, so cut the construction paper to 6" x 9".
2. It is a good idea to keep a scrap box of odds and ends in your classroom. It will come in handy for this lesson.
3. No pencils! No preliminary drawing.
4. If wire or pipe cleaners are used, have a pair of wire snips to cut them. Pliers usually have a wire-cutting edge. Do not use scissors—the wire ruins them.

5. Paste is satisfactory for any kind of paper or cloth, but you will need glue for such things as wire or buttons or any nonporous material. Do not use paste brushes in glue.
6. Paper clips opened into two loops make fine hangers for suspending the mobiles from light fixtures or an overhead cord.

Can You Make a Straight Line Curve?

3-D Construction *(Suggested for Grades 4 through 6)*

Objectives

1. To provide an opportunity for working in three dimensions.
2. To experiment with straight lines to create the illusion of curves.
3. To experiment with three-dimensional space.

Materials

thin strips of balsa wood (1/8")	glue
toothpicks	newspaper

You've heard people say they can't even draw a straight line. Maybe you've said it yourself. That won't be any problem today—you'll have a straight line to begin with. The problem will be—can you make a straight line curve?

Balsa wood fascinates children. The minute they see it they'll be excited. They'll probably want to know if they can make something with it.

Curved Line. Certainly you can make something with it. You're going to make some three-dimensional constructions that have a curved line somewhere in them. No, of course you can't bend balsa wood without breaking it, so you will use only straight lines.

There will probably be several questions and comments. But you said it would have a curved line. How can it be curved if it is straight?

Well, let's stop a minute and figure that out. Have you ever seen a group of straight lines put together so that it looked as though they curved? Sure you have! They were straight lines, but they curved—at least it looked as though they curved. Go to the blackboard and draw a series of straight lines that all begin from one point and radiate outward to form a circle.

See, the outline of the circle is certainly a curved line. Draw another series of straight lines, but this time place them as though they are attached at one end to a curved string. At one end, they will be close together, and, at the other end, they will be farther apart. That's a curved line, too, isn't it? But they are all straight lines.

An Optical Illusion. On your construction you are going to find some way of making a curved line—really one that just appears to curve—by the way you arrange the lines. You will be creating an *optical illusion*. Be sure the children know what is meant by an optical illusion.

Break a piece of balsa wood into a strip 5" or 6" long, and break another one slightly shorter. If these were your lines, you would glue them together, but I will just try to hold them in place. Would they have to be attached at the tops of both pieces like that? Well, they could, but they wouldn't have to be. Couldn't I move the top of one down along the other one, like that? No, I wouldn't want to just cross them in the middle. That doesn't even look as though it were creating any space, does it?

Modern Railroad

Stand by Itself. Continue to move the two strips so that they touch at different places and create areas of different sizes and shapes. A construction can't be made of just two lines, though, so I'll have to add a third one. Break off a third piece of balsa wood. Hold two pieces together with one hand and move the third piece about with the other hand. Would it look good to attach it at exactly the same place where the other two come together? No, no! That would be uninteresting. It would look just like a tent. Remember, though, that this construction has to be able to stand by itself. And a construction needs at least three contact points in order to balance and stand up by itself. Perhaps it would be a good idea to balance your construction before you do anything else.

Move the third stick about to show that it could be attached in many places. If this were your construction, you would have to decide where to attach it. Then you could add more and more pieces of balsa wood to it until it made an interesting arrangement of spaces. Could lines of balsa cross through some of those spaces? Certainly! That would make overlapping lines and make the construction more interesting.

Toothpicks Later. So far your construction would be made of only straight lines, wouldn't it? And we said this design must have some straight lines that curve. Let's see how we could do that. Shorter and thinner—but straight—lines will help us do that. Toothpicks will be just fine. Once you have your construction finished you will arrange toothpicks so that they appear to curve. We'll see more about that later.

Give each child a strip of balsa, a tube of glue, and a piece of newspaper to cover the desk and protect it from the glue. Urge each child to think and plan before he glues anything—even before he breaks a strip.

Yes, begin with two strips of different lengths. Then glue them together. Oh, you have to hold them together longer than that. The glue has to dry before it is strong, you know. Just hold them gently in place and be patient for a minute or so. You can be deciding where the next line will go and how long it will be. Good! You have it balanced so that it will stand up by itself. Can you find some place where a line could cross through one of these spaces? Yes, that would be fine. Makes the whole thing look better! Do you have an empty area? Yes, three-dimensional designs can have empty areas just as well as two-dimensional designs. Right! That's the space that needs something added to it. See what you can do about it.

As soon as one child has a construction that is nicely arranged, have the class stop their work and gather around that child's desk. Talk for a moment about the pleasing arrangement, the three-dimensional spaces that the construction creates, the overlapping of lines as they cross through spaces.

Lines Appear to Curve. Now the next problem is to finish the construction so that you create an *optical illusion* by having lines that appear to curve. Let's see how it could be done on this construction. Find an open space where two lines do not quite parallel each other. They may both slant inward at the top but they do not come together. Lay a toothpick so that it crosses over both of them like a railroad tie. If that were glued there, another toothpick could be placed close to it, and another one close to that. And more and more could be added. Move the toothpick you are holding down along the two lines. Wouldn't that appear to curve? Is there any other way you could create an optical illusion on the construction?

There will be other suggestions. Do all the toothpicks have to be the same distance from each other at both ends? No. They might be close together at one end and slant apart at the other end. They could even start out by connecting two pieces of balsa and then moving to a third one. Certainly, they could. It would depend upon the shapes you have in your design.

More Than One Area. As you finish the straight lines of your construction, think of where you will create your optical illusion. Perhaps you can plan for it. Do you think you should add toothpicks in just one area or would it look better if they were in more than one place? Yes, it will probably look better if there is more than one area of them, but don't overdo it and crowd your construction.

Give each child a little pile of toothpicks and leave the rest of the supply where any child who needs more can get them.

Good! That is going to make an excellent optical illusion. That line really seems to curve. Yes, you may have a straight, flat area of toothpicks, too, if you like, but there must be at least one curved area. You're right! You do have to be careful! The toothpicks are so small they are hard to handle. Don't crowd your construction. When it looks just right, leave it alone—don't add another thing.

Titles. Gradually each construction will be completed. Urge each child to give his work a title. Turn it in all directions and see what it makes you think of. Oh, it probably won't look like anything real, but it will remind you of something. A good title will help to make it look even better. Give each child a small piece of white paper on which he can print his name and the title of his construction.

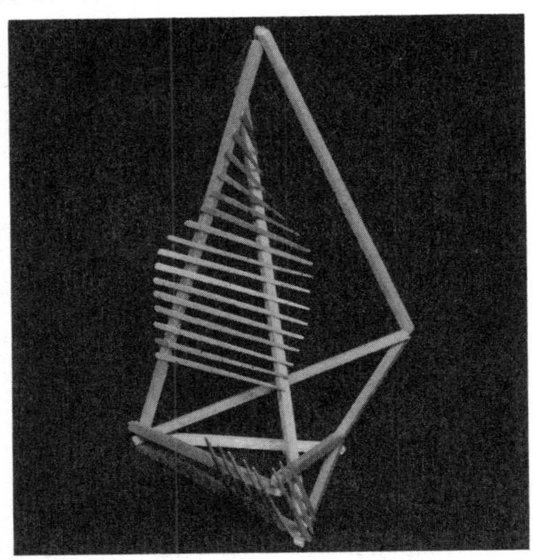

Angles

Let groups of children take turns walking about the room to see what everyone else has done. Urge them to read the titles and look at the constructions from every side. But no touching! Talk about the variety of ways that optical illusions have been created, about the use of space, about the balance between the almost-solid areas created by the toothpicks and the open areas. Then pick a place to display each construction for a longer period of time.

The next time someone tells you he can't draw a straight line, just ask him why he would want to do that. It's much more interesting to make straight lines curve!

MAKE IT EASY—FOR YOURSELF!

1. Balsa strips generally come in 2' lengths. Each child will need one to begin with and probably a second one later.
2. Use the natural color toothpicks. They will be more in keeping with the natural color of the balsa and so will create a more unified and pleasing construction.
3. If possible, give each child his own tube or bottle of glue. If necessary, two children can share one supply.
4. Once the glue has dried, the construction will be surprisingly strong. Each part must be held lightly but securely in place until the glue takes hold and dries.

Bridges and Towers

Three-Dimensional Construction *(Suggested for all elementary grades)*

Objectives

1. To introduce a simple form of construction.
2. To introduce open space as an important part of three-dimensional design.
3. To learn to view three-dimensional art from all directions.

Materials

Styrofoam 12" applicator sticks

You've wondered what it would be like to be an engineer and build all those bridges and towers. Don't daydream any longer—let's go to work!

Remember how you used to like to put blocks together and build new things with them? Sometimes they'd fall over and you'd have to begin again. It was fun, wasn't it!

Styrofoam and Sticks. We're going to build something but it won't be with just ordinary blocks. Instead it will be made of pieces of Styrofoam and sticks. Show the class the materials that are available. Let's see what we can do with them.

Have your class gather around you. Spread out the materials you will use.

The first thing you always need when you build anything is a base, isn't it? You can't put up a house or any kind of a building until you have a foundation, or base. We'll use this larger piece of Stýrofoam for a base. Push a wooden applicator stick into the base at an angle and press a smaller piece of Styrofoam on top of it.

That was easy to do; let's try it again. Would it be a good idea to have the sticks standing up straight—like that, or would it look better if they slanted slightly? Yes, it will make a more pleasing arrangement if most of the lines slant so that they help to move your eye from one part of the design to another. As you talk, add another piece of Styrofoam to the top of the second stick.

That's a good beginning, but if all the lines travel upward from the base and end with a piece of Styrofoam, it won't make much of a construction. What else could you do?

Bridges and Towers. The first suggestion will probably be to connect two of the small pieces of Styrofoam. Good! That will make a bridge across the design. You may need a shorter stick for that, so just break one to any length you need. There will be other ideas, too. One will certainly be to add another stick to the small piece of Styrofoam and build the design up higher. Good! That will make a tower for the design.

Yes, there are other things you can do to make your construction more pleasing. Try them when you have your materials. But be sure that your design includes at least one bridge and one tower.

Begin Own Design. When each child has returned to his own work area, give him his supply of Styrofoam and applicator sticks. Every child will begin immediately without any urging from you.

If all your lines just travel straight up in the air, they won't make a pleasing design, will they? Certainly—take out some and change them. Don't make too many holes in the Styrofoam, though, or there won't be anything to hold the stick in place. Break the sticks to any length you need. Good! I see a bridge already! Remember to make a tower, too. Is the top of your structure getting too big for the base? That will make it top-heavy and it may come apart. Oops—there it goes! Oh, well, that's no problem. When your building blocks used to fall over, you just put them back together again, didn't you? Do the same with these building materials, too. Oh, yes—certainly you may have more than one bridge or one tower. Just be sure to have at least one of each. Turn your constructions as you make them so that you can see them from all sides. A three-dimensional construction has to look good from all directions. Is there an empty area in your design? That's right. Can you put something there? Good! I like the way you are making sticks cross through other areas. When your construction looks just right, don't add another thing. Just look at it—and admire it!

Look at Constructions. Gradually each construction will be finished, and each child will be eager to display his work to all the class—and to see what every other child has created. So have a sharing period. The finished designs will be much too fragile to hold up, so have each child place his work in the center of his desk. Let the class make a group around a number of constructions. Talk about each one of them.

Do they all have at least one bridge and one tower? Check each one to make sure. Yes, there is at least one tower and one bridge on each arrangement. You're right! Some of them have several bridges. Can you find a different way of making a bridge? Yes, that double bridge made with two sticks right next to each other is an unusual idea.

Things That Are Different. Continue to talk about the things that are different: the tower that goes up especially high but is so nicely balanced; the part of the design that extends so far out that it had to have an extra support under it; the line that seems to curve; the crossing through spaces to create an interlocking of shapes.

Then move on to another group of constructions. Do they all have at least one bridge and one tower? What is different about these? Which one do you like especially well?

Display Them. Later you'll want to display each piece where it can be seen by other people. If there's a display case in the school lobby, that would be an ideal place for some of them. But don't crowd them—find another place for some of them. The librarian may have an empty area; she'd be delighted to have your constructions displayed there. The principal or school secretary would like one or two to make a pleasing center of interest in the office.

Wherever you look there will have been engineers at work. Bridges and towers will be everywhere, but you'll never get tired of looking at them because they're all different. There is always something new to see.

MAKE IT EASY—FOR YOURSELF!

1. Scrap Styrofoam works as well as new material. If you have some that you have previously used as inking plates, you may want to use them for this lesson. The color on one or both sides of the Styrofoam will add variety to the constructions.
2. If you are working with very young children, break the Styrofoam into small irregular pieces. Have a variety of sizes and shapes. Older children will want to make their own pieces. Give young children a base—a larger and, if possible, a thicker piece of Styrofoam—about 6" square or any irregular shape about 6" across. They will need eight or ten small pieces of Styrofoam and a supply of sticks. Give older children a piece of Styrofoam about 6" x 12" and let them make their own shapes. Have some additional materials for those children who need extra supplies.
3. Narrow dowels about 1/8" x 12" or 1/16" x 12" are available from medical as well as art supply stores. If the 12" length is not available, 6" ones can be used.
4. The finished designs are too fragile for younger children to carry home in one piece. After the constructions have been displayed in school, let the children take them apart and carry them home in a paper bag. They will enjoy using them again at home!

Sidewalk Superintendent

Balsa Constructions *(Suggested for Grades 4 through 6)*

Objectives

1. To provide an opportunity for three-dimensional construction.
2. To experiment with line and space.
3. To become more aware of rhythm and balance.

Materials

balsa wood, assorted sizes
glue
newspaper
scissors

Remember when that big building was being constructed? Everytime you went past it you stopped to watch. You were a *sidewalk superintendent.*

How would you like to go into the construction business? What would you build? Yes, you might build houses—or even apartment houses if you had a big construction business. Right! Or stores or offices or factories. Good! Construction workers build bridges and tunnels, too.

Do you stop to look at the framework of the construction as you go past a building site? It is particularly interesting if it is a tall building because you can see the lines of the framework against the sky. The lines and the open spaces make a pleasing pattern.

Make a Construction. You are going to be construction workers and build a framework that creates an interesting pattern of line and space, but you won't build houses or offices or bridges or tunnels—or anything real at all. You will just build a construction that is pleasant to look at.

Take two different size pieces of balsa wood and turn and combine them in several ways so that they create lines that move in several directions. Suppose you cut these pieces so that you had a short, thick line here and a long, thin one there. Where would you add another line?

It would be just another line sticking out if you put it here. But look—if you put it this way it creates a new shape, an open space. What would you do with this wider but thin piece? How about this piece? Oh, yes, you'd have to cut them to make them shorter. You would have to decide how long each piece should be to look good.

Let various children suggest ways they would use different sizes of balsa. Comment about the line that is created, the enclosed area that is formed, the three-dimensional spaces that result.

Easy to Cut. Balsa wood is soft and easy to cut, so you won't need any saws. In fact, a pair of scissors will be the basic cutting tool. Use the open blade of the scissors as a knife, cutting deeper and deeper into the wood each time the blade is pulled across it.

Angles

Have each child select two sizes of balsa wood for the beginning of his construction. Encourage them to return any unused pieces whenever they take a different size piece of wood. This will maintain an ample supply for everyone, rather than having unneeded supplies pile up on a few children's desks. Give each child a pair of scissors to cut with.

As the class goes to work, walk about the room to assist in any way you can. Encourage the child who is hesitant, assist the awkward child by lending a third hand, ask questions to provoke thinking, and compliment frequently.

Yes, two pieces of wood are all you can use in the beginning. You can get more when you are ready for it. Are you sure you want two pieces of balsa just the same size? Wouldn't your construction have more interesting lines if they had some variety of size and thickness?

Oh, you have to be more patient than that! Glue is weak, you know, until it dries. So hold the pieces together until the glue becomes hard. No, you don't have to press them together so hard. In fact, that squeezes the glue out. You will do better to hold them lightly. Have you tried putting your construction down on the desk to see if it balances?

That's a good beginning! You already have a new shape there, don't you! Turn your construction frequently so that you see it from all sides. A three-dimensional construction should look good from every angle. Yes, a narrow piece of balsa would make a good contrast next to that fat one. See if anyone has an extra piece he doesn't want—or get it from the supply table if you need to.

Oh, look at the wonderful space you have here! You were clever to put that line through it so that it looks interesting instead of empty. Don't pick up your construction until the glue is thoroughly dry—and strong. It would be dreadful to have it come apart.

Continue to move from one child to another. Pause just long enough to ask or answer a question, to correct some problem before it becomes serious, to use your mat knife to cut a piece of balsa, to praise a child for some pleasing part of his construction. Call the attention of the class to something different one child has done, notice the interesting interplay of lines in another, turn another in all directions to show the rhythm and motion, comment about the good balance of one and the use of space in another.

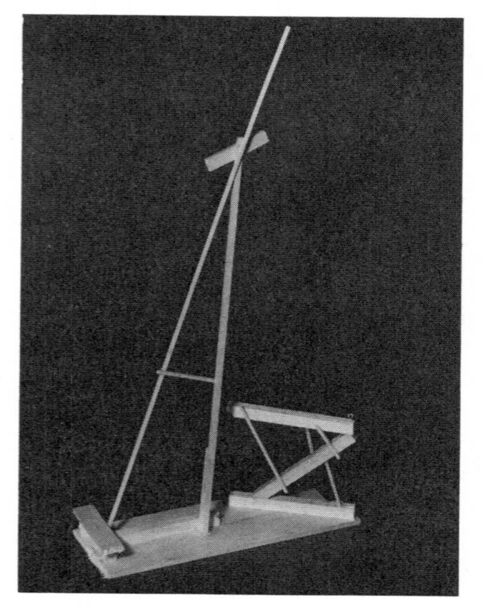

A to Z

Titles. Can you think of a good title for your construction? No, it won't look like anything real—it isn't supposed to. But perhaps some line or some shape will remind you of something. A good construction—like any good picture—will be even better with a meaningful title.

When each child has finished his construction and the materials are put away, have a quick showing. Have the class gather around one area where five or six constructions can be seen at a time. Encourage the class to find good things about each one. See that each child's work receives some favorable recognition. Then move on, going from one group to another until each child's work has been seen.

Plan an area where each construction can be displayed for a longer time. It is a good idea to place three-dimensional constructions in other parts of the school as well as in the classroom. In that way none of them are crowded, and each one is seen to its best advantage.

The librarian will be delighted to arrange a display; the principal will be glad to have a display of children's work to show to parents and other visitors. A display case in the school lobby will make a good place for several other constructions. Make a small card with the child's name and the title of his construction to place with each piece of work.

Wherever the children's work is exhibited, there will be sidewalk superintendents who gather to look, comment, and suggest. Nobody will be able to pass them without stopping to admire them.

MAKE IT EASY—FOR YOURSELF!

1. Give each child a small piece of newspaper to protect his desk from glue that may drip from the tube or his construction.
2. Each child will need an average of three or four pieces of balsa—each piece approximately 2' long. Have as many sizes as possible. They may be from 1/8" to 1" square. Other flat pieces may be a couple of inches wide but only 1/8" to 1/4" thick. The more variety the better.
3. While scissors are the basic cutting tool for each child, it will be handy to have a paring knife or two or even a jackknife available. Keep them on the supply table where older children may use them—under supervision. A mat knife will make an excellent supplementary tool if you have one. However, you should be the only one to use it. A small saw may come in handy.
4. Any good glue will hold balsa wood. Once the glue is thoroughly dry, the constructions will be surprisingly strong—but handle them as little as possible in the meantime.
5. If you have any scrap pieces of Styrofoam, some children may be able to use them as bases for their constructions.
6. Save all the scraps of balsa. They will come in handy for other lessons when a variety of materials is needed.

6
Printing

Oh, Yes, You Can!

Fingerpaint Prints *(Suggested for all elementary grades)*

Objectives

1. To experiment with a new fingerpainting technique.
2. To introduce a simple form of printing.
3. To develop a feeling of rhythm and motion.

Materials

fingerpaints
12" x 18" Styrofoam
tongue depressors
newspaper
small pieces of heavy cardboard
12" x 18" white and colored construction paper

Impossible! you say. You can't fingerpaint and stay clean! Oh, yes, you can! You won't even have to wash your hands.

Would you like to fingerpaint?

That's a silly question—but an exciting one! There will be such enthusiastic response that you will know every child wants to fingerpaint.

Clean Hands. Did you ever fingerpaint without getting even one little speck of paint on your hands? Yes, usually your hands are a mess when you fingerpaint—but not this time. No, we won't wear gloves! Well, let me prove that it can be done.

Have your class gather around you at a table. We'll cover the table so that no paint will get on that, either. What color fingerpaint would you like to have me use? Fine, I like that color, too.

Spread Paint on Styrofoam. Instead of putting the fingerpaint on a wet paper as we usually do, I'm going to put it on this piece of Styrofoam. Yes, it is a little bit like Styrofoam. I'll use a tongue depressor to scoop out some fingerpaint. I'll do that once or twice more to be sure there will be enough to cover this Styrofoam.

Put the paint on different areas. If this were an ordinary fingerpainting I'd use my hand to spread the paint, but this is no ordinary painting—and besides, I said I was going to keep my hands clean.

I'll spread the paint around with this piece of cardboard. Use the cardboard much as you ordinarily would use your hand to move the paint from place to place until most of the Styrofoam has a thin covering. Leave about an inch or so of clean area all around the edge of the Styrofoam.

Paper on Top of Paint. There's the paint, but now how do I make a picture without putting my hand in it? No, if I used the cardboard again my picture would have to stay on this Styrofoam. Then nobody else could use it. I want my picture on a piece of paper. Well, that's easy to fix—just lay a paper on top of the paint. I'll have to be careful, though, that I handle the paper on only the edges.

Now what do you think I should do? I want a fingerpainting, I have the paper and the paint, so the only thing that's left to do is ______? Right! I'll fingerpaint, but it will be on top of the paper instead of on top of the paint. That's doing things backwards, isn't it!

Begin at Bottom of Paper. Hold the paper and Styrofoam at one edge. With the other hand make a long, sweeping line. Begin at the bottom of the paper and swing the side of your hand upward in a rhythmic motion.

Looks as though nothing happened, doesn't it? But remember, this is a backwards picture. So the painting I am making is not on the top of the paper—it is on the ______? Right! On the back of the paper, the side which is lying on the paint. I have made a print.

If printing is a new idea to the class, explain that when you print you press something against an inked—or in this case a painted—surface. I pressed my hand against the paper that is on the paint, so I have made a print of the motion of my hand. It is a fingerpainting print.

From Same Place. It wouldn't be much of a fingerpainting with only one line, though, would it, so I'll make some more motions—more prints on the back of the paper. The only trouble is, nothing shows on this side, so I can't see where my print is. I'll take care of that problem by holding one finger down here where I began my first motion. If I start all my motions from the same place, they will look as if they belong together. Even though they all start from near the same place they will all be a little different.

Make another rhythmic motion with the side of your hand. Begin at the same point on the paper; but, if you went nearly straight up the first time, make this a rounding motion that swings well off to one side. Repeat variations of the motion several times, each one beginning at or near the same spot.

Some of the lines will be tall ones that go all the way to the top of the paper; others will stop somewhere lower on the paper; some will even be tiny motions that hardly get started at all. Sometimes I'll swing the lines nearly straight up, other times I'll curve or bend them to one side. Some lines even go up and then start down again. But every line flows smoothly.

Peel the paper from the Styrofoam—amid exclamations of glee! The children will be delighted with the results and intrigued with the process.

Another One. Let's try another one. Add a small amount of paint to the Styrofoam—or just spread what is there to make an even coating. Let one child choose a white or colored paper and lay it on the painted surface.

Would you like to make the first line on the paper? Where are you going to begin it? Yes, off the bottom edge of the paper. Would just off the center of the bottom edge be better than right in the middle? Then both sides could be different. Good! That was a big motion that went almost to the top. Who else would like to print a motion?

Choose another child to add to the painting. Remind him to start from about the same place that the first child used. Now sweep upwards in a big line, but this time make a different kind of motion. Now who is going to make a little line? That's a good one! Do you think this part of the picture may be empty? No one has made any lines over here yet. Good! Shall we see what your picture looks like? Nice, isn't it!

Different Colors. Explain that you will put several different colors of fingerpaint on several different pieces of Styrofoam—one color on each. The children will take turns selecting a paper and then making a fingerpainted print. After a print has been made, have the child take his picture back to his desk where he can put his name at the bottom of it and then leave the print to dry. Keep your fingers off, though! The paint will take a while to dry.

Yes, lay the paper right on the wet paint–but keep your fingers only on the edge of the paper so there won't be any fingerprints on it. Are you going to start right in the middle or off-center–and at the bottom, of course? Be sure your hand makes a smooth, sliding motion. Good! That should be an interesting print. Do you think you need to press just a little harder? It is the pressure that makes the print, you know.

Oops–you are forgetting to start from the same place. That's right, hold your finger there so that you can see where to begin. Are you making all your motions different–different sizes and shapes? Hold onto the Styrofoam and peel off the paper. Oh, that's a lovely picture! Who is going to fingerpaint here next?

Two-Color Print. Continue until each child has fingerpainted. Let's make another one–but different this time. We'll make it the same way–except we'll use two colors on the Styrofoam. Of course, the same two colors will always have to be used on one Styrofoam plate. Otherwise the colors would just get muddy and not show what they were. So on this red plate let's add some blue (or any other color you choose). On this piece of Styrofoam we'll add a bit of green, and on this one some black. We'll use the cardboard hand to blend them just a bit where they come together.

When the first child to make a two-color print has completed his picture, have him show it to the rest of the class so that they can see the effect. There will be new excitement and a renewed interest. Then let the rest of the children take turns making their prints.

One Displayed–One Taken Home. Have a sharing period at the end of the lesson. Ask the children to decide which of their pictures they think is more successful. Which one fills the paper the best without being crowded? Which one has more rhythmic lines? Which color effect is more pleasing? Which one do you just like better?

Then let groups of children show their work to the rest of the class. Later, display each child's favorite and let him take the other one home.

Oh, we almost forgot to look at your hands! See, they are still clean. You *can* fingerpaint without getting any paint on them.

MAKE IT EASY–FOR YOURSELF!

1. Cover the work area with newspaper. You will need it as a precaution and as a place to lay the cardboard that you use to spread the paint.
2. If you arrange all the painting areas in one section of the room, you will be able to supervise the work more successfully.
3. Five or six printing stations should be enough. Each one may have a

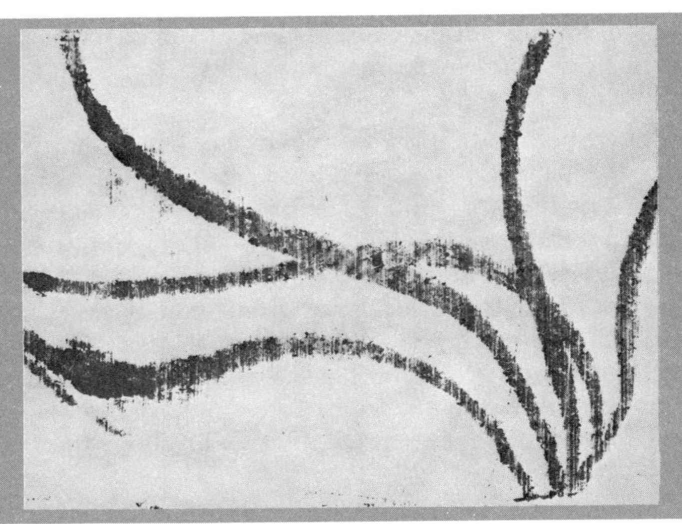

different color on the Styrofoam, or you may prefer to have only two or three printing colors.

4. More paint will be needed to cover the Styrofoam the first time. After that, a lesser amount will be needed. Sometimes you only need to wipe the existing paint smooth with the cardboard. Wipe over the paint lightly so you won't remove it with the cardboard. After a painted surface has been used many times, it tends to dry and make less satisfactory prints. Either use another piece of Styrofoam or press hard against the surface with the cardboard to remove most of the old paint—and then add a fresh supply.
5. White or light colored paper provides a greater color contrast with the paint and so results in a more effective print.
6. Older children will be able to spread their own paint on the Styrofoam, but you should do it for primary grade children.
7. Wash the Styrofoam under *cold* running water. It will remain stained from the paint, but it will still be perfectly good for future use.

That's Where They Belong!

Stick Printing *(Suggested for all elementary grades)*

Objectives

1. To introduce a simple form of printing.

2. To develop a sense of rhythm through repetition.
3. To experiment with straight lines to create a realistic picture.

Materials

9" x 12" and 12" x 18" white and colored construction paper
tongue depressors
tempera paint
newspaper

You're used to seeing tongue depressors in a doctor's office. Naturally. That's where they belong. But there's another place where they belong, too—in the art room!

Explain to your class that they are going to print a picture instead of painting one. Talk about printing for a few minutes. What do you know that is printed? Yes, newspapers are printed—and so are magazines. Look about the room for other things that have been printed: books, calendars, pictures, cards, fabric, posters.

Many of Them. Usually things are printed in order to make many of them alike. Many newspapers just alike are printed every day. All those science books are just alike. Many safety posters just like this were printed. The kind of picture you will print today will be different from every other picture—but you will print one object many times to make one picture. Explain that to print a thing, you ink (or paint) the object you are going to print, press it against the paper, and lift it. That makes it different from painting, doesn't it? When you paint, you slide the paint along with the brush or whatever you are painting with.

Let's see how printing is done. Have your class gather around you at a large table. Pour a small puddle of paint onto a piece of 6" x 9" paper. That will be my palette—the place where I have my supply of paint. I will use a tongue depressor as my printing tool.

Get Rid of Extra Paint. Dip the long, narrow edge of the tongue depressor into the paint. Spread the paint or redip the tongue depressor until all the narrow edge is covered with paint. There's too much paint on the tongue depressor to print well. It would smudge and not look good if we printed with it like that, so just get rid of some of it. Touch the edge of the tongue depressor lightly to a clean area of the palette. See, that gets rid of some of the extra paint. It is like wiping some of the extra paint off a brush when you are painting.

Press and Lift. Now let's see what happens. Press the "inked" edge of the tongue depressor firmly against the 12" x 18" drawing paper. Then lift it straight up. See, there is the edge of the tongue depressor printed on the paper. But you won't have a picture after printing just one line. Yes, you'll have to make lots of them.

Could you make a picture of real things by printing with a tongue depressor? Certainly, you could! What could this printed line be the beginning of? Yes, it could be one side of a house. To finish the house you would have to add the other walls and a roof. Can you think of any way of making short lines for the chimney or for windows? Well, no, you would have a hard time laying down only part of the tongue depressor, but there is something else you could do. Of course! You could paint on only as much of the edge as you want to print. Yes, you could do that, too. You could lay a piece of scrap paper under the part of the tongue depressor that you didn't want to print. Then that part of the print would be on the scrap paper instead of your picture.

Can You Make Round Lines? Are there other things this straight line could be the beginning of? That's right! It could be the trunk of a tree. Yes, it could be one leg of a man. Encourage children to think of a variety of things so as to stimulate their imaginations. Some of the things you have thought of have round parts to them. Could you make round lines with a tongue depressor? Well, yes, the end of the tongue depressor is slightly rounding, but it is so tiny. Is there any other way of making anything round? No, you won't be able to make round lines, but perhaps you will be able to think of some way of making them look round. When you get your practice paper you may experiment with straight lines and see if you can make them look round.

Practice Picture. Give each child a piece of 9" x 12" paper, a tongue depressor, and a palette with a small puddle of paint on it. This is just an experiment paper. Try making straight lines. Then try arranging lines so that they seem to round. Perhaps you would like to try to make some real object that has round lines. Yes, try making some short lines, too.

Good! That begins to look like a big fish. And fish have round lines, don't they! Remember to touch the tongue depressor to the palette paper before you print with it. That will get rid of the extra paint. Oh, no, no, no! Don't move the tongue depressor on your picture. That would be painting with it instead of printing with it.

Don't work on the practice paper more than about five minutes. Then take a minute or two to look at various things children have discovered. One child will have found that a thing can be made to appear quite solid by putting lines close together. Another child will have achieved the same result by crossing lines. An apparently round object has been made by a careful placement of slightly overlapping lines. Another child has made a satisfactory animal without disguising the straight lines.

If the children want to keep their experiments, have them slide them inside their desks or find some other safe place for them. If they don't want them, tell the children to lay their palettes on them so that both palette and experiment can be collected at the same time.

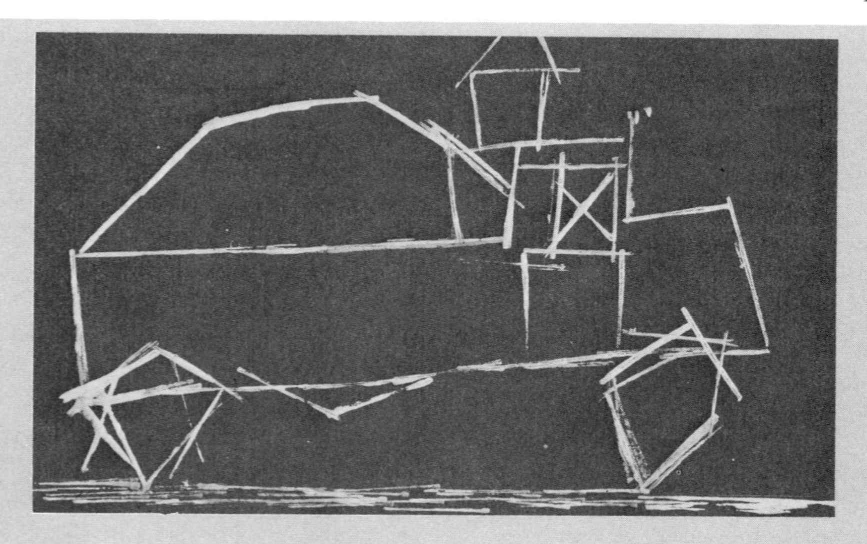

Big Dumper

New Palettes. Give each child his choice of color of a 12" x 18" paper for his picture. Have white paper and one or two other colors including a dark color. While this is being done give each child a new 9" x 12" palette. The same tongue depressors can be used again. Have two colors of tempera paint: a light color (white or yellow, for example), and a dark color (such as black or blue). If you have a light paper, you will need a ______? Right, a dark paint. And if you have a dark paper, you will need a light paint.

As soon as a child has his paint, let him begin his picture. Think of what your picture is going to be before you begin printing it. Do you think you will be able to put many things in this kind of picture? No, not at all. A picture you print this way has to be bigger and simpler than one you paint with a brush. Perhaps just one big thing in the picture will be enough. Make it fill the whole paper.

Be Different. Walk about the room as the children work. Encourage a shy child to be different. Make something no one else has thought of. Assure another that he has a good beginning. Oops, don't let the tongue depressor move on the paper. That wouldn't be printing, would it! Yes, you do need more paint, don't you. Don't put too much in your picture. Know just when to stop.

It won't be any problem to clean up. Just lay the tongue depressor on the palette and fold the newspaper (that has covered the desk) once over the palette. Let two or three children walk about the room to collect the folded newspapers. Just lay one on top of another and then put the whole thing in the wastebasket. There—everything is clean again.

Encourage each child to have a title for his picture. It will help to make the pictures more meaningful when they are shown to the rest of the class.

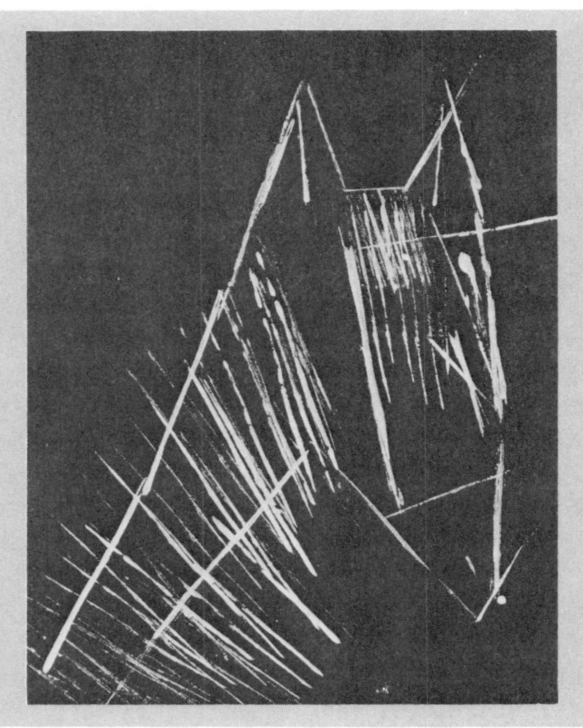

A Horse Named Phantom

When you display them, place a tongue depressor here and there with them—just to prove that tongue depressors don't have to be in a doctor's office. They can belong in an art class, too!

MAKE IT EASY—FOR YOURSELF!

1. Cover all work areas with newspaper.
2. Any reasonably heavy paper makes a good palette: manila or construction paper. (You may have some old construction paper that has become faded from being on a bulletin board. This will make fine palettes.)
3. Plastic squeeze bottles make excellent paint dispensers.
4. Each child needs only one color of paint. This allows him to concentrate on the printing technique and the idea of his picture rather than becoming confused by the problems of color.
5. Use only the narrow edges of the tongue depressor for printing. This will make it easy to hold the tongue depressor and will emphasize the line quality of the printing. If the flat solid side of the tongue depressor were used, it would make the printing process more difficult.
6. Encourage children to stand to print. For many children it is more comfortable and gives them greater freedom of motion.

Rough and Ready

Sandpaper Prints

(Suggested for Grades 2 through 6)

Objectives

1. To introduce a simple printing technique.
2. To experiment with an unusual combination of materials.
3. To realize the need for simplification in a picture.

Materials

sandpaper
unbleached muslin or white cotton cloth
wax crayons
newspaper
electric iron

You've heard of people being rough and ready. You probably like them, too! Well, this is rough and ready—ready for a picture, that is.

We're going to use sandpaper, so we'll need some _____? No, no, no! You *usually* use sandpaper on wood, but this time we're going to be different. We're going to use cloth—and crayon!

Crayon—cloth—sandpaper! Certainly! Let's see what we can do with that strange combination.

Monoprint. Have your class gather around you at a large table. Explain that this time they will make prints. Talk about what a print is. If printmaking is a new experience for them, go into some detail. Find things in the room that are printed: the newspaper, magazines, books, workbooks, maps, calendar, pictures, cloth. Many of each of these things were printed—all of them were alike. Some kinds of printing—called monoprinting—produce just one print. *Mono* means one. Older children will be able to think of several words that begin with the prefix *mono*: monoplane, monocle, monogram, monolith, monologue, monotone, monopoly!

Plate, Ink, Pressure. In any case, to make a print there must be something to be printed that has a raised surface. That is called a "plate." Two things are necessary in order to print a plate. The printing plate must be inked—must have color added to it—and there must be pressure. Let's see how we can make a plate, ink it, and press it to produce a print.

For the kind of print we are going to make this time we will begin with a material that already has a raised surface. Sandpaper will be fine for that. Let several children feel it. You can really feel that raised surface, can't you! It is rough!

It wouldn't make a very interesting print if we just inked this sandpaper plate with one color and printed it, would it? It would look just like colored sandpaper. Instead, we'll ink it with several colors and arrange them to make an interesting picture. We'll use wax crayon to "ink" the plate.

A Simple Picture. But first we will have to decide what kind of a picture to make. It should have one big thing in it and not too much else. I think I will make a tall sailboat that will just about fill the piece of sandpaper. As you talk, begin to draw a sail. I'll draw it a little off-center. It's never a good idea to put anything exactly in the center of a picture, is it? I'll make it go almost all the way to the top of the plate and I'll make it wide enough to go almost all the way from one side to the other. See, I'll round the sail a little, like that, so it looks as though the wind were blowing it. It was all right to sketch it lightly that way, but it didn't get much "ink"—much color—on the plate. That is easy to fix. I'll just push harder on the crayon. See how the crayon catches in the rough sandpaper?

I used orange for a sail so I'll need to choose another color for the hull of the boat. I would like a light color for that, so I will use yellow. Draw a slender boat under the sail. What should I do now that I have the boat sketched? Right! I'll have to go back over it and press hard against the crayon to fill in all the rough parts of the sandpaper. That is "inking the plate." Oh, yes, it has to be all filled in solid. You don't want a hole in the boat, you know. That's right. It would sink if it had any holes in it! It wouldn't make a good print, either.

Now I'll certainly need some water for that boat. Water doesn't always look just plain blue, does it? What other color could I add to the blue to make it look like deep water? Yes, green would be fine, and so would purple. I'll push hard on the blue crayon and then the green one and then the blue one again. The water should come up around each end of the boat some so that it looks as though the water is in back of the boat as well as in front of it. Continue until all the water is finished.

Eliminate Detail. Do you think I should put any people on the boat? Well, there may be people on the boat but they would be too small to show on the print. Remember, we are using crayon to ink these plates so you will have to leave out little, fussy parts. Put in only the big, important parts. Little things would just disappear in this kind of a print.

There isn't much at the top of the plate yet, so perhaps I could add a bright, red, triangular pennant, like that. I'll leave it just plain, though, and won't add any little details to it.

Flowers (plate)

Flowers (print)

Oh, yes, the sky has to be inked, too! Should it be the same kind of blue as the water? No, it will be much lighter. This turquoise blue will be fine for it—and I won't ink it as heavily as I did the rest of the plate.

Color Contrast. Call the children's attention to the fact that you have strong contrasts of color. The light yellow makes a sharp contrast with the

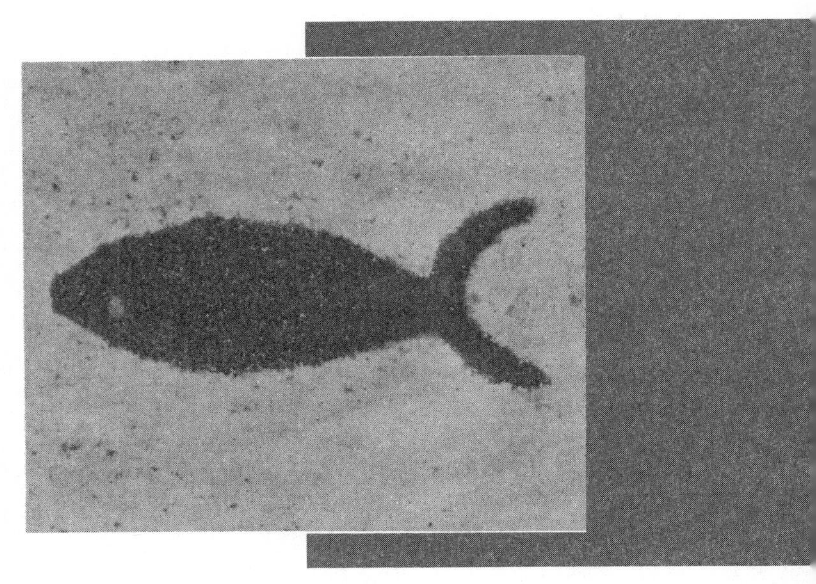

Fish (plate)

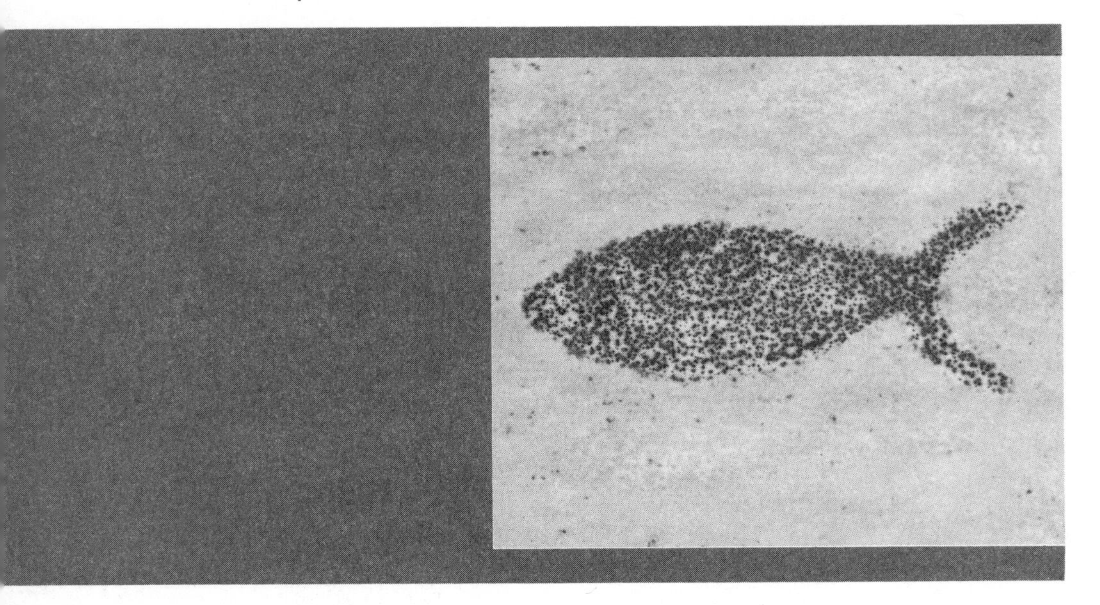

Fish (print)

dark blue and green that are next to it. The bright red and bright orange make a strong contrast with the light blue sky. The light sky makes a strong contrast with the dark water that touches it. It is important that a light or bright color touch a dark one.

Now that the plate is inked, let's print it. For that we need ______? Right! We need pressure. In this case we also need something that will melt the crayon and change it into a liquid. A hot iron will be fine—it will melt the wax and press it all at the same time.

Iron the Plate. Take your sandpaper plate to the ironing area. Lay a piece of cloth on the pile of newspaper. Place the plate face down on top of it and cover that with another piece of newspaper. Now let's see if we can print it. Press it thoroughly with a medium hot iron. It is important to have sharp, clear-cut edges to a print, so be sure you press out across the plate and onto the ironing board.

There will be great excitement as you remove the print from the plate. Let the children comment about what they see, and direct their thinking to the important points you want them to keep in mind. Yes, you can see the rough texture of the sandpaper. Can you see the little dots of color where the crayon filled in the rough surface of the sandpaper? Why was it important to have a dark color at the edge of most of the plate? Right! So that there would be contrast between the color at the edge of the print and the light cloth it is printed on. What would have happened if I had put those little people on the boat? That's right! They would have become just little spots of color and wouldn't have looked like people at all.

Opposite Direction. Have you noticed one thing that is different about the print and the plate? There is something that is just the opposite. You are right! The boat is facing in one direction on the plate and in the opposite direction on the print. Explain why that is true: because the plate and the cloth for the print were facing each other. One was face down on top of the other. Have the children place their two hands together, palms facing each other. Then open them so that only the little fingers touch. See how the thumbs are going in opposite directions. Your bottom hand was the plate and your top hand the print. But when they're separated they go in opposite directions.

What would happen if you had put any words on your plate? Sure they would! They would be backwards on the print. Yes, if you made them backwards on the plate, they would come out frontwards on the print. Perhaps this time you would rather leave off any lettering. Then you will have two pictures when you finish—the plate and the print. Certainly, the plate can be mounted and become a fine textured picture.

Simplify. Take a few minutes to talk about some ideas for sandpaper prints. Yes, a lovely, big turtle would be fine—but don't put in too much else. Each time something is suggested, comment about some way of simplifying it. A clown would be fine. Perhaps just a clown's face would be better. Then you could make his eyes and nose and mouth big enough to be seen on this kind of a print.

Give each child a piece of sandpaper and a box of wax crayons. Move about the room quickly so that you can see each child's work to make sure he gets a good start. Then you will have time to give each child a piece of cloth and later to supervise the ironing area.

Make your one important object big—almost as big as the whole piece of sandpaper. Yes, draw it lightly at first if you want to, but be sure to go back over it and put on lots of crayon. Much, much heavier than that! Oh, that's a wonderful lion! You could make his mane even larger than that. Be sure to use a darker color around that yellow and orange lion. I see an empty spot. A print shouldn't have a hole in it! That's it—fill in that spot. Yes, I think you have space enough to put one more fish in your underwater scene. Can you make him different from the first one? The top part of your plate is empty. Can you put something up high? If your plate is ready to print, let's see what the first print will look like.

Show First Print. As soon as the first print has been made, show it and the plate to the rest of the class. It will encourage the other children as well as please the child whose work is shown. Find something about it which you can commend. Then back to work again.

Once the printing has begun, you will be busy at the ironing area, but as each print is made, take time to show it and the plate to the rest of the class. Comment about something that is good.

Before long each child will have printed his sandpaper plate. Be sure to display each print. You'll want to include some of the plates, too, just to show how they were made. Yes, sandpaper is rough, but your class will be ready to use it for printmaking any time!

MAKE IT EASY—FOR YOURSELF!

1. No pencils! No preliminary drawing. Drawing with pencils encourages children to make tiny things.
2. Be sure to use wax crayons. It is the wax in the crayons that melts and carries the pigment into the cloth.
3. Any size and grit sandpaper can be used. The standard 9" x 11" size is fine. Medium or coarse grits hold more crayon and so tend to make stronger prints. ("Flowers" was done with fine grit, "Fish" with coarse.)
4. It is the crayon deposited on the sandpaper that makes the print. A fair amount of crayon must be trapped there. Before the lesson, experiment on a small piece of sandpaper so that you will be able to guide the children.
5. It is not necessary to take time to complete your demonstration plate. The children will be eager to experiment on their own. Do just enough on your plate so that the children understand the technique and so that the need for contrast of light and dark colors is obvious.

6. A thick pile of newspaper makes a fine ironing board. There should be enough newspaper so that the heat from the iron doesn't penetrate to the surface below.
7. Supervise the ironing area carefully—to make sure the iron is handled safely and to be sure enough heat and pressure are used to produce a good print.
8. Never retouch a print. Even if a small area does not print as well as the rest of the picture, don't add crayon lines to it. That would destroy the quality of the print.

The Other Side

Styrofoam Printing *(Suggested for all elementary grades)*

Objectives

1. To experiment with a simple form of multi-color printing.
2. To provide a new approach to a drawing lesson.
3. To encourage children to simplify their drawings.

Materials

12" x 18" (or larger) Styrofoam (any thickness)
12" x 18" white and colored construction paper
waterbase block-printing ink (several colors)
brayers (rollers)
newspaper
crayons

You know that there are two sides to everything. This is one time you'll be glad to look at the other side.

Have you ever drawn a picture with one color and had it come out in a different color? No? Well, you'll do it today. Have you ever drawn a picture with crayon but had it come out in ink? No? Well, you'll do it today. Have you ever drawn on the front of a paper but had it come out on the back? No? Well, you'll do it today. It isn't magic either; it's a kind of printing.

Talk for a few minutes about things that are printed—books, magazines, pictures, posters, calendars, cards. Usually things are printed to get many of them just alike. Each color has to be printed separately.

Monoprinting. The kind of printing you are going to do is a little different from most printing. It is called *monoprinting* because only one print can be made of each picture. But if you want to use several colors, it will still be necessary to print each color separately.

Have several pieces of Styrofoam. Squeeze a bit of a different color ink on each one of them, and spread it over the surface with a brayer. Let your class gather around you.

Draw with a Crayon. Let's see now—to print anything it must be pressed against an inked surface. So I'll gently lay a piece of paper on top of this inked Styrofoam. Lay it down carefully and do not move it once it is resting on the ink. But what am I going to print? There isn't anything there to press against the ink. That's easy! I'll just draw something with a crayon. Will it make any difference what color crayon I use? No, of course not, because the ink will do the printing. That's right—the crayon will just press a line to be printed by the ink.

Draw a flower, a sailboat, a fish, or any simple object. What do you suppose has happened? Yes, it should be printed in ink on the other side of the paper. Lift one corner of the paper and gently peel it from the inked block. Children will be excited and exclaim about the results.

A Rainy Day

Add a Second Color. Oh, but that's only the beginning. Now I must decide what I would like to add to the print—and what color I would like to use this time. If you have made a flower, you may want to add a green stem and a leaf or two. Take your print to the block which has the second color you want to use. Place it on the surface so that the ink side of the print is face down, against the inked Styrofoam. Be careful not to press against it with your fingers. That's right! Wherever you press, it will print–and you certainly don't want finger marks on your picture, do you!

What is the next thing to do? Of course! Draw whatever you want to be printed in this color. Press the crayon firmly against the paper to make a sharp print. Then lift the paper carefully, as you did before, and pull it away from the inked surface. Nice, isn't it!

Yes, you could add a third color if you thought it would improve your picture, but remember–sometimes a picture looks better with fewer colors. When you make your print you will decide how many colors you need to use.

Make a Second Print. Arrange the printing stations so that each color is in a separate area. This will prevent any area from becoming too crowded. In order to speed up the printing, you may want to have more than one piece of inked Styrofoam for the more popular colors. If time permits, let each child make a second print.

You will be busy during the lesson. Supervise the printing areas to make sure each piece of Styrofoam is properly inked. Each piece will need to be re-inked from time to time.

Know just what you want to draw before you go to a printing area. Then draw it carefully, because once you have pressed the crayon against the paper it is printed on the other side. Yes, you can make a solid area on your print just by filling it in with crayon, but don't overdo it. Good! You knew just where you wanted to add that second color.

Show to the Class. Continue to encourage, praise, and assist until every child has finished. If each child has made two prints, let him choose the one he likes best to show to the rest of the class. It will be an exciting time–a time for each child to be proud of his work and a time for children to appreciate the work of their classmates.

Yes, there are two sides to everything–but it is the other side you will want to see.

MAKE IT EASY–FOR YOURSELF!

1. Cover all printing areas with newspaper.
2. Have a separate brayer for each color. Use it to roll the ink in all directions in order to make a smooth coating. Too much ink–or ink that hasn't been thoroughly rolled–will print poorly.
3. Have one crayon at each printing station. The colors of the crayons are not important, but if a different color crayon is at each station, it will help the child know exactly what is being printed with that particular color.

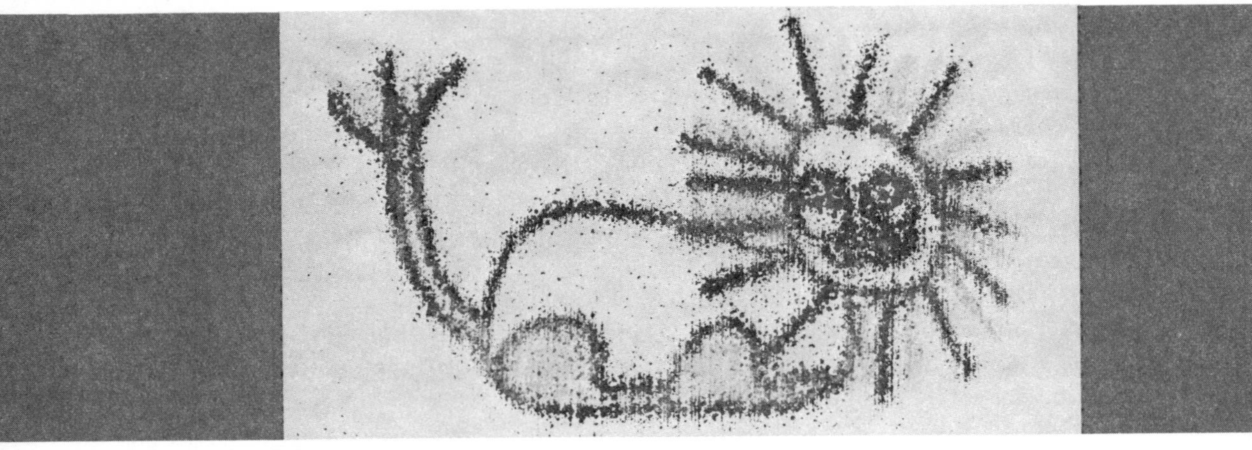

Little Lion

4. If the paper must be held in place while it is on the inked Styrofoam, hold it at the extreme edge so that printed finger marks can be trimmed off with the paper cutter.
5. Encourage children not to include too many small details as the printed line is wider and less distinct than the drawn line. A simple print is likely to be the most pleasing.
6. One color may be printed immediately after another. It is not necessary for the print to dry between colors.
7. Printing ink takes longer to dry than paint, so provide an area where prints may be spread out to dry. Don't stack them while they are still tacky—wait until the next day.
8. It will be necessary to take turns at the various printing areas. If the color printing stations are in different parts of the room and there are several stations for the most popular colors, no area will become over-crowded.
9. Waterbase printing ink can be easily washed from brayers and Styrofoam with cold water. Even though the ink stains the Styrofoam, it is reusable when dry.

How's That Again?

Monoprinting on Burlap *(Suggested for Grades 4 through 6)*

Objectives

1. To provide opportunity for working directly in a fluid medium.

2. To learn to use fingerpaint with rhythmic, flowing motions.
3. To introduce two-color design in fingerpainting.
4. To experiment using a variety of hand positions and motions with fingerpaint.
5. To produce a print of a fingerpainting.
6. To see the possibility of an unusual art combination.

Materials

fingerpaint—several colors	paper towels
newspaper	cans of water
fingerpaint paper	burlap—about 12" x 15", assorted colors

How's that again? Did you say a fingerpainting on burlap? Yes, why not! Make a lovely fingerpainting and then transfer it to burlap. You'll be delighted—and everyone who looks at it will be amazed.

Preparing to Monoprint. You won't even have to ask your class if they would like to fingerpaint—they will be excited as soon as they see the materials. So make careful preparations before the children begin work, for nothing else will contribute more to the success of your lesson.

Even before the day you plan to fingerpaint begin preparing for it by having each child bring in one of his father's old shirts. Cut off the sleeves near the shoulders. When the child puts it on backwards and buttons it in the back, it makes an excellent coverall to protect his clothing.

Be sure you have a big supply of newspapers for you will need them to cover an area of the floor where the wet paintings can be left to dry as well as to cover the work areas where children will paint. In addition, you will need fingerpaint paper, a variety of colors of fingerpaint, a paper towel for each child, cans of water, pieces of colored burlap about 12" x 15", and some half sheets of newspaper.

Demonstrating the Technique. Have your class gather around you while you give a demonstration. Oh, don't be timid! You'll love it—just as the children will—and they'll learn from it, too. Be sure you have a shirt on backwards, just as the children do. Your clothes need to be protected too, and, of course, you should set a good example.

Lay one corner of a piece of fingerpaint paper back over itself. What do you notice? Do the two sides look just alike? No, one side is whiter than the other side—it looks shiny. That's the side you paint on—the shiny side—so lay the paper well back on a table or desk that has been covered with newspaper. Use one of the cans of water to pour a little puddle of water in the center of the fingerpaint paper. Lay the palm of your hand flat in the water and quickly spread it over the whole paper. You may have to add more water, but be sure that all of the fingerpainting paper is wet—not full of puddles but thoroughly wet.

Dip your fingers into a jar of fingerpaint and scoop out about a tablespoonful. Lay it in the lower portion of your wet paper. Lay the palm of your hand flat on it (just as you did with the water) and stir it with circular motions a few times until it feels soft and smooth. Then spread it over half or more of the paper. Oh, don't just make it go straight across the paper—make it end in an irregular line, or make it slant across the paper.

See how smooth and slippery it looks! It feels that way, too. But the paper is only partly covered with paint, so let's do the same thing all over again—but this time with a different color. Dip your hand into another color and scoop out about the same amount as you had the first time. If your paper is nearly covered, you will need less paint than before, but be sure to have the paint quite thick on your paper. Stir and then spread it just as you did before, but this time it will be on the part of the paper that was empty. Let the two colors overlap each other just a bit, but don't mix them any more than necessary—your hand will do that when you make your picture.

Well, let's make that picture! Sometimes when you fingerpaint you use only one or two kinds of motions and repeat them over and over again, but this time we're going to be different. Begin near the bottom of the paper and make a big sweeping line upward to the top of the paper. Perhaps you made the line with the side edge of your opened hand, or perhaps you closed your hand into a fist and used it that way. In either case, be sure your hand moved rapidly in a big sweep and then lifted off the paper all in the same motion.

Now begin from the same spot at the bottom of the paper and swing your hand upward again. Make it a slightly shorter motion than the first one so that it doesn't go quite as high on the paper. Try it again—beginning from the same place but not going as high as either of the other two motions. Try another type of motion or hold your hand differently—and don't forget that fingernails make lovely slender lines. Perhaps you will want to make a more solid area of design at the bottom to cover all the beginning lines.

Printing on Burlap. There, that looks good, doesn't it! But there isn't any time to admire it yet, for we must hurry to print it on the burlap before the paint dries. The burlap is probably smaller than your finger-painting, so decide which is the most interesting part of your painting—the part you would like to print on the burlap. Hold the burlap flat over the painting and quickly lay it on the wet paint. Be sure not to move it as that would smudge and spoil the painting. Immediately lay a clean piece of newspaper over the burlap, then press and rub it gently with the palm of your hand. Oh, certainly fingerpaint from the hand you painted with is going to get all over the newspaper, but that is all right. That's what the newspaper is there for—to protect the burlap and to keep it from sliding as you press and rub the fingerpainting onto the cloth. You are making a monoprint—a print that can be made only once. Why do you suppose we can make only one print from our painting? Of course, all the paint will be pressed into the burlap so there won't be anything left for another print.

Let's see what has happened. Remove the newspaper and then carefully peel the burlap from the fingerpainting. There will be exclamations of, "Oh, it's beautiful!" and you will want to join in the chorus. It will be beautiful!

Assign each child to his own painting area, be sure all sleeves are rolled up, all shirts are on backwards and buttoned. Remind everyone to stand way back from his paper. You will find it easier to paint that way because your arm can move more freely, and you will be less apt to get paint on yourself.

You will be busy walking about the room giving help where it is needed. Be sure your paper is wet. You need a little more water, don't you? Oh, you need more paint than that!

Move quickly to the other side of the room, for someone will need you there. Keep your hand flat when you stir the paint. No, no! Don't draw with the tip of your finger! Use your hand. Stay at your own place. If you need help I will come to you. Yes, if you have too much water or paint, you can push it off onto the newspaper. Get that second color on quickly but don't mix it with the first color too much. Let the motions of your hand mix them when you make your painting.

Urge the children to take a few seconds to decide the best part of their pictures to print. Lay the burlap over it. That's right! Cover it with a clean newspaper and press and rub with the palm of your hand until you are sure all of the fingerpainting has been printed.

Good! That's a lovely print! And so is that one! Aren't you pleased with them!

Most of the children will be so pleased with their burlap monoprints that they won't notice what has happened to the original fingerpaintings, but after a while someone will be sure to call attention to them. Yes, look at your fingerpainting. It is changed, but it isn't spoiled at all, is it! It is lighter because most of the paint is now on the burlap, but the texture of the burlap shows on the painting. So you see you have two pictures—one on paper with the design of the burlap on it, and one on burlap with the design of the paint on it.

When the paint is dry, both the painting and the monoprint can be trimmed on the paper cutter. You will hardly know which one you like better. Perhaps you will want to display the print and the painting together. When you tell admirers that it is fingerpaint on the burlap, don't be surprised by total disbelief when they ask, "How's that again?" Just show them the proof—the original paintings with the burlap texture still showing!

MAKE IT EASY—FOR YOURSELF!

1. Have the room completely ready for fingerpainting before it is time

for the art lesson. Have all the materials distributed and ready for an orderly beginning of the lesson.

2. Arrange the room as you would for a tempera painting lesson. Push four or six desks together to make one large area. Leave one desk for supplies and assign three or five children to the remaining areas.
3. Cover all work areas with two layers of newspaper so that no paint or water will get on the desks.
4. Have two jars of different color paint and at least two cans of water on every sharing desk.
5. If the chairs and desks are separate, move all the chairs to one side of the room. This will keep them clean, make it easier to paint, and provide on out-of-the-way place for the children to sit when they have finished their cleanup. If the chairs and desks are attached, have the children stand in back of their chairs to paint, and have them remain standing until all the cleanup is finished.
6. Be sure each child has an old shirt on backwards. A piece of string or cotton roving tied around the waist holds the shirt close to the body and makes it easier to paint.
7. Always stand to fingerpaint. Stand well back from the desk so that your arm can move freely.
8. Be sure children paint on the shiny side of the paper.
9. Avoid "erasing" a design more than once or twice as too many "erasures" lessen the color contrast in the painting.
10. If the fingerpaint paper tends to move while you are painting on it, lift one edge and put a little water underneath. That will hold the paper securely in place.
11. After the children have been assigned to a work area and have seen the colors available to them, let them take turns choosing burlap. Urge them to choose a color which will furnish a good contrast to the color of the paint.
12. Lay the burlap and the extra newspaper in a clean place until you are ready to use them. There may be an extra desk nearby or a counter area or a part of the floor. But have them easily available when they are needed. Caution the children to handle the burlap only on the edges when they have paint on their hands.
13. When each child has finished his monoprint he should place it and the original fingerpainting on newspaper that has been put on the floor, and then use the paper towel to clean his hands as thoroughly as possible. Avoid letting the children go to the sink at this time to wash their hands. They can take turns later when everything has been cleaned up.
14. The final cleanup is easy. Let one child collect all the jars of paint and put the covers on them before storing them in their proper place. Have one child collect all the jars of water, empty them, and store them in

their proper place. Assign one helper in each group to pile all the newspaper from his group and then roll it (with the paper towels inside) before putting it in the wastebasket. As a final precaution, walk about the room with a damp sponge and wipe away any spots of paint from desks or chairs. There should be almost none.

Print It!

Texture Printing *(Suggested for Grades 3 through 6)*

Objectives

1. To introduce a simple form of printing.
2. To develop an awareness of the importance of texture in a picture.
3. To experiment with texture as the most important element in a picture.
4. To increase ability to create a balanced and rhythmic design.
5. To provide opportunity for individual choice of materials to create a collage.

Materials

cardboard
newspaper
scissors
brayers
glue
assorted materials: corrugated cardboard, burlap, tongue depressors, pipe cleaners, applicator sticks, string, yarn
wire clips
waterbase printing ink
glass or cookie sheets
12" x 18" white and colored construction paper

Print it? But it's a collage—and nobody prints a collage! Well, we do! Spread a wide assortment of textured materials on a large table in your room. Your class will be fascinated by them just because they are such a strange variety of art materials. Include such things as tongue depressors, yarn, wire, burlap, corrugated cardboard—and any other reasonably thin but textured materials.

Can You Use Them? That's a strange assortment, isn't it! What do you think you could do with those things? Your class may give you a variety of answers—or none at all, depending upon their previous experiences. Could you make a picture with them? Yes, you could, but what kind of picture would you make? Yes, it would probably be just an interesting arrangement of some of these things. It would be called a collage—a picture that is made of things pasted together. We will do that.

Could you print with them? Of course! You could put paint or printing ink on them, press them onto a piece of paper, and you would have a print. Perhaps you have done that before. Have you ever printed several of them at one time? Yes, you would have to glue them all together on something that would hold them in the right place while you printed them, wouldn't you? It would be called a printing plate, a raised surface that can be printed. We will do that.

Yes, we will do both. We will make a texture collage, and then we will use it for a printing plate and print it. Your class will be interested but they will have lots of questions. Well, let's see how it can be done.

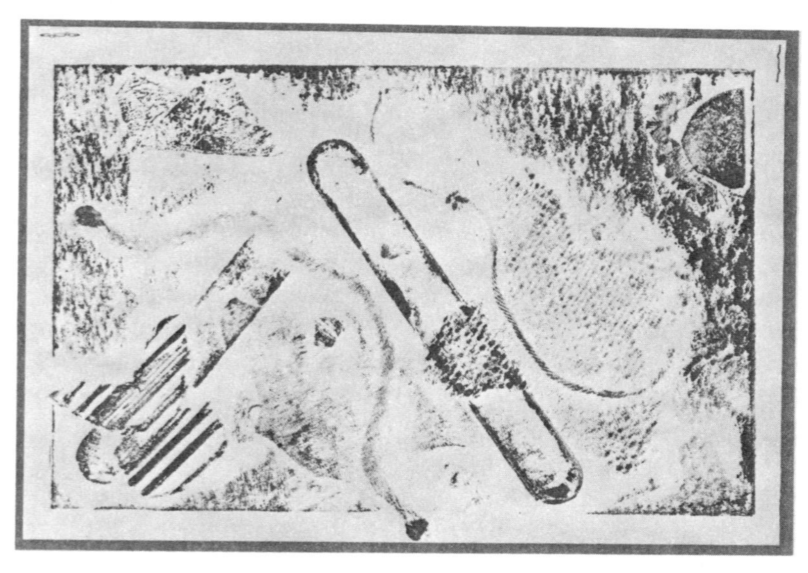

Make a Collage. Have your class gather around you at the table. Select several items from the assortment of materials. Include something which is rather large, something small, and something which is rough. Your selection might include a piece of ordinary cardboard about 3" x 5", a piece of corrugated cardboard almost as large but of irregular shape, a tongue depressor, a piece of yarn about ten inches long.

I will need something to glue these things to in order to make my collage. Choose a piece of cardboard about 6" x 8". Begin to place your four materials on them. Move them about from place to place. Does it look good to put the yarn on first and cover up most of it with the corrugated cardboard? Of course not! Do you like both large things on the same side and the smaller things on the other side? No! Not at all. It looks out of balance that way, doesn't it? Which side looks heavier? Yes, the side with the big, heavy things on it.

Continue to rearrange your materials. The corrugated cardboard will make an interesting texture to print, so let's put it in an important place. Would right in the middle be a good place? Oh, no. It would be uninteresting to have it in the center where all the other spaces would be alike, so let's place it just off center. There, that takes up a big place. Let's finish arranging all the big areas first. Then we can add the smaller things on top of them. Place the piece of cardboard so that it slightly overlaps the corrugated cardboard. Now, where would be a good place for the tongue depressor? Lay it so that its lines repeat the lines of some other part of the design—perhaps one edge of the cardboard or the ridges of the corrugated cardboard. That helps to make the line important, and it makes our eyes move easily from one place to another.

What would be a good thing to do with the yarn? Well, yarn doesn't like to stay in a straight line, so perhaps we should lay it in a freer line. Move it about in different ways. Does the yarn look good when one end goes off the edge of the collage? No, that makes our eyes go right off the collage, too. So let's place the end of the yarn where we want our eyes to go. Follow some line that has been created on your picture, and arrange the yarn so that it moves rhythmically along that line and leads your eye to some other location. See—now it helps us to see the whole picture better. Your collage may need some other material—or a second piece of something you already have—to complete it. No, you don't have to cover every bit of the big piece of cardboard—just make an interesting arrangement on it and let part of the cardboard show if it looks good. When your arrangement is finished, you will glue all the parts to the cardboard that will hold them together and form the printing plate.

Usually we have to think about color when we make a picture, but today we haven't said a word about it. Why do you suppose that is? Oh, no! It isn't because we forgot color! It's because color isn't important. But why isn't it important? Someone may remember that you said the collages would be printed. Right! And when a thing is printed you ink it any color you want the print to be. But let's make our printing plates before we think about printing them.

Select Materials. Give each child a piece of cardboard on which he can arrange his textured materials. Let groups of children take turns selecting several beginning materials. Encourage them to have one or two large pieces and to arrange them first. It is a good idea to use your largest pieces first while you still have a big area in which to put them. Arrange the first things so that they fill much of the cardboard. Make them balance but look good. Do they look interesting when you just lay them beside each other? No, they don't, do they! Move them to other areas. Then add the smaller pieces. You may have to change some of the first pieces you put in the design. Last of all add the materials that just form a line—but make that line move about wherever you want your eye to move. The line is the accent on your picture so make it an interesting one.

Print the Collage. Now we are going to print our collages. Squeeze a little waterbase printing ink onto a glass plate or cookie sheet, and spread it into a thin coat by rolling a brayer back and forth over it in all directions. Then roll the brayer over the collage—the printing plate, that is. Again roll it in all directions so that the ink will form a thin layer over everything it touches. No, it doesn't touch everything. That is because some of the things are raised higher than other things, so of course the brayer can't touch them all. But that is what will make the print, isn't it? What would happen if every bit of the plate had ink on it? Right! Every bit of the print would have ink on it, too. It would be a print of one solid color. That wouldn't be any good, would it!

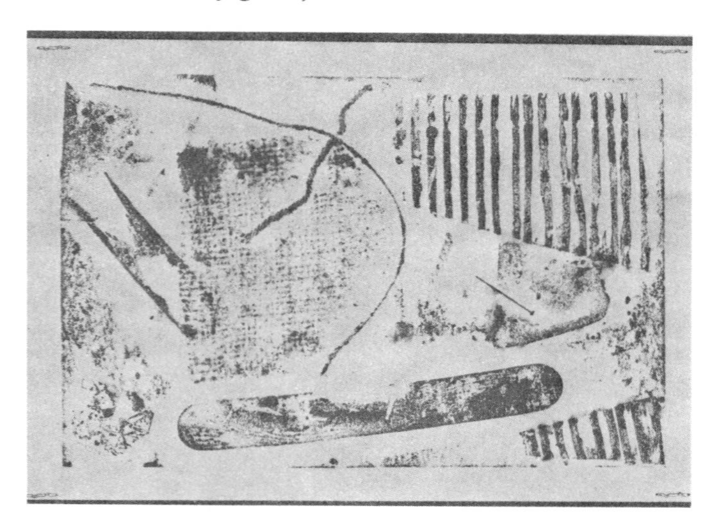

Take your inked plate to a clean area. Lay it on top of a piece of 12" x 18" drawing paper that you have previously selected. Lay a piece of newspaper over it to protect it. Rub your hand firmly over the back of it. Be sure to rub around the edges of the plate so that there will be a sharp line on the edge of the print.

Now let's see what has happened. Gently peel the paper from the printing plate. There will be exclamations of surprise and delight. The print is pretty, isn't it! And see—there is everything just the way it was on your collage. Well, it's almost the same. The texture and the arrangement are the same but everything is reversed. That is because the printing plate and the print were facing each other—they were in opposite directions.

Arrangement of the Room. Have several inking areas in different parts of the room, and assign each child to one of them. Explain that when he is ready to print his collage he will choose a piece of either white or colored construction paper and leave it on his desk. Then he will go to his inking area and ink his printing plate, return to his own desk, and place his printing plate, inked side down, on a piece of 12" x 18" paper. Cover it with newspaper. Press firmly down on all of the printing plate—especially the edges—so that everything that is inked will print. Later when the print is dry it can be trimmed to get all the edges even. Trim it on the paper cutter and leave a reasonably wide border around the print.

Each child should be able to make at least two prints. Carefully supervise the inking and printing so that each child will be successful and pleased with his work. Arrange an area where one print made by each child can be displayed. Let him choose for display the print which he thinks is the best. What will be done with the collages? Why, they'll be displayed, too. When they are dry, mount them on a white paper and put them on exhibit.

It's a collage; it's a printing plate; it's a print. Confusing? No! Just beautiful!

MAKE IT EASY—FOR YOURSELF!

1. Have enough textured materials to choose from so that each child may have five or six if he needs them.
2. Stress the fact that the colors of the things in the collage are not important. They will all become the same color when the collage—the printing plate—is inked. After the printing has been finished and the inked collages are on display, call the children's attention to them. The sameness of color makes the texture and the arrangement even more important.
3. Use the paper cutter to cut pieces of cardboard about 6" x 8" for the background of the collage. Use the scraps of cardboard—or cut other smaller pieces—as supplies to add to the collage.
4. Have a pair of wire clips to use if you need to cut pipe cleaners or any other wire. Don't use scissors to cut wire. Even if they do cut the wire the scissors are damaged for anything else. Teach children to respect materials and tools.
5. Paste could be used to adhere some of the materials—any kind of paper or fabric—but you will need glue for anything else (tongue depressors, applicator sticks, wire, buttons). It may be easier, therefore, to use only glue if you have enough of it available. Give each child a tube of glue, or let two children share a tube. Be sure the glue is dry before the children attempt to print their collages.
6. If you use glass to roll the ink onto, be sure all the edges are covered with tape. This is an important precaution to prevent cut fingers.
7. If your classroom is arranged in rows, a good plan is to have one inking area for each row. In any case, have enough inking areas so that not more that five or six children will be assigned to any one of them.

8. Cover all work areas with newspaper to protect them from glue and ink.
9. Be careful not to move the paper once it has been laid on the printing plate. If it is moved the print will be smudged. It is not important that the paper be placed exactly over the center of the printing plate as the print can be trimmed later to make it even.
10. Clean up the easy way. Assign one child to collect and wash all the brayers and another child to collect and wash all the inking plates—the glass or the cookie sheets.
11. You may want to take two art periods to complete the lesson—one to make the collages and another to do the printing.

Too Pretty for the Laundry

Chalk and Starch Prints *(Suggested for all elementary grades)*

Objectives

1. To introduce a simple printing technique.
2. To experiment with an unusual combination of materials.
3. To encourage children to work freely and rapidly.
4. To use color to create rhythm and balance.

Materials

9" x 12" and 12" x 18" white drawing paper
large watercolor brushes
colored chalk
liquid starch
newspaper
paper cups

It may have come from there, but it is much too pretty to stay in the laundry! What is it? Why, it's liquid starch—and chalk.

What Is a Monoprint? When your class sees a bottle of liquid starch, they will be curious. Your mother may use it to starch clothes, but we're going to use it to starch a picture. No, it won't make the picture stiff—the way it does clothes. It will help us make a monoprint. What is a monoprint? See if the children can figure it out for themselves. The last part of it is the word ______. Right, the word *print.* So a monoprint is some kind of print. The beginning of the word is *mono*. Do you know any other words that begin that way? Some of the older children may know the words monotone, monoplane, monologue. Explain that mono means *one* or *single.* So a monoprint means one print.

Talk about how the monoprint differs from other kinds of prints. Printing is usually a way of making many prints from a single printing plate. Books, magazines, postcards, printed fabric are examples. Someone may wonder why you would want to print just one thing—why not just use the plate for the picture. A monoprint looks a little different from the plate.

Make the Printing Plate. Have your class gather around you while you demonstrate how to make a monoprint with liquid starch and chalk. The first thing to do is make the printing plate. Usually the color of the printing plate isn't important because the plate can be inked with any color you like when you print it. But the plate we make today is just the opposite. We will put the color on first and "ink" it later.

Ask a child what color he would like to have you use to begin your plate. Green? Fine! That will make a good beginning. Lay a piece of green chalk flat on a piece of 9" x 12" white drawing paper. Push it back and forth on the paper to make a large green area. Should I choose another color now or use the green again in another place? No, it will be better to use the same color at least once more. Move the chalk to another area of your paper, lay it flat, and rub this second area. This time make a different shape, smaller than the first one. If you use the same color in more than one part of your picture, it can help your eye to move easily from place to place. And, of course, using a different shape and size makes the drawing more interesting.

Ask another child to choose a different color that will look good with the green. Brown will be fine. Let's put some of that on this edge at the top—and then we'll use the same color farther down in the picture and off to one side some. See—it helps to balance the picture, doesn't it? We could even use a little bit more of the same color in a third place, like that.

Add a third and perhaps a fourth color until all the paper is covered with areas of colored chalk. Make sure each color is used in at least two different areas of different sizes. As you add colors, talk about pleasing color contrasts; about simple shapes that help your eye to move easily from place to place; about the variety of sizes, which adds interest to the rhythm and movement of the picture.

Ink the Plate. The next part of making a print is to "ink" the plate. That is usually done with color, but this time the color is already on the plate. So all we have to do is get it wet. We will do that with liquid starch. Pour a small amount of the starch into a paper cup. Dip a large watercolor brush into the liquid and paint it over the chalk. It makes the chalk look different, doesn't it, so it will be easy to see where you have painted. Cover the whole paper with liquid starch, but be sure it is not too wet. Don't allow any puddles. Yes, some of the chalk will blur a little, but that won't do any harm.

Printing the Picture. Now for the printing part of the picture. Lay a piece of clean newspaper over your work area—right on top of the other piece will be fine as it is just to cover over the liquid starch and chalk that is there, so that they won't get your print dirty. Lay the wet printing plate face up on the clean newspaper. Now carefully lay a piece of 12" x 18" white paper on top of it. Try to center it over the plate, but don't move it once it touches the plate. Good! Now to print the plate. We want to be sure all the edges of the plate are printed—to make a sharp, clean-cut edge to the print—so use your index finger to rub the edge of the plate. You will be able to feel it as you trace around the plate. There, that should be printed, but we want the rest of the print to show, too. Use the flat part of your fingers or the side of your fist to rub the rest of the plate. Rub firmly but not too hard. We don't want to rub hard enough to push the liquid starch off the plate. That would make messy edges, wouldn't it!

Let's do one more thing to make our print even better. Turn the paintbrush upside down so that you can use the end of the handle instead of the brush. Begin to draw lines with it—long, simple lines. Keep them straight or make them move in easy, flowing curves. Connect them to create shapes or let them overlap each other as they cross the paper. Press on hard to make a line on the print—but not hard enough to tear the paper. There, that should be enough. A few simple lines that are well placed will look better than many carelessly made ones.

Print Is Reversed. The magic moment will arrive when you peel the print from the printing plate. It is always a surprise to see a thing reproduced on another paper. There will be exclamations of surprise and delight. Take a few minutes to admire the print. Notice that the printed areas are reversed from those on the plate. That is because the papers—the plate and the print—were facing each other. They were reversed, so the pictures have to be reversed. Notice the change in color. The print is lighter, isn't it? That is why it is a good idea to include mostly dark colors on the plate. If a little of the starch has been pushed out over the edge of the print, comment about it. A little won't do any harm but you wouldn't want all of the edge like that. It would make the print look messy and spoil it, wouldn't it? So be sure not to put on too much starch—and don't rub the print too hard.

Chalk and Starch. Give each child a piece of newspaper to cover his desk and a piece of 9" x 12" white drawing paper as well as colored chalk. Remind the class to use the same color more than once before using a second color. Your print will look better if the colors are repeated. That's a good start. The different areas of color are nicely balanced on the paper. Have you remembered to put mostly dark colors on the edges of the plate? The dark edge will make a better contrast at the edge of the print than a light-colored edge would. Are the edges of your shapes getting too uneven? Wouldn't the lines help your eye to move more easily if the shapes didn't have so many uneven edges? It will be easy to change the edges. Those colors should print nicely.

Give each child a large watercolor brush as you walk about the room. When you see that everyone has a good beginning with the chalk, give out the starch. Pour a little in a paper cup for each child. As soon as a child has his plate covered with chalk, let him begin to "ink" it with starch. Not too much, you know. You don't want so much starch on your plate that it has to ooze off onto the edges of the print. Good! That's a fine idea. Wipe the extra starch off with the brush. You can wipe it right off onto the newspaper where it won't do any harm.

Keep Print Clean. Be sure to cover that dirty newspaper with your clean one before you make your print. You don't want any of that dirty chalk or starch to get on your print, do you! Yes, go right ahead and make your print just as soon as you are ready for it. Be sure to handle your large white paper—the one you will make your print on—only at the edges. That part will be trimmed off on the paper cutter later. Any finger marks on the edges won't do any harm but don't get any where your print will be.

The first prints will soon appear. Hold them up so the rest of the class can see them, but don't be surprised if everyone doesn't look. Most of the children will be so busy making their own prints that they may not have time to even glance at the ones you are showing. Oh, well, their prints are

more important to them! And besides–you can make a display of all of them just as soon as they are dry.

Take the liquid starch back to the laundry? Of course not! It's too valuable for that, so just leave it right here–and use it for prints again another day.

MAKE IT EASY–FOR YOURSELF!

1. Cover all work areas with newspaper. The chalk and the starch can be washed off desks, but the more mess you avoid, the easier the cleanup will be.
2. Have children write their names on the backs of both their white papers before using them.
3. Give each child a box of colored chalk or let a group of children share a box. Or if individual sets of chalk are not available, let groups of children take turns selecting their colors from a common source.
4. If the chalk you are using is new, have the children break each stick in half before using it. A half-stick of chalk is easier to use on the side than a whole one, and it is less likely to break into small, unusable bits.

Please Pass the Potatoes

Potato Printing *(Suggested for all elementary grades)*

Objectives

1. To introduce a simple printing technique.
2. To experiment with a repeated motif to create rhythm and unity.
3. To see that art materials need not be limited to the usual media.

Materials

potatoes
paring knife
tempera paint
newspaper
scissors
6" x 9" paper for paint
9" x 12" or 12" x 18" white and colored construction paper

If you were seated around the dining room table, you wouldn't be surprised to hear someone say, "Please pass the potatoes." But during an art lesson! How's that again!

When it comes time for an art lesson, bring out a bag of potatoes and a paring knife. Watch the surprised expressions on the faces of your class. Yes, we are going to use these! Yes, for an art lesson! We are going to print with them.

Potato Printing. What is printing? No, we're not talking about the kind of thing you do when you print your name. Talk about other things children know of that are printed: books, magazines, post cards, newspapers, posters, pictures, calendars, cloth, wallpaper. When a thing is printed, many things just alike can be printed. It is a way of making many copies of the same thing.

So when you print with your half of a potato, will you print it just once? No, of course not! You will print it many times.

Have your class gather around you at a work area. Slice one of the potatoes in half. There, now it is flat on one side so I can print with it. A printing plate–the thing you print with–always must be flat like this so that it can be pressed flat against the paper or whatever you are printing on.

There is one other thing, though, that we must have before we can print. What is it that will make this potato–or anything else–print? Certainly! We need to have paint or ink to put on the printing plate before it is pressed against the paper. For our potato printing we are going to use tempera paint.

Printing Plate. Put a tiny puddle of paint on a piece of paper. Now all I have to do is gently push the flat side of the potato into the paint, dab it on the edge of the paint paper a time or two to get rid of some of the extra paint, and then print it. See, just lay it on a piece of paper and press it slightly. What do you think has happened? Well, let's see if it has printed. Remove the potato, and there it is, a colored print exactly the shape of the flat side of the potato—the printing plate!

A printing plate isn't much good, though, if you can print only once with it. Can you make another print exactly like this one? Yes, you can. How do you think you would do it? That's right! Repaint the printing plate—the flat side of the potato—by dipping it into the paint, dabbing off most of it, and then pressing it against the paper. See, there it is again! You could do that as many times as you wanted to, couldn't you?

Do you think there is any way of making a printing plate from a potato so that it would look different from this one? Yes, you could do that. You could cut a different shape in the potato, or you could cut it in a different direction. That would make the prints different—but not much different. It would still make a solid print like these, wouldn't it? Is there anything else you could do?

Someone will probably suggest that something could be cut out of the flat edge of the potato. You are exactly right! If you cut out part of the flat edge of the potato, the printing plate wouldn't be solid—so the print it made wouldn't be solid, either.

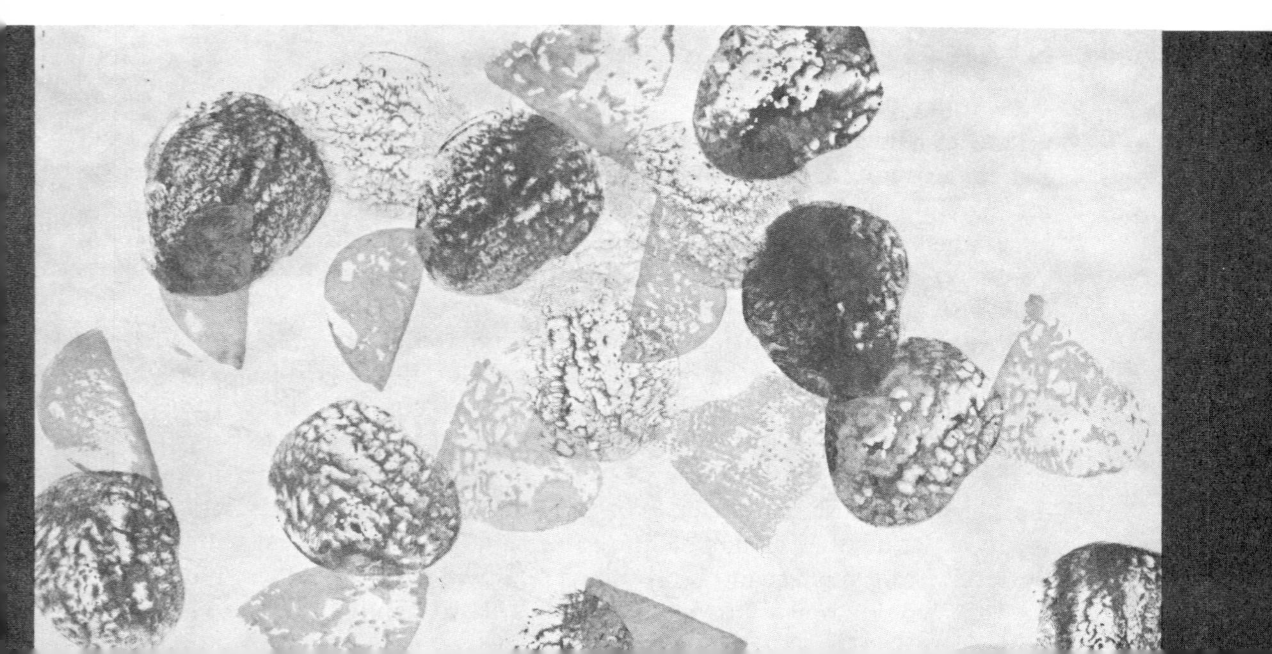

Press the painted half of the potato against a piece of newspaper several times to remove as much of the paint as possible. Then use the open blade of a pair of scissors as you would a knife to cut a piece from the edge of the potato.

That will make the print look different, won't it! Well, let's see! Re-ink the printing plate (press the potato into paint, that is), dab off the extra paint, and print it. See that! Just the shape of the printing plate. Good! I'm glad you noticed that! The print is in the opposite direction from what the shape was on the potato. That's right! It is because the printing plate had to be upside down to print—and that made the print in reverse. That is a good thing to remember when you make your printing plate.

Making the Prints. Talk with the class about ways of making their prints. Yes, of course, you can print on colored paper if you like. Be sure there is a good contrast, though, between the color of the paint and the paper you print it on. Yes, of course, you can make a solid printing plate if you like. Just the plain, flat side of your potato would be your printing plate, wouldn't it? You wouldn't have to cut it at all. Just print it over and over again until your picture looks good. Yes, of course, you can cut the flat edge of your potato to make a design on it. Use the open blade of a pair of scissors to cut the potato. Remember, though, you have a small printing plate, so of course what you cut from it will be small, too. Yes, it could be cut from the edge or from the solid part.

But isn't there one more way you could make your print? Couldn't you print with a solid plate first and then ______? Then cut it and print some more! That way you would have two variations of the same print. You could do all of it with the same color of paint, or perhaps you would like to use two colors.

Pass the Potatoes. Now it's time to pass the potatotes! So cut each potato in half and give a piece to each child. While you are doing this, let someone give each child a pair of scissors, newspaper, and a piece of paper for his "inking pad." Have several colors available for the background, and let groups of children take turns choosing the color they want. As soon as you have finished cutting the potatoes in half, give each child a little puddle of tempera paint on his "inking pad" paper.

Remember—your printing plate is small, so don't try to put too much on it. Keep the shapes you cut simple ones. Good! I'm glad some people are printing with a solid shape. Perhaps some of you will decide to leave them that way. Oops—you're cutting pretty deep! What is apt to happen if you cut very deep for your shapes? That's right! The potato printing plate may break because it is weak. So make very shallow cuts. That's the way to do it. Remember to dab off the extra paint before you print with your potato. If too much paint is on the plate, it will ooze out when you press it. That would spoil your print, wouldn't it! Certainly, you can overlap parts of your prints if they look good that way. Perhaps you will want to try that on your newspaper first to see how it looks. Yes, it would be a good idea to let the first color dry a little if you are going to put a second color over some of it.

Continue to walk about the room encouraging, assisting, complimenting—and giving out more paint where you see it is needed. When children want a second color, give them a clean "inking pad" (small piece of paper) and a little puddle of whatever color they want. Take the first pads and put them in the wastebasket so that there will be more work space on the desks. Encourage the children to stop when their pictures look just right. Don't add one thing too many!

Have an on-the-spot showing of the prints so that you can see each child's work and give him a feeling of success. Later, of course, you will want to arrange a display. You will be amazed at the variety that can come from half a potato. Now whenever you hear anyone say, "Please pass the potatoes," you won't expect to see a dish of mashed potatoes—you'll expect to see wonderful, colorful prints!

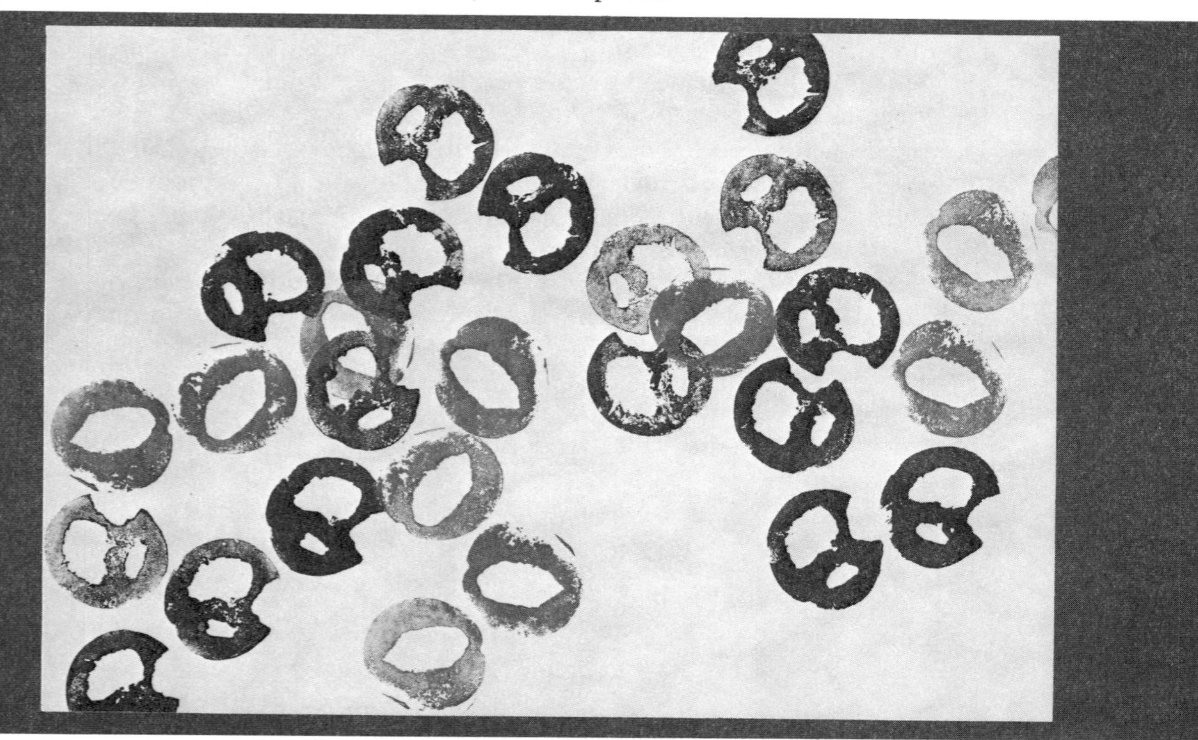

MAKE IT EASY—FOR YOURSELF!

1. Have enough potatoes so that each child may have half of one. The teacher should cut them in half in order to avoid the need for knives

and any possibility of cut fingers. Be sure to slice them straight through so that both sides will be flat.

2. Do not cut the potatoes in half ahead of time as the cut edges shrink quickly. This makes the cut edge uneven and therefore it does not print well. This is one time when it is better to prepare the material during the lesson rather than ahead of time. Have the other supplies ready and the potatoes won't be any problem.
3. Use either 9" x 12" or 12" x 18" white or colored construction paper for the background. Select colors which will make a good contrast with those colors of tempera paint you have available. Three or four colors of paper are enough. This will allow for individual selection without making it unnecessarily difficult to distribute them.
4. Cover the work areas with newspaper. Several layers of newspaper will provide a cushion for the printing and result in better prints.
5. Paper about 6" x 9" is a good size for the "inking pad." Use a new one for a second color. Throw the first one away before beginning a second color.
6. Avoid cutting letters into the potato. They are reversed when printed, and are generally not a good design in any case. Encourage children to cut simple lines and shapes into the potato. It is a tiny plate, so reduce the design to its simplest form.
7. Lines and shapes need to be cut only slightly into the potato. A shallow cut–for a slightly raised edge–will print fine. Just don't use too much paint. If too much paint gets on a plate and fills in shallow cuts, just wipe it off with a piece of facial tissue.
8. The cleanup is easy. Collect scissors, "inking pads," and potatoes. Have each child slide his newspaper out from under his print, fold the newspaper twice. Let one child collect it. If the newspaper is kept flat–not crumpled–it will be easier to handle.

7 Miscellaneous Techniques

Rabbits to Rhinos

Non-Hardening Clay *(Recommended for all elementary grades)*

Objectives

1. To provide experience with a three-dimensional material.
2. To provide direct manipulative experience with a pliable material.
3. To experiment with one method of strengthening a soft material.
4. To introduce basic clay techniques.

Materials

non-hardening clay toothpicks, dowels

A trip to the zoo is always fun. You may like to watch the playful bears—or perhaps you'd rather feed the elephants. But if the zoo is too far away for a visit today, make your own zoo. You will have everything from rabbits to rhinos!

Most of the children in your class have probably visited a zoo. Or at least they have seen one on television. Talk about the animals for a few minutes. Do you have a favorite animal? One child will like the lions. They look so heavy and yet so graceful. They are like giant cats, aren't they? Another child especially likes to see the monkeys. They're so lively

Crocodile

and chatter so much. They do such amusing things, perhaps hanging by their tails or swinging from place to place as they chase each other. Still another child prefers the alligators. When they open their mouths they have such long rows of sharp teeth. Most of the time they move so slowly, but sometimes they snap those jaws closed so fast you hardly see them. Encourage all the children to take part in the conversation.

Your Own Zoo. Well, let's make our own zoo. It will be more fun to make an elephant or a zebra than to talk about it. You may make one of those monkeys, if you like, and you may make the lion. Each of you decide which animal you would like to make.

Soften the Clay. As you talk, take a piece of clay and begin to soften it by squeezing it in your hands. Yes, you will use clay like this to make your own particular animal. You will have to get the clay soft first, too, so that you can make it into any shape you would like. See, this is soft enough now so that I can squeeze it into the long trunk of an elephant—or I can push more of it together to make a thick body for a rhinoceros—or I can curl a piece to make the tail of a monkey.

How to Attach Two Pieces. Take two balls of clay and push them together. Oops—they fell right apart, even though I pushed them together very hard. Clay just won't stay together that way. But look, if I hold the two pieces of clay together while I push a little of the clay from one ball to the other, they stay together just fine. In fact, my animal looks better, too. Now it looks like one piece of clay that shape and not just two parts stuck together. You certainly don't want your animal to fall apart, so be sure to push the clay from one part to another so that the parts will stay together.

Lion

Give each child a lump of clay and let him squeeze it to get it soft. Oh, the clay is stiff and you can't make anything out of it that way! Squeeze it in both hands, turn it around, squeeze it again. Yes, it is hard work, but after a while the clay will begin to soften. When it is very soft and easy to move, you can begin to make your rabbit or your tiger or your deer. But for now, just get the clay soft.

Strengthen the Clay. While the children are squeezing their clay, squeeze a piece of clay into a long, thin piece. Sometimes you need a long piece of clay for the legs of a horse or the neck of a giraffe or some other part of an animal. But see how weak clay is when it is thin like this. A giraffe with a neck like that wouldn't be able to eat leaves out of the top of a tree, would he! His neck would bend right over onto the ground. He would be sick. You don't want any sick or dead animals in your zoo. They all have to be strong enough to stand by themselves.

Well, that is easy to fix. You have bones in your legs and back and all over your body to help you to be strong and move about. You can give your animals bones, too. Just cover the toothpicks—or dowels for longer bones—with clay and stick them in to make legs, or back, or neck, or whatever part of the body you want to make strong.

By this time most of the children will be experimenting with their clay, so walk about the room giving assistance wherever it is needed.

Are you remembering to push the clay from one piece to another to hold them together? Good! You are an expert at making alligators! Would it help to add toothpicks to the legs of your tiger? It would make them stronger. Good! The long dowel makes a fine neck for your giraffe. But you will have to push it farther into the body so that it won't fall off. That's the way to do it. I can't tell yet what special kind of animal yours is, but I am glad he is strong. I'll just have to come back to see it later. You are doing a wonderful job of making antlers for your deer. You wouldn't be able to do that without toothpicks, would you? Fine! The lines on the lion's mane help to make it look like fur. That was a good idea.

Display the Animals. Before long the children will begin to complete their animals. Have a table or counter cleared where the animals can be displayed. As a child finishes his animal, let him bring it to the display area. Urge each child to place his so that the whole thing makes a pleasing arrangement.

When each child's work is on display, have the whole class gather around the area. Talk about the animals that can be recognized most easily because of some distinguishing characteristic: the elephant, the giraffe, the camel, the turtle, the alligator, the deer. Call attention to those that seem to move: the horse that is running, the lion with his head turned. Notice the sturdiness of most of the animals, the lines that have been drawn to show texture, the clever way the monkey's tail has been used to help balance him. Make each child feel pride in his work. Find something good about each creation.

Probably you'll find the children frequently go to the zoo—their own classroom zoo—to see the animals. And why not—there's everything there from alligators to anteaters and rabbits to rhinos!

MAKE IT EASY—FOR YOURSELF!

1. Non-hardening clay usually comes in one-pound packages that are easily divided into four strips, enough for approximately four children.
2. Non-hardening clay is an oil base clay. The more you squeeze it, the softer it becomes. The pressure and warmth of your hands makes it more and more pliable. It does little if any good to just pound it on the desk. Teach children the proper way to handle it—and why.
3. One way to arrange a display area is to place several pieces of construction paper in a colorful arrangement. Have the children place similar animals together on a single paper: all the lions together on one; the elephants on another. If all or most of the animals are different, cut the paper into pieces about 6" x 9" and use the pieces as individual "cages" for each child's animal.
4. Non-hardening clay is reusable, so when the display is dismantled, have each child remove the toothpicks or dowels from his animal and then press the clay into a ball. It will be satisfactory to use several times.

Did You Ever Need Another Hand?

Fingerpaint *(Suggested for all elementary grades)*

Objectives

1. To introduce a new and simple fingerpainting technique.
2. To observe and to learn about the mixing of colors.
3. To experiment with rhythmic motion to create a picture.

Materials

fingerpaint paper
cardboard
cans of water
tongue depressors

newspaper
fingerpaints of several colors
paper towels

You're as busy as you can be—and someone wants one more thing done. You drop a package—and you have something in both hands. Did you even need another hand?

Yes, we're going to use fingerpaint!

Not the Same Thing! There will be all kinds of expressions of delight—children love to fingerpaint. But wait a moment! Did you listen carefully? I didn't say we are going to fingerpaint. I said we're going to ______? Right! We're going to *use* fingerpaint. No, that isn't the same thing. We're not going to paint with our fingers—we're not even going to use our hands to paint with. No—no brushes either!

Let's see what we're going to do. Put your painting supplies on a large table and let your class stand in a big circle around it.

Review Procedures. Review the materials that are needed and the procedure for fingerpainting; go into greater detail if this is a first experience. Cover the desk with newspaper. Place the fingerpainting paper in the center of the newspaper. Notice that the two sides of the finger paint paper look different. The shiny side should be facing you. Fold a piece of paper towel in half and tuck it under the edge of the newspaper. Ask one child to choose two colors for you to use. Now pour a little puddle of water in the center of your paper, and immediately spread it over all the fingerpaint paper. Use your hand flat to spread it quickly and evenly. Make sure there are no dry spots and no puddles.

Use a tongue depressor to scoop out a mound of fingerpaint, and place it on one side of your wet paper. With another tongue depressor scoop out a mound of the second color and place it on a different area of the paper.

Two Colors. Why do you suppose I used tongue depressors instead of my fingers to scoop out the paint? No, I don't mind if I get paint on my fingers. In fact I am going to put my hand right onto the paint now to spread it over the paper. But what would have happened to colors if I had used my fingers to get the paint out of the jars? That's right! Some of the first color paint would have gotten into the second jar. Then no one else would have been able to have just the color he wanted.

Lay the palm of your hand flat on the mound of the lightest color paint. Stir it with small circular motions until the paint is soft and smooth, and then spread it quickly over approximately half the paper. It won't look good to have this color stop right in the center of the paper, so I'll just let some of it come way over there, and I'll end some of it way over on this side. See, it fills about half the paper—but not in a straight line.

Cover Second Half. Repeat the process of stirring and spreading the second color so that all the paper is covered with a soft layer of paint. Blend the two colors slightly where they meet. Yes, the yellow and purple have turned brown. (Blue and yellow turn to green; blue and red become purple; red and yellow change to orange. Blue and green become a blue-green; red and orange become a red-orange; blue and purple become blue-purple. Opposite colors turn brown–orange and blue; green and red; purple and yellow.)

Slide the paper towel out from under the newspaper and quickly wipe the paint from your hand. There–that will get my hands clean enough for anything except eating lunch!

Cardboard Hand. Now let's paint without using our hands. Pick up a small cardboard rectangle. This will take the place of my hand. In fact, it will give me an extra hand. See, if I hold it this way–on the long edge–it will be like my real hand when I tip it up on the side. But look–I can also make this into another hand just by turning it so that the short edge is on the paper. Yes, I will have *two* extra hands.

Well, let's see what I can do with these two extra hands. If you were using your real hand to paint with, would you always have to move it in the same way? No, not at all! You could move it in long, sweeping motions like that. (Hold your open hand above the fingerpaint paper as though your hand were tipped up on the side. Move it upward in a long sliding motion that ends in a sweeping curve.) How else could I move my hand? Yes, I could make scallops with it or even big flowing circles. What other way? Oh, yes, there are many other ways! Could you move it in straight lines? Certainly! In straight lines, in zigzag lines, in sharp points.

Stand the cardboard hand upright on one edge. Begin at the bottom of the paper and sweep it upward, using one of the motions you just talked about. Change direction slightly or change the angle of the cardboard so that the designs will be wider in some places and narrower in others. Repeat the same motion several times in quick succession.

Top First. Then pause for a moment and look at it. Why do you suppose I made the most important parts of my design near the top of the picture? If the children have fingerpainted before, they will know that it is because the lower part of the picture will be covered over and changed again and again as you add more and more parts to it. If this is not an experience which they have had before, quickly add another part lower down on the painting. Each time start from the same point. If you made sweeping curves the first time, make straight lines radiating out from the starting point or big scallops. Don't let your motions go all the way to the top this time–end them lower down on the paper.

See why you should make the tallest motions first? Yes, the parts lower down were erased when I added the new designs.

Smaller Motions Near Bottom. Add another smaller group of motions near the bottom of the paper. Comment about all the lines starting from one point. Makes the whole picture belong together, doesn't it! Have you noticed how the paint has been moved from one color area to another? Point out places where a new color has been created.

All that fingerpainting and no more paint on my hands! Oh, yes, there's some on my cardboard hand, but that can be left right on the newspaper and thrown away. I won't need that extra hand any more!

Lift the fingerpainting by the two corners closest to you and lay it on a newspaper on the floor. Fold the dirty newspaper—with the cardboard hand and paper towel inside—and put it in the wastebasket.

Distribute Supplies. Assign each child to a group of children with whom he will share water and paints. Have an extra desk on which shared materials can be placed. Be sure each child is thoroughly covered by his smock and that all sleeves are pushed up above the elbows. Let each child select a piece of cardboard, and give out the other supplies: newspaper, paper towel, fingerpaint paper.

You will need to be everywhere at once for the next few minutes. Your paper isn't wet yet—add some more water and spread it quickly. Yours is too wet—push the extra off onto the newspaper. Keep your hand—*one* hand!—flat and stir the paint before you spread it. Can you push one color a little farther over so the paper isn't divided exactly in half? Wipe your hands on the paper towel right away.

Yes, of course, you may begin using your cardboard hand. Work rapidly before the paint begins to dry. Make your hand move in big, rhythmic motions. Good! Go all the way to the top of the paper first—even off the top. Remember to begin each motion from the same place on the paper. When it looks just right, stop! Don't add another thing.

In order to be more orderly and to avoid accidents, let one group of children at a time carry their finished paintings to the newspaper that is on the floor.

Cleanup Easy. The cleanup can be easy and orderly. Let one or two children collect the cans of water and empty them. Let another one or two children wipe off the rims of the jars of paint, put the covers on tight and place them in the proper storage area. Let another child fold the newspaper that covered each sharing desk, and then discard it. Have each child fold the newspaper that covered his desk, and have one child from each group put the folded papers in the wastebasket. As a final precaution, have each child look at his chair before he sits down to make sure no paint has been spilled on it. You may want one child with a damp sponge to walk about the room to wipe up any spots of paint. There will be surprisingly few.

You were as busy as you could be—and all of you needed a third hand. Don't you wish it could always be so easy to have another hand!

MAKE IT EASY—FOR YOURSELF!

1. Cover all work areas with newspaper to protect the surface and to make cleanup easier.
2. A big shirt worn backwards makes a fine smock. Cut off the sleeves above the elbows.
3. Cut the paper in half for very small children—kindergarten and Grades 1 and 2. The full-size paper is too large for children to reach all parts of it easily.
4. Have each child write his name on the back of his paper before he begins his painting. Remember—the shiny side is the painting side of the paper.
5. Cut heavy cardboard with a paper cutter into pieces approximately 3" x 5". Have a variety of sizes, some slightly smaller and some slightly larger than the 3" x 5" size.
6. Place three colors of fingerpaint on each sharing desk. This will permit each child in the group to make his own combination of colors.
7. Be sure children stand well back from their desks to paint. This helps to keep them clean—but, even more important, it makes it possible for them to move their arms more easily in rhythmic motions. *Always* stand to fingerpaint.
8. Use only one hand to spread the water and to stir and spread the paint.
9. The painting may tend to move while you are working on it. Lifting one edge and putting a little bit of water under it will help hold the paper in place.
10. The edges of the paper will curl slightly as the paintings dry. When they are thoroughly dry, pile them together, turn them upside down, and place something heavy on them overnight. Then trim the edges slightly on the paper cutter, and mount the paintings on a larger piece of white paper.

Wear It Proudly

Tie-Dyed Smocks *(Suggested for Grades 3 through 6)*

Objectives

1. To experiment with a new technique.
2. To make a personal art smock which will be worn during future art lessons.

Materials

large white (or light-colored) cotton shirts
heavy string
scissors
newspaper
liquid dye
several pails (or large cans) of water
tongue depressors
several pairs of tongs

You'll wear it proudly! After all, you designed it–it's yours, only yours!

The old white shirts you've brought in to wear for art don't look much like artists' smocks, do they? But that is easy to change. We'll *tie-dye* them–and then we'll have extra-special smocks, pretty enough to wear any time.

Modern as Tomorrow. Explain a little about tie-dying. It is a centuries-old form of art that has been highly developed in the eastern countries around Java. Yet it is a form of art which periodically becomes a favorite–so it is as modern as tomorrow. The technique is summarized by its name: tie-dying. The material is tied–and then it is dyed. Just as simple as that! The dye colors all the cloth except where it is tied–it can't get into that part.

The people of Java are experts at tie-dying, and they make all kinds of intricate designs. Sometimes they tie their shapes by sewing fine thread

Shirt tied and ready for dying

into the cloth and then pulling the thread tight to bunch the cloth together. Well, we're not experts, so we'll do our tying an easier way.

Form a Circle. Take an extra shirt—or even a plain piece of white cotton cloth—and hold it at one point between two fingers. Let the rest hang down. Enclose this part of it by forming a circle with the thumb and fingers of your other hand. Slide this circle part-way down the material so that it gathers the folds together.

If I tied the cloth here, can you tell what kind of a shape this would create? You're right! After it was dyed and untied, we would have a circle. But before I tie this, I should make sure that the cloth is draped evenly so that the dye will get to all the parts of the circle. Remove the hand that is encircling the cloth and drape the folds evenly. There, that should be better.

Cut off a piece of string about two or three feet long. Place it at the point to be tied. Leave an end about six or eight inches long, and begin winding the rest of the string around one point in the cloth.

String Wound Tightly. Oh, it won't do any good to wind it loosely, will it? Certainly not—the dye would go right under the string and get on all the cloth. The string has to be wound so tightly that no dye can get under it. See? Each time the string goes tightly around the cloth, it is right next to the last row of string.

Circles of Various Widths. How much string should I use? All of this piece? No, not necessarily. Right! Use as much as you think you need. If you want a narrow white circle left after your smock is dyed, wind the string around the cloth only two or three times. If you want a wide white circle, wind the string many times to cover a wide area. Then, when you have covered just the right width, tie the string tightly. Tie it in a knot once and then make a big bow.

Why do you suppose it is better to tie the string in a bow rather than a hard knot? That's right! After the smock is dyed, you will have to take off the string. A bow will make that easier to do. Will it do any harm to leave rather long pieces of string hanging, like that? No, not at all! In fact, it will be a good idea because they will be easy to find and untie after the cloth has been dyed.

Would you tie only one big circle like that? No, of course not! It wouldn't look good to have just one tie-dyed area on your smock. There should be many of them. Could you tie more circles all the way up this same bunched-up piece of cloth? Certainly! That would make other white circles inside of this big one—and each circle would be smaller and smaller right up to the tip. Each circle could be a different width, too, couldn't it?

After you had one circle or many circles tied on this one area, would you be ready to dye the smock? Why not? Right! Because there would still be many more places where you could tie other circles. A picture wouldn't look good with just one shape on it, would it! Neither will a smock. So tie more and more areas until there isn't any empty space left.

There is another simple way of tying cloth with string. Can you think of what it is?

Tie Straight Lines. Someone may suggest that you could gather the cloth into a straight line and tie it. If no one sees that possibility immediately, show it to them by gathering the edges of a sleeve (that has been cut off above the elbow). See, if that were tied there, it would make a ______? Right, a straight line all the way around the sleeve. You could do that wherever you could gather the material straight across—even straight across the back. You may want some straight lines as well as circles on your tie-dyed smock.

Tying. See that each child has a supply of string. Balls of string can be shared by several children. Watch carefully for a few minutes to be sure each child is wrapping and tying the string tight enough so that no dye will be able to get under it. Then, as you continue to walk about the room, cut off any long sleeves so that they will end slightly above the elbows. Long sleeves get in the way when children are painting or doing

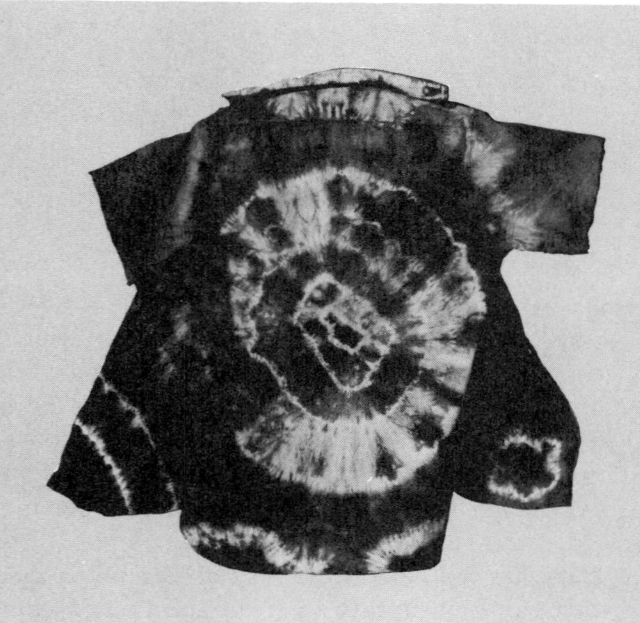

other art work. They drag in the paint, smudge the work, and are a nuisance.

Good! That should make a big, important circle on your smock. Will you tie more areas of it to make smaller circles, too? Are you sure you are tying it tight enough? Well let's see! Oh, my! If the end of the scissors can go under the string easily, the water and dye will go under it, too! Yes, unwrap it and make it much tighter. A straight line along the bottom edge? Yes, that would be a fine place for it. Yours is beginning to look like an octopus, isn't it! That long piece with so many circles on it should look just fine. Oh, yes, you can find more places to tie it! Perhaps they will be little circles, but the more you tie the shirt, the better it will look when dyed.

Two Lessons. As soon as each child has finished tying his smock, put everything away until the next art lesson. You will find it more satisfactory to do it this way. If you attempted to do the dying during the same lesson, the children would be so eager to get to the dye that they would tend to do a less satisfactory job of tying their smocks. In addition, your attention would be divided. Some children would be tying while others were dying, and you would not be able to supervise all the work adequately.

Once the class has had this initial experience of tie-dying, you may want to give them an opportunity to try it again on another project. The next time they should be familiar enough with the technique so that they could do both tying and dying during the same lesson.

Adequate Preparations for Dying. Make adequate preparations for dying the smocks. Be sure you have all the required materials. You will need a big supply of newspaper—enough to cover a large table or counter area and to give a thick section to each child. Have at least three or four colors of liquid dye, a pail or large can for each color, and two extra pails of clean water. You will need a tongue depressor or stick to stir each color of dye and at least one pair of tongs for each color used.

When the great day arrives, explain the entire dying process to the class. Several children (about the same number as colors of dye) will take turns working at the dye area. The cloth must be wet before it is placed in the dye, so the first thing to do is to put the smock into the first pail of clear water. Push it back and forth so that all of it gets wet and then lift it out of the water. Squeeze it to wring out the surplus water so that it won't dilute the dye.

Dying. Show the class the colors of dye that are available. Explain that they may dye their smocks all one color (probably the best way for the first dying attempt), or they may dye them with two colors. Yes, if you were experts like the Javenese you would use more colors on the same smock. But since this is a new (or at least relatively new) experience we will not use more than two colors.

If you use only one color, place your wet smock into whichever color you choose. Keep your hands out of the dye. Use the pair of tongs beside the dye to move the smock about in the liquid. Let it stay a minute or two until you think it has absorbed enough color. Then carefully lift the smock with the tongs. Hold it right over the pail so that the dye drips back into the container. When it has almost stopped dripping, slide your pad of newspaper under it, and take it to the last pail of clean water.

Rinse Off Surplus. Whenever you dye anything, there is a surplus of dye that isn't absorbed into the cloth and needs to be washed away. Put your smock into the last pail which has just clear water in it, swish it back and forth a few times with the tongs, and hold it over the pail until it has nearly finished dripping. Then quickly slide your pad of newspaper under it and lay the smock and newspaper on the floor (or counter space) which has been cleared for it.

No, the dye won't wash off when you put the smock in the last pail. The clear water will get rid of only the loose dye; the dye which has penetrated the cloth will stay there. No, it won't do any harm to use the same water for several smocks—even if they are dyed different colors. Yes, we will get clean water from time to time.

Two Colors. If two colors of dye are to be used, much the same process will be used except that the dying must be done in two stages. The smock should be dipped first in whichever color will be used the least. Only those parts of the smock to be dyed the first color should be held in the dye. Then hold these parts out of the second color dye as the rest of the smock is put into it. Rinse the smock as though it were all the same color.

Take time to answer questions and to repeat instructions that may not have been understood. You want all the children to feel secure before they begin to work with the dye.

Supervise Carefully. Select several children to begin dying their smocks. Have the rest of the class watch, so that if additional instruction is needed they will hear it and so that they will become more familiar with the technique by observing others using it. Stay close to the dye area and supervise it carefully. As one child finishes, let another child take his place.

When every child has dyed his smock, clear away the materials. Empty the water and dye into the sink, rinse and put away the pails. Rinse, dry, and put away the tongs. Pile up all the newspaper that was on the dye area and discard it.

The smocks must be left to dry, so there will be no sharing period at this time. That will have to wait until the smocks are dry, untied, and ironed. It will be hard to have enough self-control to wait, but when the great day arrives it will be an exciting time. No shirts—smocks, that is—will ever be ironed with more affection and pride!

Each child will be anxious to display his tie-dying skill, so let each one try on his smock. No, no! Put them on the other way—a shirt buttons down the front, but the smock buttons down the back! You won't have any trouble getting a child to wear his smock after this. He will wear it proudly!

MAKE IT EASY—FOR YOURSELF!

1. Avoid printed or dark color shirts. They are designed already. White shirts are the best for this lesson although very light-colored ones can be dyed satisfactorily. The fathers of many children will have old white shirts which will be ideal for use as smocks. Avoid jersey shirts. They dye well but are less satisfactory as smocks.
2. Any kind of string can be used, but a rather heavy cord is most satisfactory. It can be wrapped and tied more tightly without fear of breaking.
3. Use an indelible felt-tipped marker to put each child's name on his smock. Inside the collar is a good place—out of sight, yet easily found.
4. If you do not have enough pails, the giant-sized cans available in most school cafeterias are large enough to be satisfactory.
5. Tongs like those used at home to lift corn or lobsters from boiling water are fine for this lesson. Enough children will be able to bring

them in to have plenty available. Keep the children's hands out of the dye—it will avoid future problems.

6. Urge the children to wear old clothes the day they are to do the dying—or have a few extra shirts available for use as temporary smocks.
7. Assign a helper to empty the last pail of clear water after it has been used four or five times. The first pail may need to be refilled once or twice.
8. Arrange the dye area so that the pail of clear water to wet the smocks comes first. Then have the pails of dye in a row so that all of them can be used at the same time. Place the other pail of clear water at the end of the row for rinsing. Have it closest to the drying area so that there will be little movement necessary from the dying to the drying areas. If your classroom has an outside exit, arrange the area so that the rinsing pail is close to the door. Then the children can go outside to let the smocks drip before leaving them to dry.
9. If you can arrange to attach a clothesline outside your classroom, have clip clothespins and let each child pin his tied and dripping smock to the line.
10. Smocks can be untied and ironed while they are still damp or left until they are completely dry.

It Won't Wash Away!

Sandcasting *(Suggested for Grades 4 through 6)*

Objectives

1. To build upon a familiar and natural interest.
2. To learn about a new material and how to work with it.
3. To have the experience of working directly in a pliable medium.
4. To experiment with creating a sculptured form.

Materials

sand
containers for sand
pail of water
paper cups
plaster of Paris
container for mixing plaster of Paris
paper towels
tongue depressors to stir plaster

You've built castles in the sand—but they washed away. Sand castles always wash away! But you can build something else in the sand—and it won't wash away.

It's a fine day—just the kind of day that would be fun to spend at the beach. You could dig in the sand and create all sorts of things! Yes, it would be fun, but we can't do it today. We can't go to the beach, that is. But we can dig in the sand and create things.

Show the class the sand you have. See—you will be able to make wonderful things in that! Let's find out how to make things in the sand—things that won't fall apart the way they do when you make them at the beach.

Turtle

Work Outdoors. It will be best to work outdoors where there is more space and where you won't have to worry about cleaning up the classroom. Give each child a container of damp sand. A heavy cardboard box will do, or any other container that will hold three or four inches of sand. The sand should be just damp enough to hold a shape but not wet enough to ooze water.

Play in the Sand. There's your sand, so you go ahead and play with it for a while. Isn't it easy to pretend you are at the beach? If you were really at the beach, you would probably dig out the sand in some places and pile it up in others. That is fine at the beach when we're making ordinary sand things, but we aren't at the beach and we aren't going to make ordinary things! This time we are going to dig out the sand to make a hole, but it is going to be a special hole. It is going to be the shape of some real thing.

Simple but Real. Talk for a while about what kind of real things children could dig from their sand. Each thing will have to be something simple, and you will be able to dig out only one side of it. You could make a fish, for example. That would be a simple shape that would be easy to recognize, and you could just dig out one half of the fish.

Well, let's see how we will make our real thing before you decide what else you could make.

Have your class gather around you. Begin to dig out the shape of a fish. Form the shape of the mouth and the tail. Round out the depression in the sand until it looks as though you could lay a real fish in the hole. Oh, half the fish would be above the sand because you are only digging out half of the real thing.

Can you think of any way to give the fish an eye to make him look even more real? Certainly! All you have to do is press a round place into the sand where you want its eye to be. Will the tail be as deep in the sand as the side of the fish? No, because the tail of a fish isn't as thick as its body. Make the hole look as much like a fish as you can. Then gently pat the clay until the sides are smooth and firm.

That's fine for a hole the shape of a fish—but a fish isn't a hole, so we will have to fill it with something. We will use plaster of Paris for that.

Mix the Plaster of Paris. Pour into a container a quantity of water at least equal to the amount it would take to fill the hole in your sand. Slowly pour plaster of Paris into it, constantly stirring the mixture. Continue to add the plaster until the mixture is slightly creamy. You will probably be surprised by how much plaster of Paris you have to add. There may be a slight warmth to the mixture because of a chemical reaction which takes place.

Pour It Carefully. When the mixture is ready to use (creamy and smooth), pour it slowly into the fish hole. Pour it carefully so as not to disturb the sand and change the shape of your fish. Fill the hole all the way to the top.

Now there is nothing to do except wait until the plaster of Paris has hardened.

Nothing in the Sink. In the meantime let's see how you will clean up after you have poured the plaster into your shape. *Don't let even one little bit of plaster get into the sink.* The containers we used for mixing the plaster of Paris will be thrown away. No plaster from them will get into the sink. Dip your hands into a pail of water if you have plaster of Paris on them, and then wipe them on a paper towel. Put the paper towel in the wastebasket. The pail of water will be emptied in a suitable place in the schoolyard. No plaster from that will get into the sink.

Talk about what has been happening to the sandcasting. Yes, the plaster has begun to harden. When it is completely hard, we will take it out of the sand. What will it look like? There will be sand stuck in the plaster. In fact, you may want to pour some water over the sandcasting to remove most of the sand, but a little of it stuck to the plaster will look good. What will be the shape of the sandcasting? Yes, it will be the shape of a fish—just the same shape as the hole in the sand. Will both sides be alike? No. One side will be flat—the side you can see now, but the other side will be rounded.

Make Something Real. Now let's get back to playing in the sand, but this time make something real. What can you make besides a fish? Yes, a flower with the stem will be fine. So would a turtle or rocket or clown's face—or other things, too. You decide what you would like to make.

Certainly, you can change your real object if you want to. Just flatten the sand and begin again. Oh, that isn't a simple shape. Long, thin legs of an animal are apt to break off when they are made of plaster of Paris. Perhaps you had better make the horse out of another material some other time and make a plainer sandcasting. Good! Pack the damp sand until it is smooth and firm. Make the hole deep enough so that all parts of the plaster of Paris will be at least a half-inch thick. Some parts will be thicker than that. If the plaster of Paris is too thin in places, the sandcasting will break apart. Are you ready to pour the plaster into your mold?

Mix Your Own. As each child completes his sand mold let him mix his plaster of Paris. A paper cup—or a small can that can be thrown away—will be a fine mixing container. Approximately equal amounts of water and plaster of Paris make the right consistency. Have a measure in the water and another similar one in the dry plaster of Paris to make it possible to get the right amount of each material quickly and easily. Have each child stir his mixture until it is smooth. Then let him pour it into his sand mold. The rest of the plaster of Paris will harden in the container and the whole thing can be discarded.

How long you have to wait before removing the plaster sandcasting from the sand depends upon how thick the plaster of Paris mixture was. It will be wise to wait several days.

Removing the Sandcastings. When you are ready to unmold the sandcastings, return to the schoolyard again. Dig into the soft sand around the plaster and gently lift the sandcasting. Carefully push away the surplus sand. Then dip the sandcasting into a pail of water to remove the balance of the loose sand. There will still be a layer of sand embedded in the plaster and it will give your object a pleasing color and texture. Hold the object carefully—with both hands beneath it if it is a reasonably large one—to support the plaster and keep it from breaking.

Later when the plaster of Paris is completely dry, you may want to add a felt backing to the flat side so that it can be used as a paper weight or table decoration. Or you may want to glue it to a board for a background. Be sure to use a strong glue.

See—these are different from anything you ever made in the sand before. All those things washed away. But these won't wash away—not even when you dip them in a pail of water.

Butterfly

MAKE IT EASY—FOR YOURSELF!

1. Work outside if possible. Spilled sand or water or even plaster won't do any damage outside, but inside it could be a considerable problem.
2. Have all your materials organized before the beginning of the lesson: containers for sand; damp sand; plaster of Paris; containers for mixing plaster; pail of water for rinsing hands; paper towels.
3. Explain the whole process in the beginning so that each child knows what to expect and the reasons why he will be doing—or not doing—certain things. Be sure he understands why certain precautions are being taken. Once the plaster of Paris is mixed there will be no time for explanations—it must be used immediately.
4. Press the sand firmly together to form the mold.
5. A few drops of vinegar added to the water will slow the setting process of the plaster of Paris. This is an advantage when you are working with a number of children at one time. More water will not thin plaster once it has begun to harden. If it hardens before it can be used, throw it away.
6. Don't let *any* plaster get into the sink! Plaster will become hard even in a pool of water. It is a good idea to cover the sink with a piece of newspaper as a reminder not to wash hands or containers there.

7. Don't worry if a layer of water forms on top of your mold. There wasn't enough plaster of Paris in the mixture, but what was there has sunk to the bottom and will harden. When the plaster is firm, tip the mold and pour off the excess water. (Outside, that is!)
8. Allow plenty of time for the plaster of Paris to dry before removing the casting from the mold. Dried plaster is less likely to break than wet plaster.

8
Miscellaneous Materials

Close the Door

Individual Choice *(Suggested for all elementary grades)*

Objectives

1. To provide opportunity for freedom of individual art expression.
2. To encourage children to pursue the kind of art they like best.
3. To introduce the three basic kinds of art: realistic, non-objective, and abstract.

Materials

An assortment of whatever materials you have available: paper, fabric, cotton roving, wire, Styrofoam, clay, crayons, paste, glue, scissors, newspaper

The children will close the door—and you won't have a thing to do! Hard to believe? Well, try it!

What do you know about an artist's studio? Yes, an artist may sometimes exhibit his work in his studio, but more important, it is the place where he works. It is the place where artists create their art.

Puppet

How Artists Work. Talk with the children about how artists work. Every artist has a kind of art work that he likes best to do. It may be painting or sculpture or something else. Nobody tells him what to do; he has to decide that for himself. Artists seldom paint or sculpture or draw at home. They don't like to be disturbed by people. They don't want to have to hear the doorbell ring or to have to answer the telephone. They want to be all by themselves so that nothing will bother them. Usually they have a studio away from home where they can go. They close the door and go to work.

Today you are going to be an artist. You are going to have your own studio. Oh, it will be a very little studio, only about this big. Use your hands to indicate a space about the size of their desks. In fact, you are in it right now. All you will have to do is close the door—and lock it, if you like—so that no one can disturb you.

Variety of Materials. No, no—don't close the door to your studio just yet. Let's see what supplies you will have to work with in your studio. Have a variety of basic materials spread out on a large table. In addition, you may indicate where there are certain other supplies which children may use if they wish. Don't give any indication of what they might do with them. Don't even let children ask any questions about how the materials might be used. Just assure them they may use anything they want in any way they like.

Now, remember, when you close the door of your studio, no one is to come in and bother you about anything. So you cannot even share materials today. In fact, I won't come into your studio, either, unless you invite me to come in. If you really need some help, you may raise your hand and I will know you are asking me to come in. Otherwise, I'm not even going to look at you. I won't know what you are making.

Close the Door. So, everybody in your studio, close the door, and go to work. If you need me, you may invite me to come in, but otherwise I won't even see your work until it is all finished. Then you may tour other studios to see what has been made.

Many of the children will actually make the motions of closing a door and turning the key. Then there will be complete silence as each person concentrates on his own work.

You sit down off to the side of the group—and relax. There won't be anything else for you to do. Just be aware of the quiet activity and let your presence reassure each child that you are there if he needs you. Rarely will anyone even ask you to come to his studio. If someone does raise his hand, quickly and quietly go to him to see what he wants. Answer his question as briefly as possible and return to your own place again.

Have children clean up their work areas as soon as they have finished.

Tour the Studios. Now for a quick tour of all the studios to see what each child has done. Let groups of children take turns walking about the room to see all the many things that have been made. You will want to join the groups, too. Let children make comments about things they find particularly interesting.

Three Kinds of Art. You have been just like adult artists. They make three kinds of art work. Oh, they may paint or draw or model or sculpture or construct. But whatever type of art they do, they make things in one of three ways.

Some artists like to make things look real—just as real as they can. That kind of art is called ______ ? Someone may say "realistic." Write it on the blackboard. Find someone's realistic picture. Hold it up for the class to see, and talk about the real things that are in it. That is a good example of a realistic picture. Show another realistic picture—if possible, one that was made from different materials.

Other artists don't like to make anything real in their pictures. They like to make just colors and lines and shapes—but nothing real. Do you know what that kind of art is called? There is nothing real in it—no objects in it. It is called non-objective. If you take off the last letter of non, you have a word. Right! It is "no"—so no object. If you add a letter to non, what word would you have that still means no? Good! Add an "e" and you have "none." You can even change the last letter of non and have a word that also means no. Certainly! Change the last "n" to "t" and the word is "not." So no matter how you change it non-objective means no real thing in the picture. Some child will have just put shapes and colors together. Show his work. See, it is a non-objective picture. Find one or two more and show them.

But there is a third kind of work that some artists make. It has some real things in it, but the artist changes them so that they aren't entirely realistic. Some of the children may know the word "abstract." If they don't say it at once, tell them what it is and write the word on the blackboard along with "realistic" and "non-objective." There will be examples of abstract pictures among the children's work. Show several of them to the rest of the class. It may be a short man with a huge head, or buildings that you can see through. Whatever it is, talk about the way some realistic part has been abstracted.

Each Kind Is Good. One kind of art is just as good as another. An artist has to decide which type he likes to make.

Have each child decide whether he has made a realistic picture, an abstract picture, or a non-objective picture. Then have a quick showing of all those of each type. Make each type of art equally good—and find something about each child's work to praise so that every child will end the lesson with a feeling of success and accomplishment.

Antique Car

Lines and Shapes

Have an exhibit of the three types of art and display every child's work in its proper place. See what can happen when an artist goes into his studio and closes the door!

MAKE IT EASY—FOR YOURSELF!

If you motivate each child to work in his own studio, you have made it easy—for yourself! Just supply the materials—and stay quietly to the side.

How Do I Look?

Self-Portraits *(Suggested for all elementary grades)*

Objectives

1. To become more aware of the differences that establish individuality.
2. To provide the opportunity for a choice of materials to create a desired effect.
3. To increase the ability to see.

Materials

18" x 24" white or manila paper
tempera paint
easel brushes
cans for water
egg cartons
newspaper
colored construction paper
paste and paste brushes
scissors

"How do I look?" you ask when you are all dressed up in a new outfit. But it is the new clothes you're talking about—not really you. Let's forget the clothes and just look at us.

Do any of you look exactly like anyone else in the room? No—every one of you looks different from everyone else, don't you? What makes you look like *you* and different from everyone else? Your clothes? Oh, they're not really a part of you. They're just something you wear. Even if every one of you had on the same kind of clothes you would still all look different, wouldn't you? You don't look a bit like him—or him—or him. And you don't look at all like her—or her—or her, do you? What makes the difference? That's right! You have dark brown hair and she has blond hair and he has light brown hair. Hardly any of you have just the same color hair. Yes, you do have straight hair and he has curly hair—and your hair just curls on the ends. Besides that, you wear your hair in different ways. You have long, long hair—and yours is very short. You have bangs—and your hair is pushed back from your face. The boys comb their hair differently, too.

Other Ways You Are Different. Get the children to observe as many things about hair as they can—the color, the texture, the length, the style. Then shift to another difference. Eyes are different. They can be a variety of colors, and they are shaped differently, too.

What other ways do you look different from anyone else? You're right! Faces are different shapes. Some people have long faces—just as some people grow taller than other people. Find someone who has a long, thin face; find someone who has a round face; find someone with a different shape face. People come in all shapes and sizes, don't they? Their faces do, too!

Me

Still Other Differences. By this time children will find other ways they differ from each other. They will see that noses are different shapes and sizes. Mouths are shaped differently, too. Even a front tooth may be missing here and there. That makes you look different from someone else—and even different from the way you will look when another tooth grows in that empty place!

So what do you look like? You look like *you*—and nobody else!

Bigger Than Life Size. Explain that the children are going to make pictures of themselves—pictures bigger than life size. You will have to pretend that you have a giant magnifying glass over your face, so it makes you look bigger than you really are! Hold up a piece of 18" x 24" white or manila paper. Your face will be as big as that!

Choice of Materials. Have a variety of materials from which the children may choose. Some of them may want to use tempera paint—only that. So have a variety of colors, some egg cartons to put paint into, and some large paint brushes. Other children may prefer to use only construction paper for their self-portraits. Have a variety of colors from which they may choose. They will also need scissors, paste, newspaper, and paste brushes. Have all these materials close together in one section of the room so that they will be easily available. Other children may want to combine their materials—paint for some parts of the self-portrait and construction paper for other parts.

Give each child a large piece of paper—18" x 24" manila or white paper—and an imaginary magnifying glass. Remember—these pictures are to be much bigger than your face really is! We want to be able to see how you are really different from everyone else.

Choose Materials. Let five or six children at a time choose the beginning materials they will need. Those getting paper may select their own colors while you supervise and distribute the paint. The children may tell you the colors they want, and you pour a small amount of each color into the egg carton sections. (Egg cartons make wonderful palettes.) As more or different supplies are needed, allow the children to return to the supply areas and choose what they need.

As the children work on their self-portraits, you will need to walk about the classroom assisting where needed. Someone will need to be urged to use his "magnifying glass" and make his picture fit the paper. Remind another person that he wears glasses, and this helps him look different from someone else. One child's hair is long and straight; another's is curly and doesn't quite cover her ears.

With children using different combinations of materials, it will be easier if each child does his own cleaning up as soon as he completes his picture. Have a specific place for each material to be put—scissors, paint, brushes, and all the rest.

Have a how-do-I-look showing at the end of the lesson. Let one group of children at a time take their self-portraits to the front of the room. Hold your pictures just below your faces, so we see two of you—the "you" and the "magnified you"!

Call Attention to Differences. Talk about how each child has made his picture look the way he really looks—the way he looks different from

Me

another person. Call attention to the things you discussed earlier: the color of the hair, the hair styles, the eyes, the nose, the mouth, the shape of the face.

Don't expect the self-portraits to be photographic. They won't be. But they will be more interesting than a photograph. They will be personal—and surprisingly like the persons who made them. They will say, "I look like this."

MAKE IT EASY—FOR YOURSELF!

1. Make it important and desirable to look different from everyone else. Wouldn't it be dull if we all looked alike! Talk about differences long enough for the children to become observant of the things that make each person an individual.
2. A variety of materials can be handled without confusion. Keep each type of material in a different part of the room. Materials that will be used together should be displayed together—for example: 12" x 18" colored construction paper, paste, scissors.
3. No pencils! Pencils tend to make children work small. You will do better to eliminate them completely.
4. Papier mache-type egg cartons make excellent palettes for tempera paint. They can be broken in half to provide space for up to six colors—or divided in thirds for four colors. At the end of the lesson, pour the surplus paint into the sink, stack the cartons, wrap them in newspaper, and discard them.

5. Water for washing brushes is not necessary for this lesson. Just wipe the brush on a piece of newspaper before changing from one color to another.
6. Keep the cleanup well organized. Have a specific place for children to put each item when they finish with it. Leave the brushes on a paper near the sink so that they can be all washed at one time later. Have children empty surplus paint into the sink and stack their cartons on a newspaper at the sink. Do not wash *anything* during the cleanup period. In another section of the room have the storage containers for scissors and a place to put paste brushes. Have a wastebasket nearby for scraps of paper.

That's Easy to See Through!

Transparencies—with a Theme *(Suggested for all elementary grades)*

Objectives

1. To use familiar materials in a new and exciting way.
2. To experiment with a combination of transparent and opaque materials.
3. To learn to plan a picture so that it fits the shape it fills.

Materials

wax paper
electric iron
construction paper
newspaper
wax crayons
large cardboard—several pieces
small paper big enough for child's name

Have you ever said that a thing was hard to understand? Of course you have! But here's something that's easy to see through right away.

Exposing New Uses for Materials. Your class will be fascinated when they see the combinations of materials you have ready for them for an art lesson. They're used to crayons and construction paper—but wax paper and an iron? Surprise them even more by tearing off a piece of wax paper nearly two feet long—and tell them that will be the paper for their picture. Fold it in half to make a long narrow piece only six inches wide.

That's going to be a picture? Yes, you will have a tall, thin picture, or it could be a long, thin one. Can you think of something that would fit a tall, thin picture like this? Yes, it could be a tall palm tree with coconuts at the top. And even a monkey climbing up the side! What else would look good in a picture this shape? Fine—tall sail boats would look good, wouldn't they? The sails would have to be tall and narrow. Perhaps there could even be two or three of them. Some would be way in the distance, wouldn't they?

Suggest the possibility of a group of several similar things arranged downward in the picture. What would look good that way? Oh, yes, there are lots of things—flowers, butterflies, leaves.

Hold the paper the other direction so that it is long but only six inches tall. Ask the children what this suggests to them. Someone may think of a giant whale spouting water while other fish swim nearby. That would make a nice picture, wouldn't it! Another person may suggest a city skyline at night with stars and a half moon above. Since it is at night, there could be lights in some of the windows, and they would make the buildings look more interesting.

There will be other suggestions, too, for both long and tall pictures. Urge each child to think of his own and not make the pictures that someone else suggested. They are their pictures, aren't they, and every artist thinks of a picture that is his own.

Making a Transparency. Why do you suppose we are going to use wax paper for our pictures? How is wax paper different from other kinds of paper? Yes, it is shiny because it has wax on it, but you can also see ______. Right, you can see through it. It is transparent. So we are going to make pictures we can see through. If you make a picture you can see through, will you fill all the space with construction paper? No, of course not! The picture wouldn't be transparent any longer because you can't see through construction paper.

Explain that only the most important parts of the pictures will be cut from construction paper and arranged inside the folded piece of wax paper. That will leave all the space around these pieces transparent so you can see through the wax paper. Yes, the parts you cut from construction paper will be like silhouettes in your picture. The color paper you use won't even be important because when you put your picture in the window—so the light goes through it to make a silhouette—the construction paper will all look almost the same, won't it? It will just look dark. Yes, there will be a little difference in color, so perhaps you will want to use just two or maybe three colors. Light colors will look slightly different from dark colors when they are held up to the light.

Cutting Out Parts. Have white drawing paper and a half-dozen or so colors of construction paper from which the children may choose one or two or three colors they want in their pictures. Cut some 12" x 18" paper in half the long way so that it is in long, narrow pieces only 6" x 18". This will encourage children to make the thin parts they need. A pair of scissors will be the only other supply each child needs at this time.

They will need to have you nearby encouraging them and reminding them to make it tall—make it thin. Or make it long, but make it thin. Good! That's a fine beginning! Those sails are really tall and narrow. The boat will have to be a little one, won't it, to fit on the thin piece of wax paper. Oh, be sure you put the parts of your picture on only one half of the folded wax paper so that one side can be folded over your picture when it is finished. Could you move some parts of your picture so that your eyes would move downward as you looked at the butterflies on your tall piece of wax paper? Be careful not to make those buildings fill too much of your picture. You want it to be transparent, you know. Yes, it would be a good idea to make them narrower.

Holding Parts Together. Before long someone will have the parts of his picture nicely arranged and will want some paste to hold everything together. Paste? On wax paper? Oh, no, that wouldn't stick—and besides, paste wouldn't look good in a transparent picture. How else could you hold your picture together? Glue? Oh no. That would be just as bad as paste, wouldn't it? What else could you use?

Someone will probably suggest the iron, or maybe some curious child even asked about it before this. That's right—we are going to use the iron to hold the picture together. How can that be done? You are right! If you fold the other side of the wax paper over the top of your picture and then iron it, it will make it all stick together. The heat from the iron will melt the wax and seal everything. Of course, the two pieces of wax paper have to touch each other if they are going to seal things inside. So be sure none of your construction paper touches the edge of your picture. Otherwise it will fall out because there isn't anything to seal it in place. That would be a dreadful thing to happen! You are right! There shouldn't be any construction paper overlapping in this kind of picture. Every part has to be separate so that wax paper is all around each piece and can seal it right in place. We wouldn't want anything to move when we held it up to the window. You may need to change some parts of your picture slightly so that everything is separate and nothing goes quite to the edge of the wax paper. That's right, move it in a little.

Adding Crayon Scrapings. We will fold the wax paper over later, but don't do it yet. There is one more thing we are going to put inside our pictures to make them look even better. What other material do you see that we haven't used yet—besides the iron, that is? Of course, it's those crayons. Crayons add color, but we won't be able to draw with them the way we usually do. Instead, we will scrape off little bits of them and let

In the Deep

them drop on the wax paper. Open a pair of scissors so that you can scrape off the crayon just as you would use a knife to scrape carrots or potatoes. It will be just the same, except these crayon peelings will look prettier!

What color crayons will you use? Why, that will depend upon your picture. You might want to add some green and blue or maybe purple for water for that whale to be swimming in. Or you might want to add several lovely gay colors as a background for those flowers of yours. You decide what would look best in your picture and then scrape off some so that the shavings drop just where you need some color.

Again walk about the room helping children who are having trouble, complimenting others, and encouraging those who are hesitant. Oh, don't cover the whole picture with color, but add enough so that it will be important. When it is ironed, the wax in the crayons will melt too, and the color will spread out to look even better than it does now. Add the color just to the open areas of the wax paper.

Ironing the Pictures. Before long some children will be ready to iron their pictures, so prepare an ironing area. Have some large pieces of cardboard available so that as a child finishes preparing his picture he may slide a piece of cardboard under it. That will serve as a tray to keep his transparency from falling apart. Carry it to the ironing area, slide out the cardboard, put a piece of newspaper over it, and iron the whole thing.

What do you suppose has happened? That's right! The heat from the iron has melted the wax—in the paper and in the crayons—and has sealed everything together. Will the parts of the picture be able to move around now? No—we certainly hope not! If all of them were separate with some of the wax paper around each one, they won't be able to move at all. What do you think has happened to the wax crayon? Yes, the heat melted that wax, too, but do you think the color all stayed in the same place?

Everyone will be anxious to see the first transparency. There will be a chorus of *Ohs* and *Ahs* as it is held up to the window. It's even prettier than you thought it was going to be, isn't it! Part of the reason it is so lovely is the crayon that melted. No, that didn't stay in the same place—it spread out. We have to be careful when we iron our pictures—just enough to seal them and spread the color a little bit but not too much.

No one will want to look very long—they will be eager to finish their own pictures so they can hold them up to the light. You will be busy supervising the ironing. Be sure all parts are ironed enough to be sealed, but don't let them be ironed so much that the colors of the crayons spread too far. Too much ironing might even loosen the picture as some of the wax could be absorbed into the newspapers.

Weren't they fun to make! They were easy, too, but most of all they are fun to look at—or should we say "to look through."

MAKE IT EASY—FOR YOURSELF!

1. Cover work areas with newspaper to prevent crayon shavings from getting on the desks.

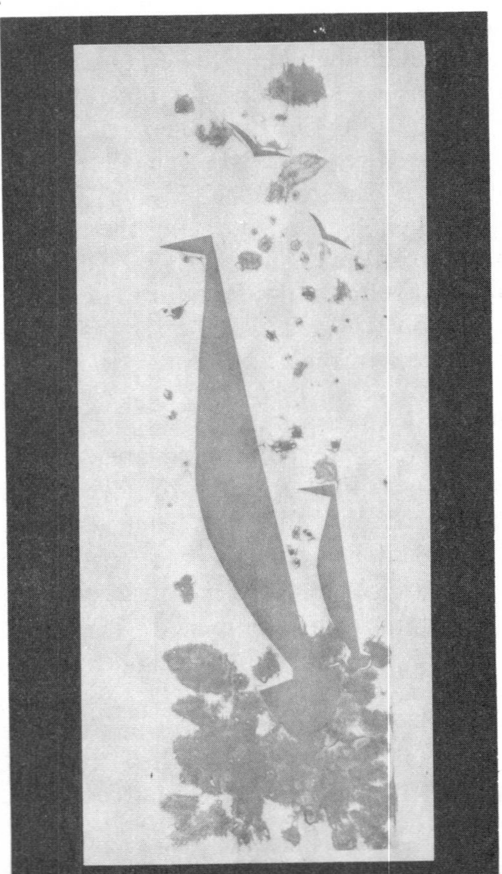

Sailing Days

2. Keep the cut paper part of the pictures simple. Remember, things that are overlapped will not hold together, and variety of colored paper is not important.
3. Use only wax crayons for the melted color. It is the wax in the crayons which will melt and let the color spread. Scrap crayons are satisfactory for this kind of work and will save your better crayons for other lessons.
4. Heavy cardboard makes satisfactory trays to carry work from children's desks to the ironing area. Several pieces of cardboard are enough for a class as they can be shared.
5. Prepare an "ironing board" by making a pile of newspapers thick enough so that the heat from the iron won't penetrate to the surface below. Keep the newspapers opened out flat to make a smooth layer.
6. Give each child a tiny piece of white paper just big enough for his name. Insert it near the bottom of the picture and iron it into the picture so that each child's work can be identified. (Remember to leave some wax paper around it so that it won't fall out.)
7. Don't iron too long. The wax paper sticks together better with less ironing, and the colors of the crayons are brighter and more alive. Use a medium-hot iron. Some brands of wax paper have more wax on them and seal together better.
8. Carefully supervise the ironing so that there won't be any burned fingers, and be sure that the iron is always left in a safe position—and that the plug is pulled out when everyone has finished.

Buttons to Bugs

Felt and Button Creatures *(Suggested for Grades 3 through 6)*

Objectives

1. To create something for personal enjoyment.
2. To see the possibilities for changing a simple shape into a variety of objects.

Materials

buttons
felt
newspaper
glue
scissors
pins

They look like ordinary buttons to you. But they're more than that. They'll change from buttons to bugs—or beetles—or flowers—or fish—or frogs—or just about anything you can think of.

You've seen the little wiggly rubber or plastic creatures that you like to play with or stick on the end of your pencil, haven't you? Well, we're going to make some, and you can put them on the ends of your pencils if you like.

What Could It Be? Let's see how we are going to do it. Select a bright-colored, large button that will be easy for all the class to see. Explain that the children will add bits of felt to change it into anything they like. What could it be? Certainly, it could be a flower. This button would make a fine center for the flower. Then all you have to do is add petals all the way around it. Would you put the petals on top of the button or underneath it? Yes, they would probably look better if they stuck out under it.

What else could this button become? Yes, you could easily change it into a turtle. Little legs, a head, a tiny felt tail and it would become a turtle. What else can you think of that could begin with a button? There will be a variety of ideas: butterfly, bird, lizard, cat, tadpole, spider, bee, fish, beetle.

On Your Pencil. Show the class how their creatures can be attached to their pencils when they have been made. The type of button I have here doesn't have any hole through it, but it has a metal loop on the back. So, when you finish with your rabbit or whatever you make, put a pin through the loop and then into the eraser on your pencil. See, like that. The rabbit would stand up along the side of the pencil. But if you have used the regular type of button with two or four holes in it, you would just stick the pin through one of the holes and then into the eraser. And see—the thing you have made will lie flat on top of the pencil and stick out in all directions. Oops—the holes in this button are so large that the pin goes right through them. Is there anything that can be done about that? Right! Just cut a little circle of felt and put the pin through it and then through the button. That will keep the pin from going right through the hole. Perhaps you can use the felt as part of the design.

Let each child select a button and one piece of felt. While they are taking turns with that, give each child a half page of newspaper, a pair of scissors, and glue. Do all your work on the newspaper to keep the glue off your desk. Yes, of course you may have more than one color of felt, but take just one for now. Most of you will need two or more colors, but you will need only tiny bits of them. Where can you get those little pieces? Certainly! Look around and see who has a color you want—then ask if you may have some of it. That will be better than cutting into a new piece

Duck Pollywog

of felt just for a speck of a color. If no one has the color you want, you may return to the supply area for another piece of felt.

Try to imagine just what you want your creature to look like, and then cut out each piece. Yes, it is probably a good idea to glue the parts to the button as soon as you cut them. Remember, you are working with tiny things this time, so be patient. Good! That's a fine start! Are you going to add some other colors to the butterfly's wings? Doesn't a spider have eight legs? Yes, you can add another one to each side. That was a good button to choose for the center of a flower.

As you walk about the room, continue to encourage and compliment each child. Leave a pin at each desk. As the first few creatures are finished, hold them up for the rest of the class to see. Doesn't this bird look like it's really flying? And isn't this the tiniest turtle you ever saw!

May Wear Them. Some children may prefer to wear their button and felt creations instead of putting them on their pencils. Use them whichever way you like.

Before long the room will be alive with all kinds of creatures. Let groups of children take turns walking about the room so that they can see what every other child has made. It will be an exciting and surprising time. What you thought were merely buttons turned out to be all kinds of things—bugs, beetles, turtles, tadpoles, fish and frogs.

MAKE IT EASY—FOR YOURSELF!

1. Have a variety of buttons—different shapes, sizes, and colors. You will get a good assortment if you ask children to bring them from home.

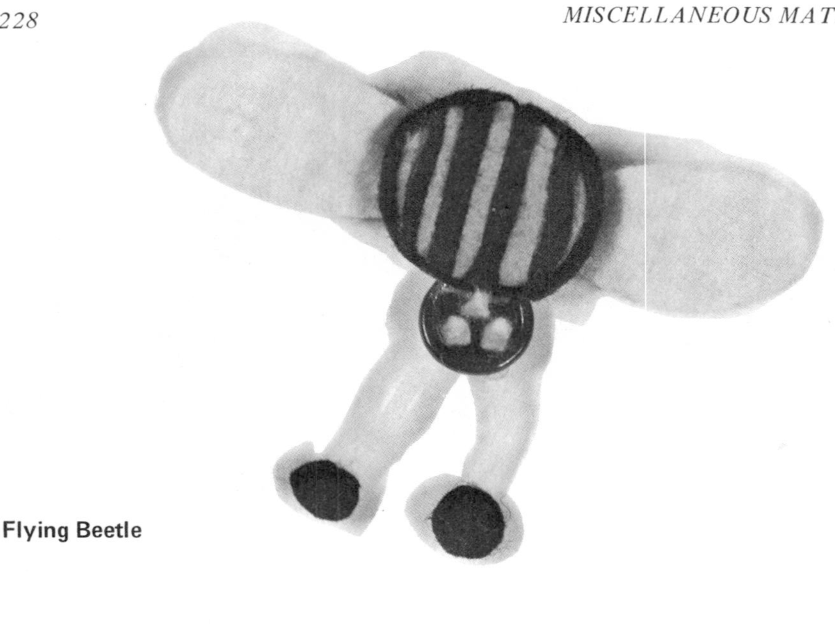

Flying Beetle

Dog

2. Bright and dark colors of felt show up best on small things of this kind. Cut the felt on the paper cutter into pieces approximately 3" x 4".
3. Scissors that are used for paper soon become dull and difficult to use to cut cloth. It is a good idea to save a second set of scissors to use with cloth only. Mark them in some way so that they are never used for paper.
4. Don't draw on the felt. Think of the shape, then cut it.
5. Save even tiny scraps of felt. They can be used for another lesson.
6. To keep the pin from bending as it is forced into the eraser, push it a short distance into the center of the eraser. Then turn the pencil upside down so that the pin head is flat on the desk. Hold the pin with the thumb and forefinger of one hand while pressing down gently on the pencil with the other hand.
7. Be sure to use glue. Paste does not hold to a nonporous surface like buttons.

Just Because It's Little

Crayon on Cloth *(Suggested for all elementary grades)*

Objectives

1. To experiment with familiar materials used in a new way.
2. To introduce the concept of a center of interest.

Materials

wax crayon	felt
white cloth	glue
newspaper	scissors
electric iron	

Don't think it's unimportant just because it's little! You've heard about good things coming in small packages, haven't you?

You're going to use your crayons to make a picture, so of course, you'll also need a piece of ______. No, not paper! This time we're going to be different—we're going to need pieces of cloth. Yes, your crayon pictures will be made on cloth!

Any Kind of Picture. What kind of picture can you make on cloth? Why, any kind you like. So you decide what you want it to be. Think about it so that it will be something you would especially like to make. While you are doing that, let's see how we can make this crayon picture on cloth.

Have your class gather around you at a table or desk. When you make a crayon picture on cloth, it is almost—but not quite—like making a crayon picture on paper. Oh, you rub on the crayon in the same way, but see!—cloth doesn't stay still the way paper does. So you will have to stretch your fingers apart to hold the cloth still and flat while you work on it.

Fill in the Parts. Begin to sketch a simple picture—an underwater scene, a flower, a clown, anything at all. Should the picture just be left with an outline like that? No, of course not! When you make a picture on paper you fill in all the things you draw. So fill them in on cloth, too. See, like that. It is a little harder to make the crayon smooth on cloth than it is on paper, though. Could you push harder on the crayon in some parts of your picture than in other parts? Yes, you can. In fact, it will help to make your picture more interesting if you rub quite hard on the crayon in some places.

So far, using crayon on cloth has been much like using crayon on paper, but there is one thing that is going to be very different. When you have finished drawing your picture on paper, the whole thing is finished. But when you have finished drawing your picture on cloth, the whole thing is not finished. You still have one more thing to do.

Iron the Cloth. Take your crayon-on-cloth picture to an ironing area which you have prepared previously. Lay it on the pile of newspapers which forms the ironing board. Lay another newspaper over it and press the top newspaper with a medium-hot iron.

Show the class what has happened. The crayon doesn't look quite the same, does it? No, it doesn't look waxy any more. The color is smoother and looks a little bit like paint. But look what has happened to the back of the cloth! Yes, that's right! The color has gone right through the cloth to the other side of it. Why do you suppose that happened? Someone will probably be able to figure out that the heat from the iron melted the wax and let it soak through the cloth. The color in the crayon went right through with the liquid wax. Explain that the color is now permanent, so the cloth can be laundered when it gets soiled.

Give each child a piece of cloth and a box of wax crayons.

Have you decided just what kind of picture you would like to make? Of course, it has to be your picture, so it has to be different from everyone else's picture. Yes, the cloth does move when you rub the crayon on it. That's why you have to hold it still. Good! Putting something big on first is a fine beginning. There will be plenty of space for the smaller things. Wouldn't your picture look better if you pressed harder on the crayon in some places? You know, the crayon looks a little bit lighter after it is pressed. That's the way to do it!

Show to the Class. As the children complete the crayon part of their pictures, let them take turns at the ironing area. Show the first few ironed pictures to the rest of the class. Everyone will be delighted, and the slower children will be encouraged to complete their work.

When the first few pictures have been ironed, ask the whole class to stop work for a few minutes and gather around you again at the table. Have the children bring their ironed pictures with them.

The pictures look good, don't they? But they are going to look even better—because they aren't quite finished yet. Sometimes an artist finds a small, unimportant part of his picture and makes it more important so that people will be sure to see it. We are going to do that, too, by finding something in each picture that is small but that would be fun to make more important.

Show the class some small pieces of colored felt. Explain that they will use the felt to make something to add to their pictures.

Something Small. Let's see how that will be done. Can you find something small in this picture of the clown's face that would be good to repeat in felt? Good! That's a fine idea! See that little flower that is bobbing out of the clown's hat? Well, you could make another flower—perhaps a tiny bit bigger—out of felt. Where would be a good place to put it in the picture? Yes, you could put it on the front of his clothes as if it were stuck in a buttonhole. Then when you saw the felt flower you would also notice the little flower in his hat. The felt flower would be different from the rest of the picture and so it would attract your attention to it. Artists would call it a "center of interest."

Find Center of Interest. Look at several more pictures and talk about possible centers of interest for each one of them. Make it some small, seemingly unimportant part which can be repeated in felt to make it into an important center of interest.

The Honey Worker

Now back to work again. After a child has ironed his picture, let him choose the felt to make his center of interest. Have him cover his desk with a piece of newspaper so as to protect it from the glue before he makes his felt object. Tubes or bottles of glue should be available for making the object and for attaching it to the crayon picture.

Have a quick showing as soon as all the pictures are completed. It will be a proud and exciting time, but it will also be a time for learning. Make children aware of the added interest in a picture by making one small part more important. Sometimes a thing can be important just because it is little!

MAKE IT EASY–FOR YOURSELF!

1. Use only wax crayons. There must be wax in the crayons to melt and carry the color through the cloth.
2. Have as much variety as you can in the color. If possible, use boxes of crayons with twenty-four colors.

The Flowered Clown

3. Apply different pressures when applying the crayons to different parts of the picture. Apply reasonably heavy pressure in some places, but don't press so heavily that it leaves a thick coating of crayon. This would cause a surplus of liquid wax which—with the color—would spread into adjoining areas.
4. Prepare an ironing area by making a pile of newspaper thick enough to keep the heat from the iron from penetrating to the surface below. Have several additional pieces of newspaper so that occasionally a fresh piece can be placed on top of the picture to be ironed.
5. No pencils! Draw with the crayons.
6. If you have saved pieces of scrap felt, they will be fine to use. If you are using new pieces—which generally come about twelve inches square—cut them into smaller pieces about 3" x 4".
7. Scissors that are used for cutting paper become dull quickly. It is a good idea to keep a second set of scissors to use for cloth only.
8. Glue should not be applied all the way to the edges of the felt as the liquid glue spreads when the parts are pressed together.
9. Let each child start with just one color of felt. When he needs other colors let him share extra pieces which other children have. Or, if necessary, let him return to the supply area for more colors.

What's He Like?

Caricatures *(Suggested for Grades 5 and 6)*

Objectives

1. To experiment with an unusual combination of materials.
2. To encourage children to exaggerate for emphasis.
3. To use line to express an idea.

Materials

thin wire	wire snips
6" x 9" colored construction paper	scissors

You hear about a new person. The first thing you ask is: "What's he like?" You meet someone for the first time. "What's he like?" you wonder.

Do you like to meet new people? Then do you like to tell someone else about them? Did you ever try to tell about a person without using words? Oh, yes, you could! Artists do it all the time. One way they do it is by drawing a caricature.

Exaggerate. Talk about the meaning of caricature. It is a picture or a description of a person or a thing. It exaggerates something particular about that person or thing.

In what way might a person look much different from someone else? Yes, he might be unusually tall or short. How else would you describe a person? Yes, you could describe his nose. It might be extra large, or perhaps pointed, or an unusual shape. If you were making a caricature of him, you would exaggerate his unusual nose. Right! Some people have large eyes, or tiny eyes, or eyes that seem to be only half open.

When an artist makes a caricature he thinks of something about the person that is different, and then he exaggerates it. Usually it is something about the person's face that the artist exaggerates. Can you think of something else that makes a person different? Yes, a person with a long beard would look different. Right! If a person had ears that stuck out, that would be a good thing to exaggerate in a caricature.

Bugs Bunny

What Is Different? Ask the children to think of someone they know. What is there different about his face that would help you to recognize him? Bring out as many suggestions as possible: hair that sticks out in all directions; bushy eyebrows; constant scowl; squinting eyes; long neck; large mouth. Or perhaps a person talks a lot or is always smoking a cigar. That would make him look different and could be used in a caricature of him. Remember, when an artist makes a caricature, he thinks of some feature which he can exaggerate. A caricature doesn't look exactly like the person but it can be recognized because of the part which is exaggerated.

Explain that the children's caricatures will be made of wire and construction paper. The most important part—the face—will be made of wire. So it will be easy to make the big nose, the ears that stand out, or whatever other thing it is that you want to exaggerate. See, you can bend the wire easily in big round shapes or pointed shapes or tiny shapes, and it is no problem at all to change a shape if it doesn't come out just right the first time.

Hillbilly Joe

Simple Body. But the caricature face will need a body. That part will be less important, so cut a very simple shape from a piece of construction paper. It may be a tall person or a short one; it may be fat or skinny. Then you will have to attach it to the wire head. How can you do that? Paste? Oh, no! Paste doesn't stick to wire. Glue? Well, yes, that might stick, but we're not going to use it this time. No, no tape, either. In fact, we're not going to use anything at all. You will have to find some way of attaching the wire and the paper without the help of any adhesive. How can you do that? Well, you try it and see.

You decide who you would like to make a caricature of. Yes, it could be a *real* person who is well known, or it could be a *kind* of person such as a policeman or a soldier. But whoever it is, you must be able to exaggerate some part so that he will be easily recognized. Yes, you could even make an animal caricature. Oh, no. It wouldn't just be any dog or any horse or any elephant. That would be like making just any person. It would have to be a famous animal caricature that you could recognize.

Give each child a piece of wire two or three feet long. Let each one begin his caricature as soon as he has decided upon a subject. Some children will get started immediately, but others will be hesitant. Can you think of someone you have seen on television whom you recognize by some different facial feature? Certainly! That would be fine. Just be sure to exaggerate it.

Yes, you may get more wire if you need it. Of course you can take it apart to change it. This time try to exaggerate some special feature even more. Good! I can tell who he is! Are you ready to make the paper body? Then get a piece of construction paper and a pair of scissors. Would your caricature be firmer if you made some part of it more solid? Yes, you could twist the wire back and forth to make it stronger. Have you planned how you are going to attach the wire head to the paper body? Yes, the wire could be inserted through the paper. Right! Or it could be wrapped around the paper. Decide which way will be best for your caricature.

Display Game. Gradually each caricature will come to life and be recognized. Give each child a small piece of white paper on which he can print the name of his person or animal. Then tack the pieces of paper on a bulletin board in order to make a long list of names.

Let each child tack his caricature to another part of the bulletin board. Then play a game. Let each child in the room try to select one name and place it with the correct caricature. Each child will be pleased when his creation is recognized and correctly labeled. No one will have to ask: "What's he like?" The answer will be right there in front of him.

MAKE IT EASY—FOR YOURSELF!

1. Encourage all the children to take part in the preliminary discussion. Verbalizing it first will help them to visualize it later.
2. A caricature should not be realistic. Some prominent part should be greatly exaggerated.
3. Any soft wire is satisfactory. Coated doorbell or telephone wire is brightly colored and pleasing to look at, as well as being flexible but firm.
4. Cut the wire in pieces about two or three feet long.
5. Encourage the children to use the whole piece of wire rather than cutting it. Make the caricature out of one continuous piece of wire. Do not add separate pieces of wire for individual parts such as eyes or ears. If two long pieces of wire are needed, be sure that they are firmly joined by twisting the two ends together for an inch or more.
6. Cut off pieces of wire from the caricature only if it is absolutely necessary. Use wire clips or the cutting edge found on most pliers. Do not use scissors—the wire nicks the blades and ruins them.
7. No pencils! Think what the body should look like, and then cut it without any drawing. The body should be simple enough to cut in one piece.
8. Leave the paper scissors with the supply of paper. In this way each child may take a pair of scissors when he selects his paper. If scissors were given out ahead of time, it would be a temptation to use them to cut the wire.

Lines--and Color

Still Life *(Suggested for Grades 4 through 6)*

Objectives

1. To develop the ability to see and to draw simple objects as they really are.
2. To introduce a simple watercolor technique.
3. To experiment with a combination of materials.

Materials

- 12" x 18" white drawing paper
- white wax crayons
- charcoal
- watercolors
- large watercolor brushes
- cans of water
- newspaper
- facial tissue
- simple objects such as vase, bottle, apple, glass, cup and saucer, pitcher

What does an object look like to you? Oh, yes—it may be a person, a rabbit, an automobile, a pair of shoes. Those are just the names you give to some particular shapes. But they really are just lines—and colors.

Have you ever made a picture that looked even better than the real thing? Oh, yes, of course you can do that!

Use Simple Objects. Show the class a simple glass. You can draw that, can't you! But when you finish your picture of the glass it will be even prettier than this real one because it will have colors on it. Show a simple but graceful bottle. That wouldn't be quite as easy as the glass, would it? But if you look carefully you will be able to draw that, too. Then you will add color to it so that it will be a better looking bottle than this real one. Show them the other still life objects you have. No, you won't draw all of them—just two or three that you think look well together.

Comment About Objects. Make several groupings and place them in different parts of the room where they can be seen by all the children. As you make the arrangements, comment about some part of each object in order to focus the children's attention on details rather than on the object as a whole.

It is a tall bottle, isn't it—taller than it is wide. You would use your paper the tall way, too. Did you notice that the sides of the glass slant in slightly from top to bottom? Both sides of the apple aren't exactly alike, are they? Notice the handle on the pitcher. See how it seems to grow out of the side of the pitcher. It isn't just stuck on, is it! See how the vase flares out at the top.

Draw What You See. Tell the class that each person is to choose whichever arrangement he prefers and then draw it with white crayon on white paper. No, the crayon lines won't show much—not now, that is. Suggest, however, that the children draw lightly at first so that they can make any changes that are necessary. Try to make the drawing look just like the real objects.

That's a good beginning. If you hold the crayon loosely it will be easier to draw. Good! You noticed the rim around the top. Does the vase slant in or out at the bottom? Yes, it does slant out, doesn't it? So you need to make a change on your drawing. Doesn't it look as though the two things overlap? But yours are far apart. Fine! Now that it looks just the way you want it to look, you may go over the lines and make them heavier. No, they still won't show much—not yet, that is.

When each person has finished the crayon drawing, have the class gather around you at a table. Have on the table a crayon drawing you have made of one of the objects.

Make Them Round. The vase and the apple and the cup—and all the other things you have drawn—are round, but your drawings are flat. We are going to try to make them look round, just as the real things do. Talk about the way the light strikes the objects and seems to create new lines on them. With a piece of charcoal draw a line that accents your crayon drawing. Make it curve inside your drawing. Draw several lines. They will be mostly on one side of the object—just as the light strikes mostly one side of the object. But there will be a line or two on the other side, too, to help it look round. Be sure each line curves in the same direction as the outside crayon line.

See—it does make the drawing appear to be rounded in all directions! It

Still Life with Grapes

seems to be three-dimensional—just as the vase and other things are three-dimensional.

Add Charcoal Lines. When the children have returned to their own work areas, urge them to observe carefully the objects they have drawn. Where will you put the charcoal lines?

Oh, don't be afraid to draw longer lines than that! The lines closest to the edges will be long—almost as long as the crayon lines. Yes, there will probably be a line or two at the bottom to show the rounding shape of that part, too. Sketch lightly with the charcoal, and then you can darken it later. Good! It looks as round as the real bottle does.

Again have the class gather around you. So far your pictures are just black and white, but we said in the beginning that they would look even prettier than the real objects because they would have color on them. Well, let's do something about that.

Watercolor Over Drawing. Dip a large watercolor brush into water and then into watercolor paint. When the brush is filled with color, quickly spread it over the crayon and charcoal drawing. See, the paint makes the crayon line show! But we must work quickly before the paint begins to dry. Dip the brush into water and then into the paint again. When you have a large area of one color, change to another color and continue to fill the paper. Softly blend the edges where the two colors meet. Work rapidly until all the paper has been covered.

Bottles and Teapot

Let's take a look at it. Yes, the white lines show now. And the charcoal lines accent the white drawing and seem to make the objects stand out from the paper. They do look better than the real ones, too. The color makes sure of that! Yes, some of the colors on the background seem to belong to the objects because they have somewhat the same shapes, but the colors don't just fill in the drawings, do they?

Everyone will be eager to add the color to his own picture, so give each person the necessary materials—newspaper to cover the desks, paints, water, and a large brush.

No, no! Don't wipe the water off the brush! You need lots of water to spread the paint quickly. It won't do any harm if it drips. That's the way to do it! Load the brush with paint and then spread it quickly. Work rapidly so that the paint doesn't dry on the edges before you add more to it. Two or three or perhaps four colors are enough. Are you following the shapes of the drawing somewhat?

Clear Away Supplies. Let the paintings dry while the supplies are cleared away. Then let the children take turns walking about the room to see what everyone else has done. Call attention to particularly good crayon drawings. Compliment other children for the roundness of their objects. Notice the pictures that have especially pleasing watercolor washes. Make each child feel that he was successful.

Well, they do look like vases and pitchers and glasses. But really they're just lines—and colors. And they are lovelier than the real things, aren't they!

MAKE IT EASY—FOR YOURSELF!

1. No pencils! Use only crayon and charcoal for sketching.
2. Use wax crayons so that the wax in the crayons will resist the watercolor.
3. Encourage the children to sketch lightly and then darken the lines. This will permit freer use of the crayon and charcoal and result in better pictures.
4. Give each child a piece of charcoal as you walk about the room to help with the crayon drawings. Collect the crayons while the children are using the charcoal. This way you can provide materials for the children as needed, and get them out of the way when no longer needed. It will provide more work space and make the final cleanup easier.
5. It may help children visualize the roundness of the objects if they are allowed to feel them. Let them put their hands around the objects.
6. Urge children to stand while painting. It encourages using the brush loosely and lightly and permits greater freedom of motion.
7. Clean up the watercolor the easy way. Have each child wash his brush in his water container and then wipe the brush on the facial tissue. This

draws out the dirty water. Empty the water containers into the sink and immediately wipe out the container with the tissue. This cleans and dries it. Let one child collect and store each of the basic supplies: boxes, brushes, and water containers. Let each child fold the newspaper and have one child collect and discard it and the tissues.

8. The finished pictures will be more pleasing if the paper is trimmed on a paper cutter to the size of the crayon and charcoal drawings. Then mount the pictures on slightly larger pieces of black paper, and remount on larger pieces of white paper to frame them.

Do Something

Gesture Drawing *(Suggested for Grades 5 and 6)*

Objectives

1. To experiment with a new technique.
2. To develop ability to sketch quickly and freely.
3. To use line as a means of showing motion.
4. To experiment with color as an accent.

Materials

12" x 18" white drawing paper	cans of water
black felt-tipped markers	paper cups
large watercolor brushes	newspaper
colored tissue paper	polymer

You know how you feel when you get bored. Everything seems so dull and ordinary. You want to *do* something!

When you play a game do you just stand still? Certainly not! You run; you throw a ball—or catch it; you bend; you jump; you kick—you *do* something. But what do the people in your pictures do? That's right! Usually they do nothing—they just stand there! Today we're going to change that. We'll make them do something by doing something ourselves!

Won't Draw an Outline. When children draw people, they usually do as much erasing as drawing—and the people end up looking stiff and stilted. We'll do something about that immediately—we'll draw with black felt-tipped markers. *Every* line that's made will stay there and will show.

But don't worry about that. You won't just draw an outline, so there won't be any one right line.

Well, we need someone to do something for us so we can see how to draw it. Select a volunteer and have him pose in the front of the room. Yes, you may get a baseball bat if you like. If you are holding the bat it will help you to feel more natural. Good! Hold it over your shoulder as though you were ready to hit a ball. Wouldn't your feet be a little farther apart? Can you stay that way for a few minutes?

Covered with Lines. Ask your class to pretend that all over the boy who is posing there are lines that help your eye to move from one part of him to another. Would the lines on his arms be straight? No. They would be curving, rounding lines that help your eye to move around his hands and up the arms. They might circle around the elbow and curve quickly up to his shoulder. Move your hand in loose curving and circling motions that move swiftly and lead your eye in the shape and motion of the arm.

Is his head moving? No—at least it shouldn't be! That's unimportant to our motion picture, so if you were drawing it, you might just make a circle. You wouldn't even put in eyes or nose or mouth. They don't do anything!

Baseball Player

Do his legs move? Well, he's really standing still, but his legs seem to have motion in them, don't they? One leg is even bent some. If you were drawing them, you would sweep your marker in swift-moving lines that carried your eyes in the same direction. Oh, it wouldn't be just an outline! Your eyes don't just look at the edges of his legs—you see everything.

Quick Motions. When you look at him, your eyes move in quick motions over all of him. When you draw a picture of him, you will let your marker move in quick motions over each part of him.

Give each child a piece of 12" x 18" white drawing paper and a black felt-tipped marker. Make it clear to the children that you do not expect them to make an exact likeness of the person posing. You won't even be able to recognize who it is. But you will recognize the motion he is making. You will create a picture that has movement.

Another Pose. Choose another child to pose, or let the same person relax a moment and then pose again. Warn the class that they will have just two or three minutes, so they must work rapidly.

Just make your marker move in the directions that those imaginary lines move. Don't try to draw an outline; draw motion—so you have to make motion with your marker. Good! That's the way to do it! Those swirling lines help our eyes to move in the same direction on the paper that our eyes move on his body. Short lines don't let our eyes move much, so there isn't much motion. Don't worry about the outline—there won't be any! Let's stop and try another one.

A Second Picture. Have another child come to the front of the room and pose. Warn him to make it a pose that will be easy to hold for several minutes. In the meantime, give each child another piece of white drawing paper. Then again urge the class to move the markers in loose, flowing motions that show the movement in the lines of the person posing. Compliment the child who uses big, continuous lines. Urge the timid child to hold the marker loosely and move it faster.

When the class has finished, collect the markers at once so there won't be any temptation to retouch the sketch. Hold up several pictures that have captured the feeling of movement. See, it isn't the outline that we care about—it's the motion that the lines create. Take one or two of the pictures to a large table, and have your class gather around you.

Good Enough to Make Better. They're all good enough to make us want them to look even better. We'll do that with color. No, we're not just going to fill them in with color. We'd have a hard time doing that because there isn't any outline. Besides, we're going to do something much more interesting.

Select two or three colors of tissue paper. Tear off a long, irregular piece and lay it over part of one leg. See—the color helps our eyes to move along that shape. It doesn't fit the shape of the leg exactly but it has the same upward motion. Tear off a rounded piece that has somewhat the same shape as one arm, and lay it in place. It looks good—and helps our eyes to move in that same direction. Let several children tear off other suitable pieces of tissue paper and place them.

Does every bit of the figure have to be covered? No, of course not! You are just making the lines look good and making them even more important. Now let's see how we get the tissue paper to stay in place. No, I'm not going to glue it to your picture. You will put on your own shapes. I'll just show you how to do it on a plain piece of paper.

Explain that the children will use polymer to glue the tissue paper to their pictures. If using polymer is a new experience for them, explain that it is a synthetic material that can be mixed with paint or used as an

Playing Ball

adhesive—as they will use it this time. Warn them that once it is dry it is waterproof, so of course, if even a drop of it gets on a desk or on clothing, it must be wiped up immediately with a damp sponge.

Brushes in Water. Special care must be taken of brushes, too. They must be wet before they are put in the polymer and they must be kept in a can of water all the time they are not in use. Drop the brush in the water while you are talking.

Wipe off the excess water from the brush, dip it in the polymer, and paint an area of the paper with it. Lay a piece of tissue paper on the wet area, and immediately paint over it with the polymer. Repeat the process several times. Let some tissue paper overlap other pieces of tissue paper. Each time you add a piece of paper, be sure there is wet polymer under it and over it—all of it. It's a good idea to work rapidly with polymer, too. Yes, you may finish both drawings with colored tissue paper and polymer.

Place cans half full of water in several places throughout the room so that each child will have easy access to one. Give each child a brush and a small amount of polymer in a paper cup. Let groups of children take turns selecting two or three colors of tissue paper.

Remember to tear shapes to fit a particular place so that they will help your eyes move. Good! You have a pleasing combination of colors. Oh, you have to work faster than that so that the polymer doesn't begin to dry before you add the tissue paper. Don't you think a longer piece of tissue paper there would help your eye move quickly up that long shape? Yes, you may want to add some tissue paper to a part of the background. It could make the extra space more interesting. But don't try to fill anything completely. Don't forget to paint over the tissue as well as under it. Yes, when you finish, leave your brush in the can of water. It must stay there until it is thoroughly washed.

One by one, the pictures will be finished. Have children clear away their materials and leave their two pictures on their desks to dry. Let groups of children take turns walking about the room to see all the pictures. Encourage them to comment about especially good things they see.

When the pictures are dry, you will want to display them—at least one from each child. Your room will be changed into a busy place with action everywhere. Nothing will be dull and ordinary—you already have done something!

MAKE IT EASY—FOR YOURSELF!

1. You are not working for correct proportion in this lesson, so don't stress it. If some child does achieve good proportion, comment on it, but don't make it something which interferes with the child's effort to

show motion. Don't try to teach too much. Make it possible for each child to be successful.

2. Cover the desks with newspaper. The ink in felt-tipped pens is likely to penetrate through drawing paper. The newspaper will also be needed when you use polymer.
3. Some colored tissue paper bleeds when it is wet. This can be advantageous, but if you wish, you can prevent much of the bleeding by painting the polymer over the edges of the tissue paper first and then covering the rest of it. This prevents brush strokes from pushing the dye out beyond the tissue.
4. Distribute the polymer in small paper cups. Just a little polymer is needed. The paper cups are light and tip over easily, so have the children hold them while using them. At the end of the lesson, return the extra polymer to the large container, stack the paper cups, wrap them in newspaper, and discard them.
5. Be sure brushes are wet before they are put into polymer, and return them to the cans of water whenever they are not in use. Wash them *thoroughly* several times when the work has been completed. Keep them in water until they are clean.
6. Polymer comes off your hands easily by rinsing them in warm water and then rubbing them or peeling off the film. It is not necessary to use soap.
7. If polymer is not available, you can substitute a solution of one part Elmer's Glue-All to one part water.

Index